# THROUGH THE FIRE

## Let Faith Arise

Job 23:10

 *Devotions by Tasse Swanson*

ISBN 978-1-0980-7536-1 (paperback)
ISBN 978-1-0980-7537-8 (digital)

Christian Faith Publishing
832 Park Avenue
Meadville, PA 16335
www.christianfaithpublishing.com

Printed in the United States of America

Dedicated to Art Carlson and Barbara Livingston, who I met while living in Israel. Their dedication, reverence to Jesus, and influence on me in the early years taught me how to walk in faith. To Pastor Larry Ehrlich, who helped guide me through the fire. And my daughter Emily Talbott who has walked through with me. Their faith, love, and courage have been an inspiration.

It is my prayer that this book will speak to your heart and encourage you in difficult times and in the usual days of life. May it offer you the peace of Christ that comes from total trust in our loving, sovereign God. The devotions are not daily but seasonal. You can move at your own pace and according to your seasons.

A warm thank you, Sue and Jim Nordby, Emily Talbott, and my husband, Lance, for your editing, time, and wisdom.

# Contents

Coming to Faith.................................................................................13

Spring

The Word of God Speaks.............................................................17
Ash Wednesday...........................................................................18
The Cock's First Crow ................................................................19
The Day Jesus Was Dead ............................................................20
The Curtain as His Robe ............................................................21
Thank You for the Weakness of the Cross ................................22
The Daniel Fast ..........................................................................23
A Cross for a Throne ..................................................................24
Carrying Your Cross ...................................................................25
The Thief Who Understood .......................................................26
The Divisive Cross......................................................................27
Firstfruits....................................................................................29
A Different Kind of Faith ..........................................................30
A Letter of Invitation.................................................................31
A Song of Praise.........................................................................32
A Sovereign God in a Clay World .............................................33
Abundance .................................................................................34
Being With .................................................................................34
Blank Pages................................................................................36
Bulldozers for God .....................................................................37
Inevitable Change.......................................................................38
Concentric Circles......................................................................39
Delayed Justice ..........................................................................40
Daniel's Blessing ........................................................................41
Eternity in Our Heart................................................................42
Faith or Fear?.............................................................................43
Fish, Bread, and Water...............................................................44
God of All Comfort....................................................................45
Golden Bowls Full of Incense, Which Are the Prayers
    of the Saints ..........................................................................46

He Reigns, He Rains ...................................................47

Hearing Heaven's Bells Ring ..................................48

House of Mirrors.........................................................49

I Tell You the Truth....................................................50

Intentional Rest..........................................................51

Inside Out Kingdom .................................................52

Jesus Knew... So.........................................................53

Keeping the Feasts .....................................................54

Laying down Palms.....................................................56

Learning from David .................................................57

Master Artist................................................................58

Messy-ology.................................................................59

Our Gift of "Wait" .....................................................60

Position of Prayer.......................................................61

Proclaiming God's Protection .................................62

Raw Courage...............................................................64

Red Threads of Presence ...........................................64

Refusing Comfort.......................................................65

Struggles as Gifts .......................................................66

Running Home ...........................................................67

Secondary Use ............................................................68

Selah..............................................................................69

Remembering...............................................................70

Shelter in Place ...........................................................71

Spirit of Fear or Spirit of Victory ..........................73

Take Up Your Baggage and Follow Me...................74

The Comfort of Discomfort .....................................75

The Currency of Heaven ...........................................76

The Idol of Worry ......................................................77

The Magnificent Ordinary .......................................78

The Song of Moses .....................................................79

Through the Valley .....................................................80

Trading Hopelessness for Truth...............................81

Unintentional Fruit ...................................................82

Bitter Waters Made Sweet.........................................83

Why Israel?..................................................................84

Summer

The Word of God Speaks............................................89
Riding the Carousel..................................................89
Road Map for Your Trip............................................90
One Eternal Thing ...................................................91
On Our Knees, Pulling Weeds....................................92
Garage Sale Jesus .....................................................93
Dormant Seeds........................................................94
Creating Blooms......................................................95
Campsites................................................................96
A Personal Psalm .....................................................97
A Duet ....................................................................98
A Cup of Cold Water................................................99
Absolutely Sure......................................................100
Psalm of Rest ........................................................101
Ambiguity .............................................................102
Belonging..............................................................103
Book Bindings.......................................................104
But During the Night.............................................105
Chariots of Fire......................................................106
Color Guard ..........................................................107
Come with Me .......................................................107
Empty Jars and Oil ................................................108
Even Still ...............................................................109
Fleas, a Fragrant Sacrifice.......................................110
God's Priorities No Matter How It Rolls...................111
Guarding your Heart ..............................................112
And When He Was Betrayed... He Took Bread..........113
Here's to Hopin' .....................................................115
HSGPS...................................................................116
In the Whittler's Hand............................................117
Invited...................................................................118
Just a Few More! ....................................................119
Leaning In .............................................................120
Learning Our Vocab Words ....................................121

Meaningful Beauty ...............................................122
Measuring Up........................................................123
Mining for Gold....................................................124
Our Invitation to Blessings .................................125
Prayer, Powerful and Effective.............................126
Promised and Not Promised ...............................127
Ready Moments ...................................................128
Reflective Faith ....................................................129
Resting in the Storm ...........................................130
Sowing for Christ ................................................131
Stones of Remembrance.......................................132
Sarah and Her Children of Promise ....................133
Standing in Faith .................................................135
Surrender..............................................................136
Temple Courts......................................................137
The Cost of Freedom...........................................138
The Dinner Table ................................................139
The Great Exchange ............................................140
The Jail Was Securely Locked ..............................141
The Mother's Heart of God .................................142
The Vulnerable Heart of God ..............................143
They Hurried Across ...........................................144
To Speak or Not to Speak ...................................145
Trip Wires ...........................................................146
Unknown Territory..............................................147
Walking in the Valley of the Middle Way............148
We Needed a Rugged Cross.................................149
There Is Purpose..................................................150
Score!...................................................................151
Your Agenda or Mine? ........................................152
Sweet Forgiveness ...............................................153
Waiting for Contentment ...................................154

Autumn

The Word of God Speaks.......................................................159
Running Home ..................................................................160
September 11 ....................................................................162
Tabernacle in the Wilderness .............................................163
Cloudy November ..............................................................164
The Trumpet's Call ............................................................165
Awake, North Wind! ..........................................................166
A Land Flowing with Milk and Honey ...............................168
A Willing God....................................................................169
Be Ye Holy as I Am Holy.....................................................170
Betrayal .............................................................................171
Broken or Bitter? ...............................................................173
Calling Us Beyond..............................................................174
Climbing to Our Fortress ...................................................175
Comfort and Rest...............................................................176
Enemy Possession ..............................................................177
Exchanged .........................................................................178
Facing Jerusalem ...............................................................179
Forgiven Is My Name .........................................................180
Godfullness .......................................................................180
Healing..............................................................................181
Hidden Manna and a White Stone .....................................182
Humility and Authority......................................................184
Is Your Soul at Rest? ..........................................................185
Joshua................................................................................185
Rebooting Our Lives ..........................................................187
Just as He Was ...................................................................188
Leaning into the Wind .......................................................189
Little Foxes ........................................................................190
Mount Sinai ......................................................................191
Overcoming Shame ............................................................192
Present Tense God ..............................................................193
Resting ..............................................................................194
Seek His Face Always..........................................................195

Standing in God ...............................................................196
The Bride and Her Groom ...............................................197
The Cross of Completeness ..............................................198
The Faith of a Humble Woman .......................................199
The Head and Not the Tail...............................................200
The Lord Knew ..................................................................201
The Parenthesis of Time ...................................................202
The Patience of Seven-Layer Jell-O.................................203
The Restfulness of Belief...................................................204
The Sacrifice of Hope ........................................................205
There Is Always Time ........................................................206
Top Down ..........................................................................207
Used by God ......................................................................208
Walking on High Places....................................................209
When Sins Collide..............................................................210
Winner's Circle...................................................................211
Kingdom Commodities......................................................212
Walls of Jericho..................................................................213
Clueless ..............................................................................214
Zipporah's Intercession ....................................................215
Wired to Worship..............................................................217

## Winter

The Word of God Speaks...................................................221
Treasures in Darkness ......................................................222
The Manger.........................................................................224
Writing Our Own Habakkuk ...........................................224
Christmas Joy ....................................................................225
Christmas Alive .................................................................226
Tidings of Comfort and Joy..............................................227
The King of the Universe in a Feed Trough ....................228
That the King of Glory May Come In..............................229
Christmas and Beyond.......................................................230
A Season of the Soul .........................................................231
Bittersweet.........................................................................232

Repairing.................................................................234
Heart Cleaning.......................................................235
Only One Resolution ...........................................236
Ski Tracks ...............................................................237
God as the Author of Romance ..........................237
Post-Valentines, Present Love..............................238
First Miracle ...........................................................239
A Leader and the Cross........................................240
A Safe Place ............................................................241
A Scepter and a Sword .........................................243
Becoming the Beatitudes .....................................244
Broken Pieces ........................................................245
Thick Darkness .....................................................246
The Love of God ...................................................247
Walking in the Truth of Christ ...........................248
Entrusting Ourselves and Others .......................250
God as Central .......................................................251
God's Glory on Earth ...........................................252
Hope and Trouble.................................................254
I Am a Weaver .......................................................255
Justice Reigns.........................................................256
Deep Calls to Deep ..............................................257
Leanness of Soul ...................................................258
Living in Technicolor............................................259
Mercy or Justice....................................................260
Never, God .............................................................261
Now Come and Go Back.......................................262
Points of Brokenness.............................................263
Priorities—Our Training Ground .....................264
Red Herrings of Angst ..........................................265
Securing My Lifeline.............................................266
Standing in Difficulty...........................................267
Terezín.....................................................................268
The Fire That Burns .............................................270
The Hovering of God's Spirit...............................271
The Real Big Bang.................................................272

The Silent Songs of Heaven ................................................. 273
The Wind ............................................................................ 274
This Is the One I Esteem .................................................... 274
Tor-Mentors ...................................................................... 276
Trump Suit ........................................................................ 277
Utter Sovereignty .............................................................. 278
Thank You for the Bitter .................................................... 279
We Always Have Time ........................................................ 281

# Coming to Faith

My hope is that this story of God's work in this life is an encouragement to you to seek a deeper relationship with Him. I was raised in a kind family. We were not a family of faith, but we did go to a church in my younger years. At this church we were encouraged to seek the truth. I took this to heart and did search for the truth. I looked in science and believed firmly in evolution; I looked in philosophy, taking many philosophy classes in college. I seemed to have more questions than answers and would frequently seek out people to talk to about these question, who God was and why Jesus was even in the picture. My grandmother sent me a letter that included the scripture "Seek first the kingdom of God and His righteousness and all these things will be added to you" Matthew 6:33. I took this to mean that all understanding would be added to me as I sought God, so I did. I had no understanding of my sin or heaven, but I wanted the truth, and I wanted to know more about God. A friend at that time stuck with me and made a big difference in my life. Slowly, through her and many others, God brought answers and understanding. One evening, I asked Jesus to come into my heart. I did not have all my answers, but it was enough to know that Jesus is alive and wants to dwell with us. He has answered with love every question I have been willing to ask with an open heart. His love and care have been with me through the divorce of my parents, infertility, and the death of two spouses by the time I was forty-seven years old. I have found His family to be our family, His wisdom available to us through His living word, the Bible. He is our shelter and our song. Eternal life is ours through the gate He opens in our hearts.

These devotions are my "treasures through darkness" that I am offering to you from Isaiah 45:3, so that ...*you may know that it is I, the Lord, who calls you by your name.*

Spring

# The Word of God Speaks

Precious in the eyes of the Lord is the death of
his saints.

—Psalm 116:15

We were on our way back from a trip to Boston to see if we could get a lung resection for my husband. He was diagnosed with meso-thelioma about four months prior. There was no hope to have his lung taken out. It was not helpful because the cancer had developed in two other regions of his body; it was in three body cavities.

*Death is not an unfortunate mistake in life; it is part of life*

On the plane home from this fateful trip, he was sleeping while I was seeking comfort from the Psalms. I happened to open it to 116. There, I received no comfort, but I did feel that I had heard from the Lord the footpath I was to take.

Death is not an unfortunate mistake in life; it is part of life. God was inviting me on board His train. That death was precious. God loved His saints and therefore loved their death as much as their life. I was far from that way of thinking, but it did set a course for me to see beyond my own feelings of loss and despair and to see my husband's death as precious to Jesus.

He did not pass for another seven months. I never told anyone about that scripture. We were praying for life and healing, which I believe is what we are to do. But when the door closed, this was his funeral bulletin verse—an invitation to all to see death not as an enemy but as a precious part of life.

# Ash Wednesday

Set a mark on the foreheads.

—Ezekiel 9:4

We read in Ezekiel that a man in linen was commanded to "set a mark on the foreheads of the men who sigh and moan over all the abominations that are committed in the midst of it" (Jerusalem) (Ezekiel 9:4 AMP). It was called the mark of righteousness. The ones without the mark on their foreheads were to be slain, every one of them.

At the Ash Wednesday service, I went for communion and focused on the coming days leading up to Easter; I wanted to keep Jesus central. I received the mark on my forehead and left the communion rail. Walking away, I began to see everyone around me with the mark on their foreheads, the symbol of the righteousness of Christ in each one of us. I thought of the mark of righteousness in Ezekiel as I saw wave after wave of believers, many of whom I did not know, being marked with the sign of the cross. It was a powerful moment that stayed with me.

Our acceptance of Christ and choosing His worldview of salvation and righteousness spares us the destruction that is talked about in Ezekiel 9. This mark sets us far apart from those who do not believe. We are different; we are marked for Christ. In the Jewish history of Christianity, the scene told of in Ezekiel foreshadows the righteousness we have in Christ as symbolized by the cross received on our forehead on Ash Wednesday.

In the Hebrew language, the word for *mark* is the same as the ancient word for the letter *t*. So when the mark was applied, it formed a *t* or, in our perception, a cross. These men and women who wore the sign of righteousness were wearing a cross on their foreheads.

We are blessed to be marked for Christ. May we wear that mark with boldness, understanding, grace, and love for those who have yet to accept the mark of Christ on their lives.

# The Cock's First Crow

Immediately the rooster crowed the second time.
Then Peter remembered the word Jesus had spoken to him: "Before the rooster crows twice you
will disown me three times." And he broke down
and wept.

—Mark 14:72

Peter was warned of his humanity, but the momentary zeal in his
heart clouded his judgment. He could not believe that he would fall
so far as to deny his Lord and the lover of his soul. This zealous disciple even followed Jesus to the house of the high priest where Jesus
was questioned. He appeared to be the only one there.

Jesus offered a warning call before the denial was expressed.
There are so many times in life when I have felt the quiet nudge of
the Holy Spirit. So often it is for things that I think at the moment
are not important and then later find out they were—things even as
simple as a morning nudge to check the parking rules and an evening
parking ticket. Jesus gave Peter a chance to redo his destiny and obey
at the rooster's crow. That is what I hope all of us can learn to do.
Listen for the early warning signs and respond in faith, not knowing
why or the outcome. I have tried to remember to ask myself, What is
the result of this nudge? If it is not sin, then obeying the nudge seems
to be a response in faith.

Yet even as Peter stood by the fire and said among the servants
he never knew Jesus, Jesus had a redemption plan in motion. He
would cause Peter to live up to his name; the rock would be redeemed
at a fire in the Galilee, having erred twice but redeemed three times as
Jesus called him to feed His sheep (John 21:17). Peter would go on
to speak courageously to the church and write two books that were
included in our New Testament. He was a restored and strengthened
man.

Larry Randolph said, "When God predetermined our destiny,
He factored in our stupidity." The combination of humor and seri-

ous need are delightful and well represented in our friend Peter. And not in him only. It is for all of us who seek to obey and to live the fullness of the life to which we are called.

So, faithful followers, as we continue to make mistakes, remember, our errors cannot outwit the cross. Hallelujah!

# The Day Jesus Was Dead

The Saturday between Good Friday and Easter

Jesus's body was dead on the Saturday between Good Friday and Resurrection Sunday. In His spiritual state, what He accomplished in this gap of time reigns supreme in all the earth! Saturday is the day of rest; it is the first thing on earth that God called holy. Genesis 2:3 NIV states, "Then God blessed the seventh day and made it holy, because on it he rested from all the work of creating that he had done."

But on this day of rest, the day He was physically dead, Jesus did the work of taking back what the enemy had taken in the fall from heaven. The keys to eternal life for His followers and the resurrected life in Christ were returned to His possession. On this day, He descended, and we are told He also ascended. Ephesians 4:9 states that Christ our Lord descended into hell after He offered His life on the cross "because He also descended first into the lower parts of the earth." He fought hell and original sin on this day, and He won.

How odd that on the day of rest, He won the battle, that by being dead, He defeated the foe. He fought with heavenly weapons, rest and death to the flesh. There is a lesson for us to learn. What a miracle was accomplished on this day between the two high and holy days—Good Friday and Resurrection Sunday—the miracle accomplished with only heavenly tools.

What a day that must have been to witness from the heavens. What an army must have been present, as Jesus rested in death to win the supreme battle over original sin, over the fall of the angels from heaven, and secured for all time salvation to all who believe.

During this day, His disciples must have struggled. They stayed locked in a room, huddled together, confused, brokenhearted, not having any idea that the end of the story would be miraculous. Salvation became available for all mankind, for all eternity. During this period of unknowing, there is one thing they did. They stayed together. They leaned on one another in their need and confusion. They may have tried out several explanations and offered opinions, but they waited and stayed together.

As we walk in the places of not knowing, remember that rest, trust, and giving up our own ways can open the door for the hand of God to move.

# The Curtain as His Robe

Tore your robes and wept in my presence.

—2 Chronicles 34:27

I have always felt drawn to the moment when the temple curtain tore as told in Mark 15:38. It happened at the moment when Jesus breathed His last. I wonder who saw the curtain tear, what they said, what they told the next priest on duty. "I had a rough shift…uhh… big storm, and…uhh…the temple curtain got a little torn. Well, a lot torn, actually, completely torn, and I saw it rip from top to bottom." All kidding aside, it was a wild, unpredicted, and strange moment from a human standpoint.

The tearing has piqued my interest for a long time. The beautiful, thick curtain tore open to reveal the shining golden holy of holies. Perhaps at that moment, the Father Almighty rent His garment as His Son died. The massive curtain, more like a rug it is said, tore from heaven down to earth. The holy of holies suddenly opens for all to see. The heart of God was revealed—a shining golden holy heart exposed to the pain and vulnerability of the world as He observed His one and only Son die.

We know that one priest came to believe in Jesus because of the rending of the curtain. He told someone and knew the timing of Jesus's death. It is recorded and remains a moment in time unlike any other moment.

It is easy to ascribe to the Lord glory and strength, power and majesty, but the thought that God tore His garment in agony presents a god who feels extreme emotion, grief, and vulnerability. Being made in His image shows us that God does feel sad, very sad, and allows Himself to be vulnerable to us His children. In this, too, His greatness is revealed.

# Thank You for the Weakness of the Cross

My power is made perfect in weakness.

—2 Corinthians 12:9b

As Jesus was hung and died upon the cross, He looked weak to those around Him. It looked as if the bullies had won. He was fully man, and upon the cross, He was weak and most to be pitied. Many proclaimed messiahs had gone and passed before Him. The disappointment must have been palpable, a miracle worker now broken upon the painful cross. What was hoped for, the One to save Israel from the Roman rule, was dying what seemed a senseless death—a young man of thirty-three, never married, no children, His followers scattered.

The weakness was my weakness. It is easy to relate to the sadness of weaknesses, dreams lost, and hope on hold. All our weaknesses died upon the cross that day; so did discouragement, senseless death, and broken dreams. Jesus was the embodiment of those things that day on the cross. He did not shy away from the pain that sank deep inside his heart. He went there! He felt it. He, even for a moment, was totally separate from His Father. The rending of the temple curtain was nothing compared to the rending of His heart when He cried, "Father, why have You forsaken Me?" He was forsaken at that moment; this was not a drama, a play He was acting in. This was raw, real pain.

All that was on the cross, mine to bear no more. The hopelessness of shame and grief were taken upon Jesus. I am grateful for the weakness of the cross; I feel that weakness. Some days the bullies seem to win. But they don't! I do not need to be afraid of weakness, sin, shame. Those died when Jesus came to life. They were buried in the tomb and stayed there. God's glory came to life and lived. Let us make no room for fear and weakness. We have a strong tower we can run to, ever ready to take us in. We have blood-bought righteousness that gives us entrance.

> The name of the LORD is a strong tower: The righteous run to it and are safe. (Proverbs 18:10 NKJV)

Please meet me there.

# The Daniel Fast

> Whoever drinks the water I give him will never thirst. Indeed the water I give him will become in him a spring of water welling up to eternal life.
>
> —John 4:14

For Lent, I took the encouragement from leadership to do the Daniel fast. I did it for ten days. Some wonderful lessons were in store.

When I made a mistake in the fast, my knee-jerk reaction was to give up and continue to err. What a strange reaction. We are wired to descend, to give way to our less noble emotions. However, the Lord said, "Rise, let's go," as He did to His disciples in the garden after they fell asleep. He did not condemn them, shame them, or abandon them. He said, "Let us move on." He invited them back to His side to continue in His work.

At times, we have to act outside of our feelings in order to cause our emotions to be aligned with the truth of Jesus. Shame and guilt have to be two of the most difficult feelings. However, our encounters with these two uncomfortable journey mates only need to be brief. Shame is never of God. It is ridicule from ourselves or others. God never ridicules, ever. Guilt is either true or false. True guilt can be righted. False guilt is never satisfied.

God always esteems us when our hearts are turned toward Him. Even when we err, He esteems and encourages. And we can do the same for others. We can always choose to see Jesus in the other person, being gentle in reminders and believing in the best for that person each moment. That is value straight from the Father's heart. After all is said, Christ is in them and in us, and He is our hope of glory.

Drinking from the streams of living water brings life on earth and for eternity. Blessed be His name!

# A Cross for a Throne

> Come let us worship and bow down, let us kneel
> before the Lord God our Maker.
>
> —Psalm 95:6

A cross for a throne? The contrast of images pulls at our mind, the concept even more. Yet the sovereign Lord chose His earthly throne to be a cross. The object of ruling and reigning from that fateful day reveals more power on that "throne" than any earthly king could ever hope to have.

As Jesus hung on the cross, the greatest enemy of mankind was defeated; never again could Satan rule the earth without submitting to the One who, on that day, established His kingdom on earth as well as heaven. On the cross, He hung all the sins of mankind—past, current, and future. No earthly throne could support the weight of that burden. On the cross, the fate of millions was decided; the heavens would open for assurance of salvation through Jesus. Never has there been a throne with such power, nor a king who would suffer so severely for His Father's triumph.

When we ask Jesus to make His throne in our hearts, it seems the cross slips in there to truly transform our lives. Once again, the throne becomes a cross. It is more effective for "life and godliness" (2 Peter 1:3) than any throne could ever be. The relationship of sacrifice and power is one that causes the usual way of the world to pause and question. There is a kingdom principle at work in this contrast: *the deeper the sacrifice, the higher the power!* His ways are so far above our ways that our ponderings on this only begin to grasp the concept of His ways.

We are the royal priesthood bowing at the cross/throne of a gentle and powerful King.

# Carrying Your Cross

And anyone who does not take up his cross and
follow me cannot be my disciple.

—Luke 14:27

When was the last time you embraced your burdens? That sounds like hugging a cactus to me! However, we have a treasure from the Word about this. Our difficulties are often painful, and our first response is to flee. We use many fleeing techniques: busyness, distraction, and sometimes even things that become addictions. Sitting and embracing our difficulties is the last thing we want to do.

What if we made a friend of our struggles? What if we numbered them and then embraced them with thanksgiving one by one? When we fear them or ignore them, we give them power they do not deserve. When we sin, we make more trouble for ourselves, but somehow, I do not believe that even our sins surprise the Lord. He is well aware of our weaknesses, and in the process of dealing with difficulties, we come to Him. The very things we are running from are our teachers.

One time I asked the Lord how He saw a mentally challenged person in our congregation. I seemed to hear from the Lord, "He is a teacher among you." This life that seemed to be full of need was elevated as our teacher. God offers labs, not just words of instruction.

Our burdens are embraceable because God is our strength and Jesus is at our side. By the power of His Spirit, we can carry them, learning the instructions along the way.

# The Thief Who Understood

Luke 23:40

It seems there is always something new in the resurrection story. This year, the thief on the cross caught my eye. I am amazed at his understanding. Bill Bright (founder of Campus Crusade) could have taken the four spiritual laws straight from this thief's words. They are life-giving words of understanding, imparted only by the revelation of the Spirit of God. I wonder when this thief came to this revelation. He knew who he was and that Jesus was the sovereign Lord. Luke's gospel alone records this dialogue. Someone was listening in very close proximity to the crosses. The listener heard these words: "Don't you fear God?" One thief rebuked the other. He knew "the fear of the Lord is the beginning of wisdom." Somehow, hanging on that cross, he was in reverent awe of the man next to him. Reverence for Jesus is the safest place in this world, no matter what your position. This guilty man could have joined the other thief in anger and insults, but he chose the humble and truthful position.

*Reverence for Jesus is the safest place in this world, no matter what your position.*

The thief went on speaking to the other thief, "You are under the same sentence. We are punished justly, getting what we deserve." How did the thief know that Jesus came to earth and took on the sentence that belonged to us? He seemed to realize the innocence of Jesus and that the perfect pardon for us was somehow in process. We, too, are sinners. Freedom and abandon flood my heart when I fully embrace my own sinfulness. I love the line in the song "Calling Oh Sinner Come Home": God knows who I am, and He still calls me home! I don't have to pretend with Him. The payment of Christ's blood is enough for my sin! That thought thrills me.

The next line of our friend, the thief, tells us why the payment is complete: "This man has done nothing wrong." There we have it, perfect yet crucified. The thief understood and believed that Jesus had lived a perfect life. We know this man was being ministered to by the Holy Spirit. How could he have known so very well?

We know his understanding was complete when we hear the next line: "Jesus, remember me when You come into Your kingdom." He knew that Jesus had a kingdom that was of the eternal world. This whole passage is amazing evidence of the understanding that is given to a humble and observant heart. We have the understanding of salvation laid out perfectly for us by the thief on the cross. Jesus's cross stood in between the two very different thieves. One went with Jesus to glory; the other seemed to have decided his fate by his angry words. Jesus parts the sheep from the goats. We only need a humble, grateful heart of faith to be with Him in paradise.

# The Divisive Cross

As Jesus hung on the cross, there was a man on His right and a man on His left. One of these men believed who Jesus had claimed to be. This man is now with Him in paradise. On the other side hung a man who would probably never see Jesus again. The cross of Christ divides. We live in a pluralistic society; sayings like "Have it your way" and "Whatever" are common phrases that represent our acceptance of whatever that person wants as truth, without verification or challenge. Relativism is a more common worldview than a belief in absolutes.

I know many people in my life and family who believe the cross is foolishness. The acceptance of original sin is a foreign thought; a just god who does punish sin and requires a sacrifice is not on the radar of so many. We are told in 1 Corinthians 1:18, "For the message of the cross is foolishness to those who are perishing, but to us who are being saved it is the power of God."

These are poignant words: *foolishness, perishing, saved, power.* Jesus with the thieves on either side is a picture of what the cross offers and represents power. What a dividing line is drawn! It is uncomfortable; it is almost unfathomable. The cross is that dividing line. It matters that we have a relationship to the work of God on the cross. It is the difference between life everlasting and death eternal. The setting of Golgotha was actual; Jesus with the thieves is a picture of what the cross offers and represents. The cross was the divide. The one would go into eternal fellowship with the Lord; the other, to eternal separation.

Our response is thankfulness. We who have accepted the sacrifice of Jesus's death are under the power of God and are being saved. Thanks be to God! By the help of the Holy Spirit, we can understand ourselves as well-intentioned sinners who miss the mark often and need a savior.

The other response to those who are perishing is a calling to love them enough to say something. The Lord activates ready hearts. We must follow Him and speak when the opportunity is presented. It is such a challenge, for fear of being offensive is real. Yet the scripture could not be clearer.

Lord, give us bold hearts to walk through the doors You have opened with fearless love.

# Firstfruits

This Sunday is Pentecost. Fifty-three days after the temple curtain was torn, with the holy of holies exposed, the indwelling presence of God left Solomon's temple. On this day, He entered His children. The Jews of that day were celebrating the Feast of the Firstfruits, also called the Feast of Weeks (seven) and the Feast of the Harvest (early wheat). With all the celebrating going on, do you think the early followers of Jesus realized who the real "firstfruits" were? We know that Jesus is the firstfruit of all creation (1 Corinthians 15:23). And we are the firstfruits of the resurrection! James 1:18 states, "He chooses us to be a kind of firstfruits of all He created." The Lord never misses a party! He was right on time, delivering the firstfruits of the Holy Spirit to His church.

Everything He does is right on time. I wonder if we, like the first apostles, may miss many of His miraculous moments. The multilayers of Pentecost are huge. God established a time frame, and Jesus fit in perfectly as did the giving of the Holy Spirit. God delivered many layers of history and future in one huge event. The Holy Spirit was given to live in the hearts of His people. His presence and His temple were offered to dwell in the frailty of a believer's heart. It says in Numbers 28:26 that an offering of *new grain* is to be presented during the Feast of Weeks. I wonder if that was happening in heaven—we, the offering of new grain, brought before His Father's throne.

Seeing the hand of God is sometimes easy; we pray and He gives. Blessed be His name. Other times, it is layered. The timing does not seem understandable, and the magnitude of His intervention is only minimally grasped by our short attention span or lack of spiritual eyes.

Lord, please open our eyes to see even a fraction of what You do on a daily basis.

# A Different Kind of Faith

I would have despaired unless I had believed that I'd
see the goodness of the Lord in the land of the living.

—Psalm 27:13 NASB

I love the joy-filled faith of answered prayer, the moment we see the clarity of a listening god who reaches into our hearts and lives and responds in visible and visceral ways. I love the quiet answers that slowly dawn, doubt and faith mixed together as we realize it had to be God for this to happen.

But a different kind of faith comes in the long-awaited prayers, with sometimes surprising answers far afield from what we asked for. This is still faith. We can then choose to trust God's wisdom and timing, or we can turn away from Him in confusion. Working through confusion in His presence can also be an act of faith. I am so glad for a god who will reason with us but knows when to not bend. He is quiet when we need Him to be but stays near us as we weep on His shoulder. He never owes us an answer. We may ask for one, and He may answer, but not because He must.

A different kind of faith is the long faith, the unhealed faith of chronic illness or even untimely death, the faith that has chosen to not ask *why*. In those times, it is as if we enter a kind of boot camp faith. We are being trained to not get what we want and still wait on Him, have faith in His goodness, be okay with imperfection. We are being trained in things that strengthen us, for God's future plans for us are most likely far beyond what we can see.

There have been times when the Lord has been so good to me, and I have said, "If You never answer another prayer, this is enough. Your goodness is true and seen. You don't have to keep proving Your love for me. You have done that, and I am content." Later, I often have to remind myself that I have said this, but the old "want" comes back quickly, tugging on my mind and heart. Though I have meant it when I said it, I am glad the Lord's kindness and nearness did not end on that day but has carried on and on.

# A Letter of Invitation

To the ones I love,

I long for you to understand the relationship I have with the Lord through Jesus, His Son.

I long for you to know the depth of His love, how deep, how wide, and how wonderful it is to have a living relationship with a living god.

I long for you to know the peace that He desires to fill you with moment by moment every hour.

I long for you to have the complete forgiveness of everything that separates you from Him or others. His is a "cleansing forgiveness" that reaches back and forward, with arms of love and a strong embrace, while still holding to justice and truth.

I long for you to love Him who has helped me so much. He has spoken to me: encouragement, love, wisdom, truth, and grace.

He is a real god with a real personality that I cannot retrofit to my whim. My understanding would be far too small for Him.

I hope that you may be able to see past my human frailness and take hold of Him—One who loves exuberantly and who shares His depth of wisdom and delight, One who does not share His throne but who reigns in love that lasts forever, One who called your name before you were born and has good plans for your life, One who knows you deeply and loves you completely.

You know my love for Him, and because of all His goodness and my love for you, how could I not hope that you would come to know Him—a god that through His Son, Jesus, made a bridge to the world?

He has said that "none may come to Me but through Him." Please walk with me across that bridge into the fullness of a relationship with the living, loving God of the universe.

# A Song of Praise

For whoever touches you touches the apple of
His eye.

—Zechariah 2:8

I love Your land,
The land of Your people,
The land of Your Son,
The land Your eye is upon,
The land You will return to,
The land of Your struggle with man,
The land of Your fulfillment,
The land of pain and war,
The land of victory forevermore.
Thanks, we can touch Your land,
Feel its rocks,
Hear its songs,
See its history,
See its progress,
Hear the voices of their ancestors,
Hear the language of Your word.
Your golden thread of presence through the chaos and strife,
Uncompleted
Yet completed in Christ.

Our lives reflect this story, the unending love and covenant of
God, brooding over what He has called His own.

# A Sovereign God in a Clay World

He is good and He does good.

—Psalm 119:68

Spring is a busy time with lots of things happening. Many of those events include relationship and situations that can be challenging. How do we keep the faith through all the unpredictability, seeming unsuccessful outcomes, confusion, and lack of resolution?

Life is messy. We can slip and fall so easily, get mud on ourselves, and simply not find our way through the swamp. Situations come that can easily frustrate us, look hard to handle, seem hopeless, and feel that we are helpless. Even with the best of our faith at times, we cannot see things as under the power of God. Fitting God into this world seems like putting a square peg in a round hole. God may also feel the strain as we try to squish Him into our image and expectations of Him. We feel entitled to the answer of all our questions that begin with *why*.

Remembering to focus upward as we slog through life's difficulties is our saving grace and peace. God is sovereign. He is good, and He does good (Psalm 119:68). The book of Ruth and Job and the story of Joseph are poignant examples of God's sovereign plan when all the evidence appeared otherwise.

John Eldredge, in the book *Sacred Romance*, wrote, "The arrows seem like the truest part of life." They are not. The heart of the universe is still pure love, and God has it in the palm of His hand. Life can discourage us as we look at the defeats and difficulties, when we eat the bitter dust of defeat rather than the sweet honey of Jesus. As you name those "clay" areas of your life, remember, when they are set on the altar, they become beautiful works of art in the hand of the magnificent Creator.

# Abundance

There are days when the duties and events sweep the time away, and I forget to even turn my heart upward. Then there are more deliberate and precious days when I feel the ache of the human soul and seek His glorious face. That one brief moment changes everything.

Recently, I was listening to a dear sister tell about her daughter who was decorating her first home. The daughter wanted a trim on her valance just like on the one in her mom's home. This mother was considering removing the trim from her curtain and giving it to her daughter. It made me think of God's love toward us.

The love of Jesus is so abundant toward us that He looks night and day seeking ways to love us. He is like a fountain overflowing with love, trying to find recipients of His love. We waddle about our days, sometimes oblivious to this waiting love. He seeks those who are ready to receive the rich gift He wishes to pour out. A fountain ever flows; a heart ever waits. He does not always give us what we want when we want it, but He waits on high to love us.

> On that day a fountain will be opened to the house of David... (Zechariah 13:1 NIV)

# Being With

> And there was evening, and there was morning—
> the third day.
>
> —Genesis 1:13

The third day of creation began with resting. And the rest of creation followed the pattern of resting with God before beginning the work ahead. We all live a busy, to-do life. Doing is usually what calls our name first thing in the morning. But we have a higher calling; we are asked to know who we are in Him, the depth of His love, and trust that He has gone before us and made all the provisions needed in Christ. "Being" is a quiet waiting on the Lord, seeking our identity in Him before the task ahead.

It is so much more difficult *to be* than it is *to do*. When we are doing, we don't have to wrestle with thoughts of not being done, not being good enough, not valuable. When we spend time "being with" God, we have to face ourselves and our Creator. Once we embrace the utter and complete love of Christ, "being with" becomes the safest place on earth. We can rest with work undone and relationships that need repair and soak in the strength of the One who will help us.

We are created for connection before action. Even as we look at infants, eager for their parents' face and kind attention, we can understand that we are hardwired for connection. Resting and connecting. That sounds like eternity to me. It is also the kingdom now. That is how we were created and how we live most fully. If we believe that we are too busy to rest and to connect, that is hell on earth. We end the day dissatisfied and empty. Then we are called again to rest and be with our Creator in peace and sleep, to move on full of His love, direction, and energy.

A few weeks ago, I made a mistake that cost more money than I wanted to waste. I felt so guilty and turned to the Lord for forgiveness. He offered me so much more. I heard the sweet small voice of the beloved Holy Spirit whisper to me, "Do you want to choose shame or grace?" I was expecting forgiveness, and the Lord offered me so much more. In that moment, I could feel my flesh want the shame so I could "pay for my error." I had to deliberately release the shame and open my heart, mind, and spirit to the grace the Lord had for me.

> Therefore choose life that you may live!
> (Deuteronomy 30:19, paraphrased)

# Blank Pages

If it were to be written down, the whole world would
not have room for the books that would be written.

—John 21:25b

The other morning I noticed something in a completely new
light—the blank pages between the Old and New Testament. There
were empty pages cradled between two sets of God's words to us.
The blank pages thrilled my heart, something like the day before
Christmas or a child's birthday. The anticipation is a big part of the
enjoyment of events to come.

Even though the pages were blank, they were teeming with life
and anticipation.

The patterns of the Old Testament were established, frame-
works built, characters and characteristics revealed. The whole stage
was set. It was the calm before the storm, the hush of an audience
before the curtain parts. The anticipation of God's next move was
stirring behind the scenes. All kinds of thoughts, dreams, prophecies,
and promises were written and ready for revelation.

Alexander the Great, a Greek conqueror, had brought completely
new styles of thinking, culture, and art to the world. Even he was part
of the master plan. His influence allowed the writing of the gospel in a
common language, and it could spread throughout the known world
without political and physical hindrance. The Romans had conquered
the world during these intertestamental times. Communication, common government, and international travel were at an all-time high.

The holy waiting was in progress.

Then the scene opened. What a scene to be revealed for the
entire world—a baby in a feeding trough! No wonder they did not
recognize him as king of the world and of eternity. It reminds me of a
line from T. S. Elliot, "And this is the way the world ends, not with a
bang but a whimper." (The world as they knew it exploded with the
whimper of the newborn king!)

This quiet event rang loud in the heavens.

# Bulldozers for God

He who sacrifices thank offerings honors me and he prepares the way, *so that* I may show him the salvation of God.

—Psalm 50:23

We have all experienced points in our life that do not seem to contain anything to praise God about. Broken dreams, relationship strains, difficult decisions, job problems—fill in your own items.

However, that little "so that" in the above scripture tells us there is something else going on. It provides the faithful with enough motivation and reason to launch into territory we have yet to understand.

Every believer wants to "prepare the way and honor God." The "so that" in my life sometimes looks like a bulldozer plowing through mud, preparing the way for a highway that will materialize months later.

I want to encourage all of us to offer the praise regardless of the circumstance. We offer it in faith to see the "so that" come to pass in our lives and in the kingdom work we have been given to do.

God is always worthy of praise. Lifting our eyes upward in praise prepares a way in our soul to use the difficulty as a highway to God.

*Lifting our eyes upward in praise prepares a way in our soul to use the difficulty as a highway to God.*

Builders in the kingdom are vital! Today may you have the strength and the vision to bulldoze through in prayer and praise *so that* you may prepare a way to honor and glorify God. May you also be able to see God in the answers.

The bulldozer operator is often not part of the finished product, but he or she is vital to its completion. Let us be those operators in prayer and praise, knowing the Lord will never waste our efforts for His kingdom. May we have eyes to see His hand.

# Inevitable Change

He has made everything beautiful in its time.
He has also set eternity in the human heart; yet
no one can fathom what God has done from
beginning.

—Ecclesiastes 3:11 NIV

Just when we think we have a cadence, change sets in. Change is inevitable. Yet our hearts long for sameness, the security of predictability. We have hearts made for eternity, and change is not what we are made for. There is a book by Karen Kaiser Clark that states, "Life is change. Growth is optional. Choose wisely." While we are on earth, there will be change—constantly. We serve a god of purpose, so we know change benefits the saint. If we lived with no change, we would quickly get stuck on ourselves, our way, our choices and could become self-reliant and godless.

As much as we may resist change, not embracing it does not seem to offer us the best answers. Change is the vehicle that keeps us looking to and seeking God. Our wiring is for stability, and the world offers us a constantly moving target.

As we grow in grace and God-reliance, we realize that our only stability is at the foot of the throne—a place that is real, vital, and stable. The constant flux of the world can be exhausting, but He tells us, "I the Lord do not change" (Malachi 3:6 NIV). We have one solid place of perfect predictability.

So the benefit of living in this shifting, variegated world is the gift of choosing to abide in the presence of God. He could not be closer. Once we realize that, change will be constant, and so will God's willing presence. In Him and Him alone can we fully rest.

# Concentric Circles

After my second husband's death, I found myself needing a lot of support and help. Being a part of a loving body of Christ is so helpful at times like this. Brothers and sisters in the Lord seemed to form a wall around me. I had nothing to give. They seemed to have an endless well to draw from. It was my lifeline while I tried to stand up in Christ.

Slowly I moved forward, loved into wholeness again, accepted as a new entity, and made the needed adjustments. Not so very long ago, I found myself part of the wall around someone in need. It was obvious that they needed a shield of protection and love. I suddenly realized that we as the body of Christ are like concentric circles, each taking our part in the center of a loving fellowship or a part of the team that surrounds those in need. The concentric circles are ever moving, trading who is in the center and who is on the edge.

I am so thankful the Lord never expects us to do what we cannot do. He, like a loving fellowship, lets us rest and heal, then when we are able, we stand up and give again. As part of the Lord's army, we are trained and ready by our time with Him, with His Word, and in fellowship. As a good commander would, He makes provisions for the wounded and gives them time to heal on the sidelines of the battle. Jesus is that good commander, kind, able, and gentle. He, through others, loves us back into the game and uses us to comfort others in the same way we are comforted (2 Corinthians 1:3–4).

As we live in the body, make our needs known, and allow them to comfort us, we are comforted. As it says in the Beatitudes, "Blessed are those who mourn for they shall be comforted." We need to allow ourselves the time to mourn and the comfort that God offers through others and through His Son. He is so wise.

# Delayed Justice

Delayed justice is a difficult issue in the Christian life. We know God is a righteous judge and that we need to let judgment rest with Him. It is not our project to correct every injustice. We also know that God will hold us accountable in the end, but judgment is reserved for the unbelieving. I am most thankful that Jesus bore the penalty for the judgment we deserve. However, I struggle when unjust things happen and no recourse can be found. Last night was one of those nights that seemed to never end.

How do I respond to injustice while in the sweeping torrent of anger, powerlessness, and frustration?

Unforgiveness is also a denied sense of justice. When we withhold forgiveness, it is because we seek justice on our own terms. We may hold onto a grudge until we feel the offender has paid the penalty. Somehow, that repayment never seems like enough to our natural man. We believe we deserve a kindness, a sincere apology, or respect that was withheld. We are born with an internal plumb line.

We may find ourselves keeping score, furthering a sense of denied justice. When fairness is denied, it is very hard to keep Jesus as our focus. The emotions of strong injustice are difficult to tame. Anger over injustice is our God-given ability to know right from wrong. I am thankful for that gift. As with all gifts, application is the key. Asking the wrong question produces an errant answer.

The widow asking for justice in Luke 18:1–8 was seeking justice for her affairs. The unrighteous judge replied, "And will not God bring about justice for His chosen ones, who cry out to Him day and night? Will He keep putting them off? I tell you, He will see that they get justice, and quickly. However, when the Son of Man comes, will He find faith on the earth?"

Walking in faith is our job; justice belongs to the Lord. By comparison, He will do much better than we could. O Lord, please help me walk in faith so the issues of injustice pale beneath Your loving and mighty arm. If I cannot have justice, let me have faith.

Maranatha!

# Daniel's Blessing

Praise be to the name of God forever and
ever. Wisdom and power are His.
He changes times and seasons, he sets up kings and deposes them,
He gives wisdom to the wise and knowledge to the discerning.
He reveals deep and hidden things; He knows what lies in darkness,
And light dwells with Him.
I praise and thank you, oh God of my fathers,
You've given me wisdom and power.
You make known to me what we ask of you,
You make known to us the dream of the King.

—Daniel 2:20–23

As we move into this Lenten season, some of us are seeking to ready our hearts in tangible ways. Some are giving up something for Lent to remind us of Jesus and the deep sacrificial offering that we remember at Easter time. Some are doing the Daniel fast, a diet of whole grains, fruits, and vegetables only. As we approach this season, may we seek the blessing the Lord has to offer us. And may we seek to be the blessing He wants us to bring to our world. The above prayer speaks of the wisdom and power He wants to offer us as we place ourselves under His loving sovereignty.

As we seek His dreams for us, as we ask what He wants to make known to us, His light dwells in our hearts. We live in a world that lauds self-centered entitlement. It creeps into our hearts and minds, and we gain much support in "doing our own thing, having it our way, whatever you want" living. We are happiest when God is on the throne, when our hearts are aligned with Him and His ways, when we are saying "Blessed are You, God Almighty" rather than "Bless me, Lord." Then we receive wisdom and power from on high to live richly, fully, vibrantly in Him.

Let's make this Lenten season about seeking to know the dreams of the King and then follow His lead. That is a life worth living!

# Eternity in Our Heart

He has also set eternity in the hearts of men.

—Ecclesiastes 3:11

Will not God bring about justice for his chosen ones?

—Luke 18:7

Much human passion is around the issue of justice. Anger, righteousness, unforgiveness, war, and even mercy are issues of justice. We seem to be born with an inner barometer for what is right. The two-year-old saying "That is mine" is a way of expressing their sense of justice. Made in God's image, with eternity in our hearts, it tells us we are built for heaven. We are built for justice, righteousness, peace, and order. Built for eternity and living in a fallen world leaves a wide chasm in our hearts.

Designing our own sense of justice often does not work well for our hearts and minds. We can justify unforgiveness because we are trying to balance the pain scale. Claiming our rights often leads to a focus on ourselves and off the big picture of God's big design. Holding on to anger, betrayal, and inconsiderate action creates a hole in our hearts, and they cannot fulfill the longing for justice in our hearts.

God is just and cannot be otherwise. He will bring justice in a way that is most likely beyond our comprehension. However, He has given us the cross; we can see justice in the death of the perfect Son who took the hit for our imperfections once and for all time. It is an incredible example of justice. Sometimes I fall short of comprehending this and fall into my small thoughts of trying to bring about my own form of justice.

I am reminded of Jonathan Edwards, a well-known evangelist of the 1900s. He was a magnificent preacher who was the object of scandalous rumors that caused his ministry to plummet. He sat quietly in the back of the church, never coming to his own defense for two years. He waited for the justice of God to take effect. Today we remember his sermons and his faithful life; the rumors are long forgotten. He waited on earth for justice and received some, but his heavenly reward of justice, we have yet to see.

I want to trust Jesus for the areas of injustice in my life, fully placing my need in His ability. He will do it, He has promised. While we wait, let's be found in faith.

> He will see that they get justice and quickly, but
> will he find faith on the earth? (Luke 18:8)

# Faith or Fear?

Faith is the substance.

—Hebrews 11:1a

In our pastor's farewell sermon, he gave a choice to live by faith or fear. The Lord continues to challenge this choice. Fear is living in a constant state of angst, wavering in worry, anxiety, and reactions. When fear reigns, the realization is lost that there is a choice over what station is the base of operation. Living in fear translates into bumbling along thinking fear is the only choice and not recognizing the sly enemy hiding from view. The other option is faith.

So what is faith? It is the absence of fear!

Is not all worry born of fear? Is not all distress, anxiety, and pride born of fear? To capture these worries by intentionally applying faith to the situation is the road to freedom. This is not a done deal, a one time fits all, but it is a choice between two landmarks, to transform our mode of operation from this time forward.

Life does not stand still, so this application of faith is a continuously moving target. The guidance and enlightenment of the Holy Spirit is a compass. The northern star, Jesus, is a guide *through* life and pointing homeward.

Sweet warriors, rise as an army living in faith. Identify what is hiding behind fear and label it by its true name. Exchange fear for faith and peace, and the Savior will follow you all the days of your life.

# Fish, Bread, and Water

Jesus meets us at the point of our offerings. He respects the labor and efforts we put in. He seems interested in our well-meaning attempts, even if the outcome is not what we planned. When He chooses to do miracles, He often uses the offerings of humble, almost unaware people who were just setting out what they had. The earthly elements offered at the occasions of the hillside feeding of thousands were only fish and some loaves of bread and at the wedding at Cana, the jugs of water. He miraculously acted upon these earthly elements seemingly offered in simple generosity. It does not seem the people with the fish, bread, and water even knew they were performing the first step of a miracle that would be scribed and told for the next two thousand plus years.

A willing heart for the small things was all that was needed, along with the quiet dynamo, Jesus. Sometimes we think that we have to do things that are really amazing to be counted for the kingdom. It does not look that way. Anything great that was accomplished in all the ages began with the act of one person plus God. We may think that the one fish or the five to seven loaves of bread are too small an offering to matter. We may believe that much prayer must be offered, that many people need to be behind us. That is true at times. Prayer and community are essential, but not every time. The Lord acts through the hands of the willing. He watches what we do and, even more importantly, the intent of our hearts and then adds His Master's touch.

A few weeks back, our worship leader prayed a remarkable prayer at the end of the service. He asked the Lord, "Do in us what You want to do through us." We act in faith; He uses our small gifts for others' good and His glory. I wonder what the photo halls of heaven will be like.

> For the word of God is living and active…and able to judge the thoughts and intentions of the heart. (Hebrews 4:12)

# God of All Comfort

Blessed be the God and Father of our Lord Jesus Christ, the Father of mercies and God of all comfort, who comforts us in all our affliction, so that we may be able to comfort those who are in any affliction, with the comfort with which we ourselves are comforted by God. For as we share abundantly in Christ's sufferings, so through Christ we share abundantly in comfort too.

—2 Corinthians 1:3–5 ESV

In difficult times, comfort is so hard to come by. It seems we can hardly comfort others when our supply is so short. We are told in scripture that "we ourselves are comforted by God."

In asking the Lord about this dilemma, He seemed to direct me in a whole new direction. It wasn't that I was to sit and wait for His comfort to come to me in abundant supply so that it could be shared. I was to worship Him! And there, the channel would open for my heart to be comforted. "How unfathomable are His ways!" (Romans 11:33 NASB). The key to our comfort? Worship.

In worship, our eyes are completely lifted off ourselves or situations that may have caused angst. We are relieved of earthly cares and pain. We can get caught up in heaven, and in the process, our hearts find comfort.

There is another key here. It is in sharing our afflictions, not keeping our pain locked deep inside, but talking with others and Jesus about what is hurting us. In the sharing comes fellowship, and in the sharing comes comfort from earthly sources—others. We have two tools that offer us comfort: worship of the one true and loving God and fellowship with the saints.

Thanks be to God who does not leave us without comfort.

# Golden Bowls Full of Incense, Which Are the Prayers of the Saints

Revelation 5:8b

A small group of women joined to pray. There were burdens, new and very old, small and large. We began to pray. It seemed we could not get out from under the weight of these very important cares. We pressed in, again and again. The verse above suddenly came to life and with deeper understanding.

What struck me was that the fuel of this burning incense pot was the hard, painful, unresolved issues we were bringing before the Lord. The smoke was black and oily as it burned; as it rose upward to Jesus, it became a fragrant offering. The fuel of the incense was our difficulties! As they burned and rose to heaven, they became a fragrant offering to the Lord.

Jesus is pleased to receive our prayers.

Beloved, let the darkness, unresolved questions and issues become a fragrant offering unto the Lord. It changes our thinking to realize that the very burdens are the *fuel for blessing* the Lord. Redemption will come, yet it honors our God to take the things of the fallen world and burn them in prayer that become golden bowls of incense before the throne.

Women of God, let us remember to pray, even if we do not see the outcome. Our prayers will reach the heavens and are a fragrant offering to Jesus. That is enough for the moment.

# He Reigns, He Rains

Let my teachings drop as the rain, my speech distill as the dew, as droplets on fresh grass and as the showers on the herbs.

—Deuteronomy 32:2 NASB

There are times in life when God gives me just what I need when what I want is a huge supply. It is like a gentle rain when what I wanted was a thunderstorm.

He gives me the grace or strength for a moment, and then the next moment I need to call on Him again. We want onetime big broad answers so we can have the big picture and not have to check in again and again. It does not seem to work that way.

*We want onetime big broad answers so we can have the big picture and not have to check in again and again.*

"His grace is sufficient."

As frustrating as that is, I am beginning to understand that is how He wants to do it. More importantly, that is the only way we can absorb the wisdom, patience, and strength He has to offer us. He may tell us that the answer to *why* is "For your good and My glory" when we want Him to write a dissertation.

I want to hear all the answers, but I believe that all the answers would be impossible to absorb, digest, comprehend, or use wisely.

His wisdom comes down like drops of rain on the earth, watering slowly, so we can take in what the Lord offers to our dry and thirsty souls.

"His grace is sufficient."

Some of the rainstorms we have had this season have been torrential. We have had enough rain to know that the land can take in the moisture. I pray our souls are the same, that we take in the daily watering of God's word so that when He speaks or guides us, we can take in what He gives. I pray that we can be content with what He offers and know He will move again when the need and the readiness is there.

"His grace is sufficient."

I think of Mary when the angel told her she would bear the Messiah. She received what the angel told her with a completely submissive and humble heart. She knew that she might be cast out from her family, treated as a prostitute by her culture, possibly exiled from the life and family she had always wanted, even stoned to death. Yet she accepted what the angel told her and said, "Be it unto me according to your word." She asked for no reassurance or further word; she knew, and so do we.

"His grace is sufficient."

# Hearing Heaven's Bells Ring

*Who despises the day of small things?*

—Zechariah 4:10

The resonance of a church bell moves my soul. There is joy mixed with a somber presence that speaks to the heart of faith through the ages and is current to the moment. I wonder if what starts the heavenly bells' ringing is almost unnoticeable from our earthly view. Perhaps it is when a liar tells the truth or a child receives his or her first Bible or when someone who has never had a quiet time decides to sacrifice five minutes a day to read their Bible. With small acts of faith, there is rejoicing in heaven. Though we do not read about the bells that ring in heaven, we do know there is much rejoicing as in Luke 15:7–10. May we be people who can listen from earth to hear that rejoicing.

Living moment by moment while paying attention to what matters to the Father's heart is of great value. It means having an ear tuned to heaven to hear and see the things that matter most as we join our Savior in rejoicing over victories for His kingdom here on earth. It is being able to see the mustard seed and know the gigantic plant that is possible.

It is easy to miss things of value because of our quick glance or busy schedule. Watching for the little things helps us be alert to what the Lord is doing and what may bless Him, others, or ourselves. We may have the lens pulled back so far that we forget the moment really matters and that answers to prayer may be evidenced at our fingertips. Wasn't it a small boy with a few small fish and a little bread who offered the food when Jesus fed the five thousand?

Remember, when Elijah was listening for the voice of the Lord, the powerful wind tore the mountains and shattered the rocks, but the Lord was not in the wind. Then came an earthquake and fire, but He was not there either. "And after the fire came a gentle whisper. When Elijah heard it, he pulled his cloak over his face and went out and stood at the mouth of the cave" (1 Kings 19:12–13 NIV).

Often, we are looking for the big earth-shattering responses and actions from the Lord when He is speaking in a whisper. As we learn to live with our eye fixed on His hand on earth, I have no doubt that multitudes of answered prayers would become evident. God may be choosing to speak in the little things that are close to home and heart. May our ears be tuned to hear heaven's bells ring.

# House of Mirrors

There are times our lives seem like a house of mirrors at a midway. As we go through our day, we can so easily begin to compare our lives with those around us. We look at how accomplished someone is and think of all we have not done. We see someone in a particularly bright spot in their life and feel that our life is continually under a dark shadow. We remember all the Lord has poured into our lives, but still, we are not an author, speaker, mentor, or even a very successful mom or a particularly good wife. We may spend much of our day collecting evidence of our shortcomings, looking at ourselves, and bumping into walls.

It becomes a maze we wander through, a familiar "house of mirrors" where we always check our reflection in comparison to other people. Or it becomes questions, often legitimate, that we keep asking over and over again. How am I doing? What is the correct path? Or perhaps we even pick up a pleading prayer that takes on ungodly focus.

Have you ever found yourself in a house of mirrors? Was your focus on the smallness of your life?

Let's rejoice together that as Christians, there is a way out of this trap. We can and should turn to Jesus instead of focusing on ourselves, our difficulties, or our shortcomings. He will deliver us from a misguided focus just by asking Him to do so. He loves us and sees us with joy, His work in progress. He is satisfied with us today. Our usefulness to Him is His job; our job is to trust Him. We can't ensure a fabulous outcome to our lives, but we can partner with Jesus every day, even every minute.

Hebrews 12:13 tells us, "Make level paths for your feet, so that the lame may not be disabled but rather healed." We are to do that for ourselves; we are to step out of the circular paths and move forward, leveling the ground before ourselves. Our eyes need to focus on Jesus, beyond ourselves. What a relief! We have it in our power to stop any thinking that does not serve us or Jesus well. The Holy Spirit is right there when we call upon Him. He seeks an open door and enters when invited. Truly moving outside of our house of mirrors is a partnership with Jesus. There is a lovely small line in Mark 1:31 about Jesus healing Simon Peter's mother-in-law: "Jesus took her by the hand and helped her up." The same hand of Jesus reaches to us today. Thank You, our kind, gentle, sweet Savior.

# I Tell You the Truth

I tell you the truth if anyone gives you a cup of cold water in my name because you belong to Christ, he will certainly not lose his reward.

—Mark 9:41

Praying for those who don't yet know Christ can be a long process. There are a number of people who have been on my prayer list for years. Some of whom are my family members. They have watched my life and seen my faith in action. They know well where I get my strength, yet they appear unchanged in their openness toward the gospel.

In Mark 9:41, we are told that those who give to God's children, even a cup of cold water, will not be forgotten. These pre-Christian loved ones have given much to me in many earthly ways and with much love. As I was thanking the Lord for their offerings and at the same time pleading for their salvation, I sensed the Lord's heart. Much of His love for them was based on their love for me, His child.

It's similar to being a parent. If someone loves my child, my love and notice of them sharply increases. I found myself interceding for others on behalf of God's love for me, based on Mark 9:41. I prayed, "Jesus, because of my dad's love for me, remember him in your kingdom." This is what Jesus does for us!

I then felt the longing love of Jesus for my father and the sad truth of this earth. Even the Lord does not always get His way. People whom He loves deeply are left unsaved. The price of free will is most costly to the one who granted us that freedom. However, I will continue to press on to the hope of salvation, based on the love of God and the finished work of Jesus, our Savior, and I will keep asking.

# Intentional Rest

> Therefore since the promise of entering his rest still stands, let us be careful that none of you be found to have fallen short of it.
>
> —Hebrews 4:1

Does your calendar look anything like mine? Everyday has something, the daily duties unwritten, and special events noted. I like being busy, as long as there is time between to rest. However, busyness is the hallmark of America, the church, and most of our lives. It is exhausting.

In Genesis 2:2, the Lord rested from his work. He set a standard for us to follow. The Lord did not rest because His work was done; He just divinely rested.

When we were in Israel, it never ceased to amaze me how well they rested on the Sabbath. Everything came to a stop. They did not drive, cook, clean, shop, have parties, or go anywhere beyond their neighborhood. It was as if time froze for twenty-four hours. They did not even carry anything. The whole nation came to a halt. It was complete rest. I do not know if that sounds good to you or not. As I remember this Sabbath rest phenomenon, it was very hard to do.

As Christians, we live under grace and not the law. Our salvation is through Jesus, not by deeds we may do. However, we give up a huge blessing by not taking seriously our need for rest.

Intentional rest is a discipline; it is in direct opposition to our culture and our living patterns. It is not in opposition to something the Lord has for us. As we read in Hebrews, the promise still stands, both for eternity but also for today.

I want to encourage each of us to be deliberate about rest, one day a week if possible. Stop, sit, talk, do not make plans, listen, read, pray. Our soul needs to stop doing and learn again to just be. That is a challenge for myself as much as anyone else. I do believe there is a blessing untold in our divine and intentional rest unto the Lord.

# Inside Out Kingdom

For My thoughts are not your thoughts.

—Isaiah 55:8

There are times when I am amazed at what the Lord shares with us. We gain understanding that is far and above what earthly wisdom could offer. Other times, we cannot understand Him or even begin to wrap our minds around His ways. Even being able to comprehend what we do not know reveals the work of the Holy Spirit.

As we reflect on Easter, we can see how unearthly it is. The long-awaited Messiah is crucified. The death of one gives eternal life to all who seek Him. The disillusioned disciples disperse and become the foundation of the church.

There are many times I find myself wanting, hungry for something the world cannot give. When I ask Jesus how to fill the want, His answer is usually the opposite of my logic. Here are a few examples:

If you are *empty*, become hungrier (Matthew 5:36).

If you want *comfort*, become more contrite (Isaiah 57:15).

If you want *more life*, you must die (1 Corinthians 15:31).

If you are *weak*, be joyful (the joy of the Lord is my strength) (Nehemiah 8:10).

If you *want more*, give more (Luke 6:38).

If you want to *be great*, become lowly (Matthew 23:11).

If you want *life*, you must die (2 Timothy 2:11).

As humans, we want to make a formula out of even this. If we do, we will miss the point. Most of our opinions and answers reflect worldly logic. We find the enduring answers on our knees. He provides what we lack when we obey what we hear, through the Word or the Spirit. We trust that His heart is always for us. As we practice living according to God's thinking, He will open the floodgates. He is our sole/"soul" provider.

And My ways are not your ways.

# Jesus Knew... So...

*Jesus knew* that the Father had put all things under his power, and that he had come from God and was returning to God; *so*...he began to wash his disciples' feet.

—John 13:3–4

Living in the Middle East, we came to understand why feet needed washing. It is hot, so sandals are the only comfortable choice, and the soil is dry. It is not sand; it is soil, and it gets dusty! The dirt clings to your feet and dries where the sandal touches your foot. It is right to take off those dusty shoes in a clean house, but ooooh, the feet are a problem! As we know, washing feet was the job of a lowly servant. As we know, Jesus took that role.

Jesus may have surprised them on another level. They were very near the Passover mealtime. It is typical that the host goes from person to person around the table with a basin of water so they may wash their hands before the meal begins. Jesus took what was known and understood and added a twist to it. His position was secure in the heavenlies before the beginning of time. He acted both as host and servant at the meal.

Jesus's mission here on earth was ending. He knew the Father had put all things under His power, that He had come from God and was returning to Him (John 13:1–3). Knowing who He was, is and will be, He used the servant's duty to demonstrate His sovereign role. What power!

We cannot miss the analogy here. Knowing who we are, that we are loved, forgiven, cleansed, and destined for heaven gives us the power to be humble and to serve. It takes power to be humble in the face of difficult circumstances, injustice, cruelty, ridicule, or just daily life. Jesus's example demonstrates that pride only resides in our hearts when we do not understand His kingship and our position in Him.

As we enter this important season, it is my prayer for all of us that we can let the power of humility reign in our hearts from our secure position in the Lamb of God.

Lord, please give us the power and love to humbly serve.

# Keeping the Feasts

Exodus 23:14–19; 34:18, 22

The writings of Exodus remind us to keep the Feast of the Unleavened Bread, the Feast of Weeks, and the Feast of the Ingathering, also called the Feast of the Firstfruits. The Lord sets days and remembrances apart. We are not to go on as if every day is the same. Once a week, we are asked to set a day aside, a rest day for the Lord, altering what we do, not working but visiting, and reenergizing for the week ahead. We traditionally make the Resurrection Day (Sunday) our Sabbath day of rest. We are told in 1 Corinthians 5:8 NIV, "Therefore let us keep the festival, not with the old yeast, the yeast of malice and wickedness, but with bread without yeast, the bread of sincerity and truth." Jesus fulfilled the law; He did not demolish the law (Matthew 5:17).

I am thankful for the early Christians who recognized that the Lord had fulfilled each of these festivals in the celebration and resurrection of Jesus and the coming of the Holy Spirit. In our celebration of communion, we remember the *Passover* evening when Jesus had the Last Supper with His disciples. Unleavened bread was used in honor of the Passover; we still use that today in the celebration of communion.

On Good Friday, we remember the death of our Passover Lamb, who made the sacrificial atonement for our sin, and the angel of death passes over all who believe.

We also celebrate the Feast of the Firstfruits. We call it Easter. Jesus was resurrected on that day of the Jewish festival. He is—and always will be—the firstfruit of God. His mission was complete.

He has risen, and we have eternal life because of His sacrifice. He not only was the firstfruit but He also brought us in to the kingdom as the Feast of the Ingathering is fulfilled.

Let us not forget our beloved Holy Spirit. The keeping of the Feast of Weeks was fulfilled at Pentecost. And the early Christians, many of whom were Jewish and had celebrated the feasts all their lives, passed the celebrating of Pentecost down through the ages. Thus, we do celebrate the fulfillment of the feasts in Jesus, whose perfect timing was displayed in His life, death, resurrection, and the coming of the Holy Spirit.

Let us therefore keep the feasts with great joy in the One we celebrate this season—Jesus, who fulfills all things and redeems us unto Himself!

# Laying down Palms

They took palm branches and went out to meet
him, shouting "Hosanna!"

—John 12:13

As we approach the celebration of Palm Sunday, let us join with those in scripture who were celebrating a kingdom yet to be realized. Let us gather what we have and lay it before the King. He is royalty in the full sense of the word.

Yet there is another part of this day. For all the joy and majesty of Jesus's entry into the city, the day left most of the people confused and, later that week, perhaps angry. The crowds did not fully understand the magnitude of the King they were welcoming. They gathered branches and flung their coats on the road to honor Him. That same crowd turned on Him in the next few days. Some may have disappeared and have been confused and disappointed, and others stayed with Him and watched Him die. This scenario was not what they had longed for.

They were disappointed and disillusioned. Jesus did not meet their expectations. Often, we may find ourselves disappointed that Jesus did not do for us what we had hoped. Maybe someone was not healed, our job was lost, or our child met with painful rejection or illness. They, like us, had an earthly goal for Jesus and expected Him to "measure up." We might even build a case of evidence to tell Jesus how our plans would further His kingdom.

The throngs lining the roads to Jerusalem could envision many things Jesus needed to do. Yet Jesus rode in, knowing what was coming would dash their hopes. Was His heart breaking as He knew their coming disappointment? He must have been praying for them to endure it and come through with the depth of His plans for them. He knew the next few days would influence all lives in a far deeper way for eternity.

Knowing that our prayers are not always answered as we request, that disappointment will come, I hope we can fling all our lives before the King in perfect trust. He knows what we really need and what will take us into eternity with pure and trusting hearts to enjoy His presence.

# Learning from David

## 2 Samuel 7

*Taking no for an answer.* David had an exceptional ability to take no for an answer. When the Lord said not to build the temple, David obeyed. We can be reasonably assured that it broke his heart. He, of all people, loved the ark. David was the only one mentioned to have danced as it came into Jerusalem. He wanted to create a suitable place for its placement. His influence as a king had brought stability, peace, and the establishment of the nation of Judah. He had wealth and workers to build the temple, but the Lord said no. David did not argue with the Lord on this. He did not give the Lord all the reasons that he should be the one to build the temple, and he did not feel rejected by God because of the negative answer. David accepted, believed, and went on. He then collected materials for the one to whom the Lord had given permission to build. Accepting *no* takes greater faith than carrying out the *yes*.

*Waiting for God to answer.* David also had an amazing ability to leave God's plans to God. David was told he would be king and was anointed king several times, but he never tried to bring about his position by his own power, even when presented with easy opportunities to do so. David waited twenty years or more for the Lord to fulfill what He had promised. We can learn from his perseverance. His trust in God's timing, authority, and ability was walked out over twenty years. Waiting for the answer to our prayers also takes greater trust than carrying out the plan ourselves.

*Accepting rebuke without being crushed.* David had an acute grasp of his ability and penchant to sin. It seems that when he was rebuked, he was ready to accept the rebuke and repent. Often, when a rebuke, however gentle, comes my way, my first response is to defend myself, correct the rebuke, feel crushed, and much later, listen to the words that are meant for my good. David never seemed to have this lag. Rebuke did not affect David's identity before the Lord; he was a man who understood who he was and his position before the Lord of Hosts—one very capable of sin but deeply loved. As are we.

# Master Artist

Make a tabernacle with ten curtains of finely twisted linen and blue, purple and scarlet yarn, with cherubim worked into them by a skilled craftsman.

—Exodus 26:1

There is a reconstructed desert tabernacle in Israel. It was faithfully made in detail by a Jewish believer and an Arab believer who worked together to recreate what once served as the tabernacle of God for the children of Israel. The first view of this tabernacle is shockingly small and bland. The desert is so expansive that the tabernacle looks almost miniature in comparison. Yet it is made to scale and contains every piece that is described in Exodus 25, 26, and 27. The colors fit into the desert—bland. Yet in this bland exterior lies what God ordained as a place to worship Him and where His glory dwelled. Once inside the inner court, the temple curtain that separates the holy of holies is majestic for its place in history. It is through this curtain that the ages, people, and history began to speak as if God Himself was telling the story:

> I am a weaver. My beauty is in the cloth with the colors of time and texture. Events come and offer their place. Perhaps I'll weave them through; they may change colors as well as add twists and turns. Sometimes rains come and wet the cloth. It never returns to its original look, but the strands remain in their pattern and bend to shape with each other. The skill is in the process; the time it takes is sacred. The slow pace distills the colors, the weave, and the warp. Every life makes its own cloth. Every era has a pattern. Each adds a color: neutral, bright, and buff or loud, dark, and dull. Sometimes it is golden. The color or contrast supports the many ways of My purpose.

Thanks, Lord. You take the dark threads, scars, wounds, sins, and mistakes of my life. You use the gifts You have given me in their abundance. You "work the cherubim into them" and blend them into a design, beautiful in Your sight and for Your glory.

# Messy-ology

Blessed is he who is not offended in me.

—Matthew 11:6 NASB

While at a conference recently, I heard George Verwer speak. He is the founder of Operation Mobilization, a large fifty-year-old multicountry mission. When reflecting back on the last fifty years, he said he was more aware of "messy-ology" than missiology. Messy-ology is when people show up and disrupt what we thought was the plan of God. It is when the Lord keeps working through broken, apparently disjointed vessels, and His kingdom prevails. We embrace God on His throne even when we don't understand what He is doing. It is when we embrace the working of God in ways that don't quite fit our expectations of Him or of others. I like the word *messy-ology*; it is something to which I can relate.

Radical grace comes to mind. This means we are willing to stand in the gap of time and current understanding, and still trust the love of God to be in control. It is when we stand at peace even when things are not as we expect or people disappoint us. God's grace toward us describes messy-ology so well. He has been patient with us through immaturity, mistakes, unforgiveness, and resentments, and still He loves and loves. He offers us radical grace many times a day. This grace calls us to offer radical grace to ourselves and to others. Jesus stands between God and the deserved judgment. We are set free.

I am drawn to John the Baptist in prison, who was uncertain of Jesus as the proclaimed Messiah. John sent his disciples to ask Jesus about His identity, and Jesus responded by telling him what He had been doing and added, "Blessed is he who is not offended in me." I wonder if that felt helpful to John; I wonder if he even understood what

Jesus was saying. This "voice in the wilderness" was beheaded before the cross and resurrection even took place. I hope John was able to embrace those curious words that seemed to offer little understanding or support to one of Jesus's faithful followers. That is messy-ology—radical acceptance of Jesus, the Son of God, who does not owe an explanation of His plans. This is not an ambiguous grace but a radical call to trust His love. It may be messy; it may not fit our expectations. But God Himself models this radical acceptance and asks us to do the same.

# Our Gift of "Wait"

May You never answer, so I can wait on You;
I'm sure Your time and knowledge will see my issues through.
May I never know the part I play in the master plan
So that my gift of waiting rests fully in Your hand.
Sitting, trusting, and waiting, at Your feet I stay,
And struggle against the immediate that only wants it's way.
I am called to live beyond this life to wondrous love above;
The waiting of this earth will fade into His hands of love.

We often struggle with a sense of the immediate and carry the "get it done" mentality into all area of our lives. Yet our impatience does not regard the hand and wisdom of God, much like a butterfly that does not realize the struggle to break out of the cocoon is providing the strength needed to fly. God is working His patience in our hearts so that our readiness matches His perfect timing.

*God is working His patience in our hearts so that our readiness matches His perfect timing.*

We are called beyond our full understanding, beyond our knowledge, and beyond our strength. There are not many gifts that we can offer to the One who holds the world in His hands. Yet we can offer Him our gift of waiting for when His perfection will shine through us and our situation.

To the only wise God be blessing and honor and glory (Jude 1:25)!

# Position of Prayer

Father, thank you that you have heard me. I knew
that you always hear me...

—John 11:41b–42a

Jesus spoke these words from His position of favored relationship, a
relationship that He shares with us as adopted children in the family
of our heavenly Father.

Our position in Him is not about kneeling, standing, sitting, or
being face down when praying. The Lord has impressed into my heart
awareness that much of my prayer is spoken from a position that does
not acknowledge my place in Him and His victory over the world.

Instead of praying "Please help with this, please be near that," the
Spirit has been speaking that I am to take my full position of authority
in the finished work of Christ and begin to pray from that position.

The position of prayer I am learning is this:

> Lord, all I need is supplied in You. I will lean on
> Your power today and in this situation. You are
> sufficient for my need. May I have eyes to see
> Your provisions in whatever form they come.
>
> Jesus, You are full of grace and favor for me.
> Thank You. I am able in You to face and deal
> with the days' challenges. You are my comfort
> and joy. You provide me with friends, coworkers,
> and family to love me and challenge me, so I may
> be more like You tomorrow than I am today.
>
> You are a god who sees us through fire and
> rain, cold and heat, hard work and gentle rest.
> You favor Your children; You love our company
> and desire long and detailed conversations with
> us. You are never in a hurry and have allotted
> time for each of us. Your sweet presence waits,
> and Your joy overflows in love for us.

You take joy in this world. You are not troubled that it will overtake Your power. You care about the details surrounding us and wait for us to hand them over to You so Your mighty hand can act. You never take what is not Yours.

The world may be "under the control of the evil one" (1 John 5:19). But we are here, Your agents of prayer; we are the "take over kids." "For everyone born of God overcomes the world…" (1 John 5:4).

Here, Father, take this over…and You do.

Loving, gracious Father, You are amazing. Help us to pray from the position we have in Your victorious Son.

# Proclaiming God's Protection

Returning from a year in Israel has been an adjustment. It has been wonderful to see family and friends, but the recent war in Israel has directed much of our energy and focus back to Israel. Somehow, through all this, I have felt under considerable enemy attack. As I begin to write, there is great joy in my heart to share this message with you. It has been so powerful in my life; I pray it will also give you strength in Christ.

A guest at the bed-and-breakfast I worked at in Israel gave me a prayer bookmark; I have used it as a base and personalized it for myself. Praying scripture is the most powerful prayer I have found. I used the corporate "we" in this prayer as we don't stand alone but as the family of God.

> "No weapon that is formed against us shall prosper, and every tongue that rises against us in judgment, we do condemn. This is our heritage as servants of the Lord of Hosts."

Now we declare that You and You alone are the Lord our God; there is none other but You.

God our Father, Savior, and His Holy Spirit, we worship You. We submit ourselves to You, Lord, in *unreserved obedience.* If there is any sin between You and us (or me), please convict us so we may find forgiveness and cleansing in You. Having submitted to You, we do as Your word directs. We resist the devil, all his pressures, attacks, deceptions, and every instrument or agent he would seek to use.

If there are those who have been speaking or praying against us or seeking harm or evil to us or have rejected us, we forgive them. Having completely forgiven them, we annul their efforts in the name of Jesus, our Messiah, and we bless them in Him.

We do not submit to these attacks. We specifically reject and repel despair, infirmity, every form of witchcraft, condemnation, rejection, shame, fear, low self-esteem, and persecution. (Be sure and add any of your vulnerable places.)

Finally, Lord, we thank You for the sacrifice of Jesus on the cross that has given us free access to You. The curse of sin has been broken, and we enter into the blessing of life in Christ, forgiveness, honor, health, productiveness, victory, and God's abundant favor.

We place ourselves, family, property, possessions under the lordship and blood of our Savior, Jesus, the One who loves us. All praise is to Him. In Jesus's name. Amen.

That is my prayer for each of you. I would like to end with a quote from Northcote Deck: "Wherever God has placed us, and in every detail of our lives, He has ordained the land we are to possess to its very borders, and has ordained the victory to be won."

May we walk in the victory, joy, and trust God has given us through His indwelling Spirit.

# Raw Courage

I told you, you would die in your sins if you do
not believe that I am the one I claim to be.

—John 8:24

What a courageous Lord we serve! He infuriated His listeners with
the open truth. He had no fear of rejection, no fear of death, both of
which happened shortly after these words were spoken. His courage
stemmed from truth, knowing His purpose and His destiny.

What a challenge He is to us. It makes us brave to know and
hold onto the truth apart from any distraction. When we give all our
doubts and fears to Jesus, we become not only brave but the enemy
loses access in our lives. The enemy uses our fears and doubts as
weapons against our peace of mind. What we hold back from Jesus
becomes vulnerable to the world and the enemy. Fearless truth is our
best shield; a life poured out for Him is filled not only with peace
but also with protection from the world, the enemy, and ourselves.

In John 3, Jesus repeatedly makes statements of no compromise
with anything but the truth of who He is. See verses 3, 7, 13, 16, 18,
and 36!

Jesus is the only way to the Father and the only portal to heaven.
In a world filled with compromise, relativism, and negotiations, we have
a solid rock that never bends the truth of His position and our destiny.

Jesus, we believe. Help us walk in Your path of courageous truth.

# Red Threads of Presence

Acts 27:46

When Paul's ship broke up against the rocks, the crew followed and
listened to Paul and threw their food overboard. It must have been
hard to believe that they were going to live beyond this point as the
crashing surf broke apart the ship. When the ship began to break

apart, each person swam on their own or clung to a piece of the ship in hopes of drifting ashore.

Yet they all made it to shore. Not by the bright miracle they may have expected after Paul's speech to them or by their obedience to throw food overboard. It may have looked like an earthly event. The hand of God was not seen, but the fact that not one was lost, revealed divine intervention and fulfillment of Paul's words. God's hand was hardly visible.

In British Navy ropes, there is always a red thread twisted into the warp. It is nothing that could be seen from a distance, but up close, it is evident. A rope found anywhere in the world could be identified, and the presence of the British would be evident. Prisoners were said to have kept a piece of rope in their captivity to use as proof of their nationality.

There is another sea story that tells of a British captain who, with his crew, was under great danger. He told his men he was the red thread that was holding them together.

A small difficult-to-see red thread of Christ's presence can be what holds us together in times of peril or difficulty. We cannot see from a distance the hand that leads us to shore, but up close, we can see the evidence of our identity and the power that stands behind us.

# Refusing Comfort

When I was in distress I sought the Lord, I stretched out untiring hands, and my soul refused to be comforted.

—Psalm 77:2

A voice is heard in Ramah, weeping and great mourning…and refusing to be comforted.

—Matthew 2:18

There are events in our own life or the lives of others around us that are so painful that comfort seems like an inappropriate response. At these times, we may refuse comfort. Perhaps holding onto the pain is the proof we need of the seriousness of the heart's wound. It demonstrates to ourselves and others how much we care about the loss.

What if we had another way to offer proof of the pain?

What if the proof was offered by the death of Jesus? We, the world, needed an event so serious that the Son of God had to die to answer our need.

What if we came to trust God to care for us so deeply that we knew He really, personally, cared about our pain?

What if He would dwell with us there, privately, as long as we needed Him near?

What if we went to the depth of our pain with Christ so we wouldn't have to repeatedly seek from others what only Jesus can offer?

What if we allowed His presence time to fully honor the pain, to stay before Him, seeking the balm that He offers, a healing salve straight from His heart?

We know that salve does not heal instantly; it seals the wound. It keeps invading forces out and lets nature takes its course in a protected environment. It heals from the inside out. And it gives time to close the wound and protect its vulnerability.

This Lenten season, seek the what-ifs of God. He will meet you heart to heart.

# Struggles as Gifts

In the Passover ceremony, there are four cups of wine. The second cup, called the cup of sanctification, recounts the struggles the Hebrews had in Egypt. The plagues are remembered one by one. We are reminded that it is through struggle that we draw nearer to the Lord, seek Him more diligently, and listen at His feet. Sometimes our anger, confusion, or disagreement get in the way of this process, but the Lord allows even those elements to be used for His glory.

Our struggles become a gift to the Lord. When we do not pull away but press in to Him, He becomes more central and our hearts more fully rely on Him. Our prayers are gifts to Him. They are our bids for connection and our motivation to seek Him. Our need, our difficulties, our angst is precious to Him. It is the process of growth that follows the pilgrim to the foot of the cross. All glory and power in the universe are His, but not all hearts are His until they bow before Him and give Him what He does not possess: our trust during the storms of life. We acknowledge His power as we give our pain and anxiety to Him.

Having prayed and released our struggles to Him, we wait. We bring our prayers as treasure boxes to Him; we tell Him what we hope and want, then we slide those prayers like curling stones across the throne room floor to land at His feet. We wait for His way, His timing, and His response—not returning to the throne and taking them back again and again, but waiting and believing in His love, wisdom, and power.

In Luke 10:38–42, we read the story of Mary and Martha. Martha struggles with many cares and concerns, but Mary has chosen the better part—to sit at the Lord's feet in honor and nearness to Him.

> But the Lord answered and said to her, "Martha, Martha, you are worried and bothered about so many things, but only one thing is necessary, for Mary has chosen the good part, which shall not be taken away from her."

# Running Home

> At that time I will gather you; at that time I will bring you home.
>
> —Zephaniah 3:20

Home is a place of the heart. Our heart's desire for home is often bigger than the actual place. Home is where we want to relax and feel strong, loved, protected, and somewhat in control of our world. Our homes often do not fit the bill. There is normal tension and conflict. There are areas of frustration and unresolved burdens. It can easily become the center of strain and strife. Our hearts long for a place that is not here. Solomon writes in Ecclesiastes 3:11, "We have this burden; God has placed eternity in our hearts." We are built for "happily ever after," living victoriously in the promised land.

Thankfully, we do have a home here on earth.

It is our relationship with the Lord Jesus Christ. He is our peace, our strength, the lover of our soul. He protects, guides, and is the One to whom we can run. Our heart finds refuge in Him. He has made us pure through the washing of His cleansing blood; we are pardoned from having to be perfect. We face conflict and trials, but He will save us. While we wait for our permanent home, we can run home into the arms of Jesus. He is always for us, never against us. He never condemns, hurts, or resents us. So while our hearts long for our perfect heavenly home, we can live in the safe arms of Jesus.

> The name of the Lord [Jesus] is a strong tower, the righteous run into it and are safe. (Proverbs 18:10)

## Secondary Use

> They will renew the ruined cities.
>
> —Isaiah 61:4

*Secondary use* is an archeological term. If you have ever toured ruins from past cultures, you may have encountered this phrase. When a city built by stones is laid to ruin, the rocks are scattered. Jesus spoke this way about the future of Jerusalem in Mark 13:2, "Not one stone will be left on another." The next culture then starts to rebuild with the very same stones that were once tumbled. As you walk around these ancient cities, you may see a door header used as a corner post. The ruins become the building blocks of what is to come. This is secondary use.

Only recently did I begin to realize this is a picture of our lives too. The healing from former pain, sin, or difficulty is put to critical use for the benefit of God's kingdom. The rubble becomes the necessary stones for the next project in kingdom work.

When the events are going on, we may not have a glimpse of how the situation could ever be useful to us, much less crucial to our ministries, the lives of others, or God's kingdom.

I believe God is a god of "secondary use." Events from our lives that look messy and unpredictable become the very "stones" that God turns into redemption. Our understanding is not a prerequisite for this to happen; we do not need to be concerned with how it may look. As time peals onward, we may or may not recognize the process of how a certain characteristic was in place just at the right time. Nevertheless, this "secondary use" was planned and in place to bring fruit for His kingdom.

It makes me glad that I am only the stone and I can trust my Builder.

# Selah

pause and calmly think of that!

(Amplified Bible)

The book of Psalms is our first hymnbook. What a treasure that we still possess, evidence of songs sung thousands of years ago in the era of King David. The word *Selah* is used seventy-four times in the Bible, most of those in the Psalms and three in Habakkuk. Although the exact meaning is unknown, it is thought to be a musical term, probably similar to the word *interlude*. Beckoned by the ancient hymns, we do well to continue to attend to the call of Selah in our lives today. It is defined in the Amplified Bible as "pause and calmly think of that!"

*Pause*. In this fast-paced world, pausing does not come naturally to us. We need to be reminded that among the demanding events of our days, stop, Selah, and think of Him, which brings truth and a peaceful rest. Allowing for Selah puts margins in our moments and days not only as a gift to ourselves and those around us but also to the loving Lord, who attends our every move and thought with outpouring love.

*Calmly.* Calm opposes hurry. Hurry often accompanies worry. We as believers in the presence and love of Christ can ruthlessly remove worry from the fabric of our lives. What we are worrying about, we are not trusting for. We may think the opposite of worry is peace, but in truth, it is trust. Imagine us moving item by item from the camp called Worry to the lush site of Trust.

*Think of this!* We are in an era of superficial, brief communications. Stopping to think of what we have just heard or read is translated in this culture as a waste of time. It feels we are pressured to move to the next thing that bids for our attention and quick response. Being people of "Selah" is a rare commodity. Thinking on what was said, read, and felt is rare. When big or small events happen, we double the gift or the understanding if we stop and ponder on them.

Psalm 32:5b states, "You forgave the guilt of my sin." Selah. And verse 7 states, "You surround us with songs of deliverance." Selah. Psalm 24:10 says, "He is the king of glory." Selah. Habakkuk 3:13 states, "You went forth for the salvation of your people for the deliverance and victory of our people Israel…" Selah.

May we be Selah people in a world that brushes past the wonderful and deep work of the Lord.

# Remembering

The memory of the righteous will be a blessing.

—Proverbs 10:7

Memorial Day is a time to think about the importance of remembering those who went before us. Remembering is a human's godlike trait. The Lord says many times, "I remember." He also asks us to remember what He has done and to keep those memories as an accounting of His faithfulness.

Sometimes when we remember those we have lost, we feel sadness for the empty place that is left in our life. Yet the Lord wants us to allow this memory to become sweet. The thought of who they were to us, what went into their life, and who deposited those traits and strengths in their character are important to consider. These musings give us a chance to let what could be harsh and cruel memories become sweet as we hold God's hand and look back. Gratefulness can be exchanged for the pain. What did they deposit in you? Prayers, words of encouragement, children, homes, family? Remember and think back of God's work in your life.

Soldiers, family members, friends, young and old, have all paid forward both in ways we can see and ways we will never know.

Jesus told Lazarus to "take off the grave clothes and let him go" (John 11:44), setting Him free from the bindings of death.

Surely the hand of the Lord has done this. "Blessed is he who is not offended in me" (Luke 7:23).

Let's remember well the works of the Lord and let the sweetness of His love wash over our memories.

> I will give you every place you set your foot...
> (Joshua 1:3)

# Shelter in Place

This is what is being asked of our country at this time of the COVID-19 pandemic. As I was thinking about this time for our nation, I began to pray for God to swoop into many lives and speak to many hearts. I heard a testimony last night that fifty-seven thousand people came to Christ in a twenty-four-hour period through the ministry of Global Media Outreach. What a blessing in the storm!

The words *Shelter in Place* touched my heart as a deeper message from on high, something the Lord was calling all of us to.

*Shelter.* God is our shelter in the storm, a very real presence in times of trouble. We are His chicks He wants to gather under His wings. We just need to listen and be attentive when He calls. Hide out, stay close, feel His warmth and protection.

*In.* "I in You and You in me and they in me." (John 14) certainly features the *in* idea. We are to be in Christ and in the Father, not over Him, telling Him all our ideas that we think He should adopt in His ways, and not below Him, being shamed or scolded like a child. But we are to grow up *in* all aspects of Him. We are to commune near His heart, our focus being intimate togetherness, our heart's deepest desire. Then we don't face the world wanting and attempting to fill ourselves with things that can't satisfy the space He created for Himself. I wrote a little song once. It goes like this:

> Lord, I know only You can fill me,
> It's not from love or life or food,
> Only You can touch me deeply,
> I have looked and found none else.

*Place.* We have a place we belong, a place just for us, our mansions prepared for us and decorated and filled with what draws us to God. Beauty, mechanics, science, nature, and so on. Belonging is the cry of the human heart, from birth to death. I am a therapist, and almost every person I see has this at the heart of their need or the loss of it. We grew up in a family, a place we belonged, and sometimes sin crept in and caused betrayal and hurt. Those become big scars in our heart, because we are created to belong completely. Only Christ offers that in this world. We do get moments of belonging if we learn to embrace them and recognize a shadow from heaven on earth. But complete and utter belonging belongs to Christ alone. There is a saying that "wherever you are, there you belong."

The circumstances that connected you to that spot is enough to claim a stake there and to recognize that we do belong exactly where we are.

# Spirit of Fear or Spirit of Victory

And God placed everything under his feet and appointed him to be head over everything...

—Ephesians 1:22

When we live in a battlefield, it is difficult to see the victory. We know the sovereign God has won the victory in this world; death has been subdued through Jesus our Lord. We read in Hebrews 2:8 and 1 Corinthians 15:27, "All things are under His feet," yet we are aware of the battle we often live in.

As I wrote these words, I was traveling to Israel with a group from my church. There was a battle in Israel at the time. The Israeli Defense Forces had just launched an attack on Gaza in response to four thousand rocket attacks over the last two years. We were not going to be going near the area. We were as safe as any of you at home; in fact, the chances of a car accident today far exceeded any risk we may have faced (may the Lord protect us!). However, it does bring up the question of whom we trust in the midst of battle.

*Our security lies in following a sovereign God into unknown places, not in seeking the comfort of the familiar.*

Our security lies in following a sovereign God into unknown places, not in seeking the comfort of the familiar. Often, we try to find our security in seamless and flawless lives. Other times, we may hang onto the fight as if that is our calling, yet we are called out of the battle to the side of the victor. And there we find rest in His love and protection. At times, we find ourselves seeking comfort over the Lord, fighting battles that are not ours, or just worrying endlessly. All these are substitutes for Jesus. Zechariah 3:4 tells us, "Take off these filthy clothes. I have taken away your sin, and I will put rich garments on you." We wear filthy rags of worry and refuse to take the garment of praise the Lord offers to us. Somehow, we believe that our worrying will win the battle. This is not the heart of God. He wants all our trust in Him. We can act wisely, but unless we live in the victory of praise and trust, we have not won the battle.

Walking in the victory God has won for us is a challenge that will take all our lives to accomplish.

What is the victory God has for you today? What peace, what action, what stillness? May God give you eyes to see His victory in your life today, and may He bless you with peace.

# Take Up Your Baggage and Follow Me

Arriving in a new country can be confusing and disorienting. Finding that familiar face in the crowd at the airport washed me with a sense of relief. Once we collected our baggage, we began to follow our host through the airport to the van that would bring us to our new home in Israel.

Knowing we would be living in Galilee, I had decided to read through the gospels during my quiet times. I was at Matthew 10:38, "Take up your cross and follow me." As I had just followed someone through a bustling crowd in a foreign country, "Follow me" stood out.

This is a familiar passage to us but often unfamiliar in our daily life. To follow someone, we have to be very focused so we see his or her every turn. We must keep our eyes on him and not be distracted by interesting things, events, and conversations around us.

I was having a problem juggling all that baggage while attempting to follow.

When our Savior, Jesus, asked us to take up our cross and follow Him, He knew what was required of us. He asked for an increased focus on Him instead of our baggage. Once our eyes are set on Him, He becomes that whom we look at and seek. He could have said, "Leave your difficulties and follow me." If the trials of our lives were not the very tools of God—the exclusive bridge designed for our growth—He would have said to leave them behind!

What are your crosses today? Perhaps you want to list them. Do you struggle with a difficult marriage, a family member who is ill, a recent death, financial trouble, or a bad habit? These are the very tools the Lord wants to use in your life. They are the crosses that become a bridge once we turn them over to His loving care.

May we all learn to embrace our trials, pain, and hardship with our eyes on Jesus, the lover of our soul. He will use these very things for our growth and His glory. It is a privilege to serve a god who says to His loved ones, "Take up your cross and follow me." He will lead you up; He will lead you home.

# The Comfort of Discomfort

Let him who walks in the dark, who has no light,
trust in the name of the Lord and rely on his God.

—Isaiah 50:10

This has been a unique fall for our congregation. We have been having united services that are wonderful, uniting and bonding, as well as new, different, and slightly unpredictable. The need to trust and rely on Jesus has been at a high level.

It has been a season of trusting that what is being done is by the Lord's prompting even if we don't see the exact outcome. It has been wonderful and difficult at the same time—wonderful to experience the fullness of our body, which is multidimensional and multigenerational, and difficult because it has been hard to trust the Lord in the unknown.

In other areas of life, trials and stressors seem to multiply, this always requiring a conscious reboot to get my thinking into line with the reliability and goodness of the Lord. The above scripture goes on to say there are others who light their own fires and create their own torches for light but lie down in torment.

The Lord does give us understanding as we seek Him, but at times, things do not seem clear. The Lord has a right to do things

His way and not always explain it to us. It is so easy to fall into entitlement to know and understand the full workings of the Lord or to judge Him as being unkind or uncaring if things are difficult for us.

# The Currency of Heaven

His kindness leads us…

—Romans 2:4

His kindness leads us. Can you think of a better way to lead? The Lord knows our hearts respond best and most willingly to kindness. It is the language of the Trinity. How extraordinarily happy I am to have such a god! He could be any way He wished—He is God—but our God is our Father, and His every move is motivated by love.

Love is the currency of heaven. We were bought with love, the love that rather released His precious co-creator Son to this risky world. The Father's love believed in His Son's courage to become fully man and not fall.

Love held Him; He held love. Jesus suffered for love, went to hell for love, rose for love, and reigns for love.

When we are rebellious, His love stands back and lets us fight. When we are angry, His love steps in and becomes the target. He is courageous because He knows He will never fail us. He can wait for us to understand the depth of His love.

Love infused into our daily cycles makes the rhythm of life hopeful and meaningful, not just repetitive. We, above all people, are most richly blessed. We are loved; we are taught to love, with eyes wide open. Love is all around us.

His love lifts us, shelters us, slowly defrosts a frozen heart. It joins us in righteousness, as our most avid cheerleaders. His love fears for us, suffers for us, whistles for us. Love willingly loses for a while, because it knows *love wins*! This is the currency of a life in Him; this is the currency of heaven. Hallelujah!

# The Idol of Worry

Fret not yourselves—it only leads to evil.

—Psalm 37:8

I grew up in a family that worried; we worried about everything. In fact, worry was a way of loving. It showed you cared and were thinking of the other person. In coming to know the Lord as a personal savior who was interested in my life, I began to understand differently. However, old behavior dies hard. My prayer life became my way of worrying. I would fling little prayer arrows all day but never sit down and work it through to the point of faith.

Worry covers a multitude of sins; disbelief, pride, rebellion, stubborn independence, and more. I remember a sleepless night that thoughts just kept stewing in my mind. Focusing on the Lord, scripture, prayer, and praise only seemed to give me temporary relief. I was sure that if I thought about these things long enough, I could figure out what to do and a way to end the trouble. I would construct my dialogue just so and have ready answers for every response. Either you are laughing at how ridiculous this sounds or you are relating.

Thankfully, the Lord interrupted my stewing. By His Spirit, He asked me to list my concerns. (This sounded like a redundant question, as I knew He knew!) It was for me to identify clearly and simply what needed to happen. Having listed the worries, He then asked me to give them to Him one by one. I followed, and then He asked me to list them again and tell Him that I trusted Him for each of those circumstances. For some reason, that was difficult, because I realized I did not trust Him to handle these things.

Anxiety, fear, and worry had become more familiar to me than the peace, trust, and faith He wanted for me. I had developed an idol; something was taking the place of God. I came to understand that there is no grace for our imaginations and worries. God gives us grace for what is real and true. I had stepped out from under His umbrella of protection, and it was raining!

His kindness leads us to repentance (Romans 2:4). His will for us is peace, trust, faith, and joy. The truth of who He is and that He is able to guard everything that we entrust to Him is the sure foundation of our life.

This continual process builds grace upon grace. We can relieve ourselves of old habits and bring in new, faithful ones. It reminds me of directions on my shampoo bottle, "Rinse. Lather. Repeat. Do this daily for clean hair," and may I add, clear thinking. God is good.

# The Magnificent Ordinary

They recognized that they had been with Jesus.

—Acts 4:13

Jesus embodies the phrase "the magnificent ordinary." A humble birth, not of priestly lineage, He lived as a child and young adult in obscurity; many miracles were likely done in private. His disciples were as ordinary as we are. They did not see the magnitude of the three-year risk they took as they left their nets and followed a man they hoped was a great rabbi, perhaps even, they may have thought, the coming Messiah.

Jesus used ordinary words that contained concepts that rocked the ages: the Beatitudes, the Lord's Prayer, and so much more. As He spoke, His disciples were scribbling down His words on small pieces of parchment. All these were very ordinary, yet they became part of our absolutely magnificent Bible, a book that changes hearts and the world.

Worship has always fit into this category for me. Even during the most brilliant and anointed worship times, there seems to be a lid in place, as if a vibrant, brilliant light is right around the corner. I am not able to go to the heights that I sense in my soul are possible, even when I worship alone. Worship is well described as "magnificent with a large dose of ordinary." We like or don't like a song, we sneeze and distract others around us, and children call us to their needs of the moment. The trappings of this world, our earthly minds, bodies, and sin hold us from what we are created for: wild, free, radical worship of our Creator and Lord. We can walk to the edge but are held back until heaven.

Our mundane, repetitive lives move in daily small steps. Just as Jesus's followers did not see the outcome of their life with Jesus, we now know they were living the magnificent ordinary. We also live in the magnificent and ordinary. We long for the largeness of heavenly worship or a fuller understanding of the results of a faithful life. We live in the ordinary, sensing we were created for the magnificent. The day will come when "our faith shall be sight." In the meantime, may we be recognized as those who have been with Jesus.

# The Song of Moses

In a desert land he found him,
in a barren and howling waste.
He shielded him and cared for him;
he guarded him as the apple of his eye,
like an eagle that stirs up its nest
and hovers over its young,
that spreads its wings to catch them
and carries them aloft.

—Deuteronomy 32:10–11

"In a desert land he found him, in a barren howling waste." That is the state of the soul without Christ—a barren, howling waste. Jesus wants satisfaction to be our position, not the hollowness of a leaky soul. The Lord is our source and our perfect security. The Lord encircles, shields, cares for, guards, and delights in us. We are His focal point. We quickly forget our position in Christ when taunted by the world of want, the idol of more, and the push for production.

We live with a daily decision: a choice to be satisfied or dissatisfied. If we look to the world for our source of satisfaction, we will live in a perpetual state of wanting. When we live with a wanting soul, we are looking for our source from a dry well.

Security and satisfaction are available to us in Christ. When we live filled and safe, we serve not from our need to be valued and appreciated but from the abundance of our satisfied, secure life in Christ. We live as one eager to share what is ours in abundance. Once filled to overflowing, we give and live.

We read in Psalm 90:14, "Satisfy us in the morning with your unfailing love that we may sing for joy and be glad all our days." That is our calling. It is not elusive and ethereal. It is actually what Christ can do when we set down our baggage and our ideas and take up His viewpoint. Let the Lord stir up your nest; let Him draw your attention to those items that keep you stuck in insecurity and dissatisfaction. His hand is faithful to hover over you and catch and carry you to places of security, satisfaction, and abundance.

# Through the Valley

## Psalm 23

"When I walk through the valley of the shadow of death." Notice that we are to walk through! It is certain that we will have those valleys in life. The death rate is 100 percent, and we all have that as our final earthly destiny. However, we are to walk through it, not hang out there, looking for something to do. We keep moving. The valley is not our home.

Sometimes people get stuck in the valley and forget to keep walking. God is a god on the move; He is new every morning. God walks with us, next to us, sometimes ahead to whistle us onward, sometimes behind us to give a little push.

Our home is the foothills of heaven, up from the valley. We walk until we have a perspective that we did not have in the valley. Valleys close in around us at times. We lose our view of life, God, others, and our path, but as we keep moving through the dark valley, one step at a time, we do arrive out of the valley.

There are times we want to be airlifted from the valley. Wanting to escape from pain is healthy, normal, natural, but not always possible. God does do miracles at times; they seem rare. It seems to me

He wants us to learn to walk out of the valley, so the next time we find ourselves or a friend there, we will have a route out and words of faith to encourage the sojourner.

When we get out of the valley by a miracle or by the daily path, I believe what God is after is our faith. I am reminded of the widow who was asking the judge for help in Luke 18:6–9. At the end of that parable, it does not seem to matter if she got what she wanted or not. The question is asked, "Will faith be found on earth?" That is the prize. That is God's goal. That is what our hosts of Hebrews 11 are watching for. Did faith arise?

# Trading Hopelessness for Truth

> May the God of hope fill you with all joy and peace as you trust in him, so that you may overflow with hope by the power of the Holy Spirit.
>
> —Romans 15:13

While on a recent bike trip in the Czech Republic, I was struck by the beauty of the country but also by the seeming passive hopelessness of its people. As a country, they have been free from communism since 1989, but as a people, they have yet to rejoice in their freedom. There seems to be continued fear of outside rule and vulnerability. They are a humble and caring people, but a shadow of despair remains. The beauty of the Austro-Hungarian Empire still exists in the land. The architecture of the country's castles to the city homes that line the street is intriguing, a cross between Victorian, Baroque, and Gothic style. The beautiful foundations and structures are in some places painted and kept up, but much of these remain in partial ruin.

The response to their freedom appears, at best, cautious and sometimes despairing. As we live our lives in Christ, we, at times, fall into a similar pattern. We are set free, fully redeemed, and have every reason to rejoice and respond with vigor and power, yet we forget or we fear or we let our freedom be swamped by the everyday cares of life. When we saw a restored building, its beauty was inspiring, detailed, and rich, filled with color and uniqueness. We need to take up our freedom and let Christ restore us to the same rich, colorful uniqueness. When hopelessness and fear rule our lives, it creates an ongoing pattern of lack of responsiveness to the finished work of Christ in all its hope, power, and beauty. We might feel safe living our lives without hope, but it is not what Christ died for.

The Lord has planned for us a life of hopefulness. The life He offers is a life with depth, richness, color, plans for the future, and power to impact the moment and the future. As we build our hope on the love of God for us, we don't have to rest on outside sources to create hope in our hearts. As we walk daily in the earth we are called to, listening and obeying what we understand to be God's call, then we can rest assured that our small faithful offering can be used by a magnificent and powerful god who causes us to reach beyond our smallness and into kingdom events.

# Unintentional Fruit

I planted the seed, Apollo watered it, but God has been making it grow.

—1 Corinthians 3:6

While traveling in Southern India, we came upon a huge and very old weeping ficus tree. The trunk was large, but what was amazing was that the branches hung down and sprouted into new smaller trees. This reproduction of new trees must have taken years of growing on the part of the mother tree. Walking inside this tree was like being in a small jungle microcosm.

We, as disciples of Jesus, are asked to bear fruit, and as I stood inside this tree covering, it seemed to have a likeness to a Christian's walk of life. There are

*The small mustard seed produces much new growth, moved by the will of God and the winds of the seasons.*

times when we seek to produce fruit, prayerfully focusing on sharing the love of Christ, saying a word in season, or setting out with ministry in mind. However, it seems more often that I hear of a time that I did not even know when someone was looking, listening, or noticing. Sometimes days—but more often years—later I hear that the Lord had used what was said or done to instill faith in a person's life.

Beyond our own lives, we see this as a kingdom principle. A seed is planted and grows in fertile soil, then it reaches out, and fruit is borne in a new location. This seems to be a way that God moves in His kingdom. What was once a barren field now has many new trees that will in turn reach out with their branches and produce new trees. Fruit is borne even when we are not noticing or intending it to take place. The tree reaches its branches down and reproduces itself many times over. The small mustard seed produces much new growth, moved by the will of God and the winds of the seasons.

God is in charge of this unintentional fruit; He manifests His kingdom in many ways—seen, intended, unseen, and seemingly incidental. All this adds to the glory of His majesty.

# Bitter Waters Made Sweet

> When they came to the oasis of Marah, the water was too bitter to drink. So they called the place Marah [which means "bitter"].
>
> —Exodus 15:23 NLT

Thirsty travelers arrived at the oasis they had seen from afar, eager for the water their parched throats needed. When they drew the quenching sip, salt is what they tasted. Nothing helpful there; in fact, it not only made them thirstier, it drew the small reserves of water from their bodies.

In Hebrew, salty water is called bitter and fresh water is called sweet, which emphasizes an even bigger stretch between the two tastes. Israel is a desert country, and the need for fresh water in a sea-surrounded desert country makes fresh water not only neutral but sweet.

We are also thirsty travelers at times, longing for the respite, pause, clarity, and purity that a sip of cool water can offer in a stained and struggling world. We have eternity in our longing hearts. We can see the oasis in moments of prayer, wonderful worship, and sweet fellowship, but the bitter, angst-ridden, fear-filled, intolerable world sets its foot on the threshold of our hearts daily.

Moses was instructed to throw a piece of wood into the salty water. That was a direct word from the Lord to save their lives and give them strength and hope for the next miles. He threw in a "piece of wood." In the Hebrew text, it says a "tree."

We know who hung on a tree to sweeten this dying, difficult world. The cross was foreshadowed as the piece of wood went into the bitter water. The water became sweet. It is a big stretch from salt to sweet, but that is the work of "the piece of wood" in our lives. The cross gives us ability and opens potential that can be found no other way. Not only is eternity sweetened from bitter to sweet but daily life is as well. That happens when we see Jesus show up in the middle of the situation and do the unexpected change of circumstances or hearts.

How, except for a miracle, could a piece of wood sweeten the water? How, save a cross on which a sacrificial Savior hung, could a piece of wood change lives and hearts and destiny? How, save a miracle, could we be met in our wrongs, the scary places, the overwhelming circumstances? We have had the bitter water turn sweet many times in our walk with Jesus. He will do it again today. Let's keep on trusting.

# Why Israel?

It is forever curious to me why God chose and continues to choose Israel as a people. We know He loves everyone, and His plan of salvation is available to all men. "He desires all to be saved and come to the knowledge of the truth" (1 Timothy 2:4). Yet He especially set aside a nation and a people to bear His name. Reams of paper have been written about this political hot potato. But we must acknowledge His word, which does focus around Israel as a people, nation, and geographic location. It is the heritage He chose for His own Son's birth, death, and resurrection! He mentions Israel about 1,800 times in His word and Jerusalem about 2,500 times. We need to pay attention.

We know that God wants us to share in His love for His land and His people, many of whom have yet to know Him as a personal saving Lord. He wants us to prefer Jerusalem, to pray for it, and to watch the working out of its salvation and His end-time plans in it. What a god to reveal His hand here on earth not once or twice but yet again! Israel is "a nation that was born in a day" (Isaiah 66:8) (United Nations resolution, May 14, 1948). God says of Israel, "I will bless those who bless you, and whoever curses you, I will curse" (Genesis 12:3). He also extols that Jerusalem should be our chief joy (Psalm 137:6). I must confess that is not my heart, but because the Lord wants it, that is my aim.

I was discussing all this with the Lord Jesus, asking Him to help me understand and to internalize what it all means. He spoke so clearly to my heart, in words I could comprehend.

He said, "Just as I pray for your child, will you pray for mine? Would you pray for the child that I love, that she would grow up to be mature, complete, and lacking in nothing? Would you pray for my prodigal son, who has not yet returned to me?"

In response, I pray:

> Lord, would You help us to love Israel and Jerusalem as You do? We want to feel Your heartbeat and comprehend what is important to You. Thank You for praying and loving our children. Help us say yes, we will pray for those whom You have placed as the apple of Your eye. We want to be like You and watch Your glory dawn. Amen.

Summer

# The Word of God Speaks

Lay your head between my shoulders.
Let the beloved of the Lord rest secure in him, for
he shields him all day long, and the one the Lord
loves rests between his shoulders.

—Deuteronomy 33:12

There were angry days even though I had committed myself to trusting God for what had happened.

One particular day, I was upset and talking with Him about all the negative fallout from my second husband's death. The Lord said to me, "Lay your head on My chest and pound as hard as you want. I can take all your anger, but... please don't walk away."

*"Lay your head on My chest and pound as hard as you want. I can take all your anger, but... please don't walk away."*

This touched my heart in such a deep way. The God of the universe was almost begging me to not walk away from Him. He loved me. I had the power (or was given) to break His heart. He invited my emotions, even my blame; He did not worry about those issues. He has broad shoulders and can handle all that, but He has a tender, vulnerable heart that He has given away to His children. It did not take a long time for me to rest my head on Him in my mind, before His love and care started to saturate me. What a god we serve!

# Riding the Carousel

Carousels are joyful and full of summer memories. They go 'round and 'round. The joy is in the beauty and the predictability, not the destination.

Lately, I have realized how often our thoughts can be like a carousel ride. We repeat the same patterns over and over, never arriving at a destination and sometimes not even enjoying the ride, though we board many times a day.

Thoughts that repeat themselves often are those worrying kind of thoughts—fears, guilt, shame, sin, regret, hopelessness, or difficult circumstances that never seem to change. We could call it the defeat-and-repeat carousel. We feel stuck and have all the reasons well rehearsed.

Before we can get off the defeat-and-repeat carousel, we need to realize that we have again bought a ticket!

The scripture in Isaiah 49:4 states this pattern well, "I have labored to no purpose; I have spent my strength in vain and for nothing." It goes on to say, "Yet what is due me is in the Lord's hand, and my reward is with my God."

I want to invite you to a new carousel. It does have a destination, and the ride is enjoyable. Your struggles will not be ignored; you can board with them and hand them to the attendant. He is the Lord Jesus. Our Savior is eager to be our helper and guide. He intercedes before the throne of God on our behalf day and night. We can trust the Lord for His care. Victory will soon follow what we have released to Him. He will help us turn the struggles into trust. "God Is Able" and "He Is Good" are the songs that play as you ride with Him.

# Road Map for Your Trip

Inscribe a map. Set up road signs and guideposts. Make a straight highway in the wilderness. Write a scroll of everlasting witness, a scroll of remembrance. Sounds like a trip is being planned!

There is a fabulous set of scriptures about planning our trips of life: Jeremiah 31:21, Ezekiel 21:19, Isaiah 62:10, Isaiah 57:12, Isaiah 40:3, Isaiah 35:8, Habakkuk 2:2, Isaiah 30:8, and Micah 3:16a.

Having plans is on the Lord's heart for each of us. Just as you plan your vacation, ask Him for His road map. Write down what you know. Let Him slowly fill in the details. Our role is to be patient as He reveals it bit by bit.

Our being rather than our doing is His focus. He wants us to walk by faith in reliance on Him. We start thinking of all the things we can do for God and places we can go; His focus is our heart. He wants to travel with us along the way. It is more about the companionship than the destination.

When my daughter and I were praying about living in Israel for a year, I heard the Lord say, "Walk in that direction." It was not a promise; it was an action of moving toward what I thought He was saying. Most of life is like that, moving toward our understanding with purpose but with openness and a sense of the critical importance of our waiting on Him. He will deliver!

Happy trails!

# One Eternal Thing

Summer flies by. We Minnesotans know how to squeeze every minute out of good weather. The pace gets fast and fun. Time with the Lord can easily fall to the back burner. However, fellowship is at a premium. We took a trip to visit some in-law relatives. As we sat and talked after a separation of about seven years, we realized that time had not put any distance between us. It is a miracle of the heart the Lord gave.

Those relationships that are timeless show up, ones that never fade, and are full of years and memories. In all the busyness of life, these relationships are what we take to heaven. Relationships with fellow believers are eternal. Of all the trappings of life we put time into, relationships are a piece of earth we will find in heaven. There is comfort that we are doing eternal work we will recognize when we get home.

The Trinity, a triune relationship, further identifies that the Lord is all about this relationship pie. Relationships are equally challenging and rewarding. In the measure of life, our relationships are perhaps the most valued piece of our existence. Our living relationship with the most high God, His beloved Son, and His Spirit is the source on which all human relationships build.

Love one another as I have loved you. (John 13:34)

Love, the currency of heaven and earth.

# On Our Knees, Pulling Weeds

He is like a well-watered plant in the sunshine,
spreading its shoots over the garden.

—Job 8:16

Gardening season is in full bloom. It is such a yearly miracle to see the transition of the last month. Weeds are also having their heyday. For all the beauty, there is also work. Gardens, if left to their own devices, will default to weeds or to the strongest plant, which will eventually take over the space once cleared for planting. Weeds will creep into tiny and large places, encroaching on once-sunny open spaces. As A. W. Tozer said, "This is the law of the wilderness." In Job 8:18–19, we read about this process of weeds taking over the once planted areas. "When it [the plant] is torn from its spot, that place disowns it… Surely its life withers away and from the soil other plants grow." Tending our gardens is serious business.

Our hearts and lives are not much different. Onetime experiences aren't enough to last us for a lifetime. Left to ourselves, we also default to "weeds" and things of the flesh. I recently listened to an oldies radio station while riding in the car. I may be more sensitive to music than most, but I have been singing what I call "junk" songs for weeks, even the first thing in the morning. How quickly I defaulted! Our obedience is like an umbrella. If we stay under it, we stay dry. It is God's protection for us. Whatever we put outside of His protection gets wet or worse. In Bruce Wilkinson's book *Secrets of the Vine*, he talks about how vines "trail down naturally" and that they need to be staked or tied to stronger vines to learn to trail upward. "Gardening" our hearts daily is the only way to keep the weeds of life from encroaching. Keeping our thoughts and actions in check and pulling those small weeds before they take over is our place as the gardeners of our lives.

In the Bible, there are two gardens, both places where the will was set. Eden was a place of will for Eve and Adam; they made their willful choice and set many "weeds" into motion. Jesus, in the garden of Gethsemane, also faced a position of the will. He chose the better way: "Not my will but thy will be done." Two gardens, two choices, both affected the world in profound ways.

And so we tend our gardens and our lives, on our knees to pull the weeds. May the gardens of our lives be bright with color, fullness, and health and be weed-free. Weed on!

# Garage Sale Jesus

Last weekend, we had a garage sale as a fundraiser for my daughter's mission trip. Many people had donated things for us to sell. Our garage was loaded; it felt damp and dank in comparison to the sunlight outside. There was junk we hoped would sell and a few treasures. As I prayed for His presence at the sale, I saw Him looking for treasures in darkness.

In that dingy, dark place, He found us among a lot of stuff and even junk that we had gathered into our lives and hearts. Perhaps we were broken or stained, at best unremarkable for kingdom purpose. He found us with a glint in His eye; He saw our destiny, a vision of a perfect place for us in His kingdom.

Jesus made His purchase and bought us back from hell. The previous owner: sin and Satan. He lifted us up, brought us into the light, and then came the payment. We were not a bargain purchase, but we were His treasure in darkness. His riches would be poured into our lives. He would remove the trappings, then clean and repair our hearts. And from the darkness, He would bring us into His marvelous light.

# Dormant Seeds

For behold, the winter is past, the rain is over and gone. The flowers have already appeared in the land; the time has arrived for pruning the vines, and the voice of the turtledove has been heard in our land.

—Song of Solomon 2:11–12 NASB

Seeds await their turn. They may be dormant for years, just waiting for the right conditions for their growth. They can exist in completely lifeless conditions depending on the seed and the fruit that will spring forth from it. It can be bone-dry for years on end, and suddenly, a flower will appear. As with rice, those seeds can be waiting for flooding to cause them to germinate. Perhaps they need long days, a warm or cold climate, a season of the year, drought or fire, as with the jack pine.

We are often well aware of our spiritual gifts, ones that flow freely from us, whether they be mercy, service, or cheerful giving. There may be seeds in your heart that have waited for a particular season of life or need in the body of Christ. They have been dormant, quietly waiting for the Savior's call. You may have had very little awareness or need for these seeds of fruit. These seeds were deposited at your birth and waited for their appointed time in your life to grow and mature into fruit. It may be a call for a season of your life or perhaps, like Grandma Moses who began painting at the ripe age of eighty-eight, it will continue for the rest of your life.

The Lord knows what events of our life will call forward the fruit He has appointed. We are never out of season with Him. As we dwell in Him and trust Him for the events of our life, we will be ready for the call. Using the lens of faith, the fruit will appear in the land at just the right time, not because we are so good and ready but because He is able to bring life from what looks barren, flowers in the desert, and purpose and strength at the right time in your life.

# Creating Blooms

It is I who created the blacksmith who fans the coals into flame and forges a weapon fit for its work. And it is I who has created the destroyer to work havoc.

—Isaiah 54:16

I am the Lord, there is no other. I form the light and create darkness; I bring prosperity and create disaster; I, the Lord, do all these things.

—Isaiah 45:7

This is a big stretch to see the Lord in these ways. We are very familiar with the verses that tell us that "no weapon forged against you will prevail," at times the Lord makes life difficult and later we see His glory in our growth.

*"There are some flowers that only bloom in the dryness of the desert."*

When we bring it into familiar, more comfortable surroundings, we can begin to understand. When my child was learning to walk, I remember counting fifty falls in the first few hours of learning. But I didn't go pick my child up. I watched with pleasure and compassion. Schools assign huge homework loads to even young children. Gardens get the rototiller and hoe before being planted. Why should our growth in Christ be any different?

I remember walking in the Judean Desert at the end of the summer season. It had not rained for six months. Not a drop. There was a beautiful flower blooming very close to the rocks it grew among. The guide casually said, "There are some flowers that only bloom in the dryness of the desert." Somehow, I felt like that flower. I had just lost my first husband, and life felt very dry and barren. Rocks and obstacles seemed dominant in my life. Yet the Spirit of God seemed to say to me that blooms would come from this barren time.

Have you ever felt like the Lord hired out a rototiller to till the garden of your life? Somehow, I believe that may be what has happened. We know from Exodus that God caused an evil spirit to attend to His work of freeing the children of Israel. I have come to believe that Satan is merely a pawn in the hand of the Almighty God. God is sovereign over Satan. Satan needs His permission to act (Job 1:6). This idea challenges me, yet when we look at the scripture, we see it to be true. God is after our growth and His glory. Often, that growth comes at a price, just like anything that is valuable. A garden cannot grow right and beautiful on a field that has never been prepared and worked. The enemy cannot touch our lives without God's permission. We can rest in that because we know God's heart is for our growth and His glory.

# Campsites

And they camped at…
(repeat 42 times)!

—Numbers 33:3–48

Summer is upon us; we are making plans for trips large and small. It is exciting to make plans. Sometimes our plans work well, and sometimes we are disappointed or even thwarted. Planning without foreknowledge is often challenging and requires trust in the all-seeing God, whether it's for camping trips or other areas of life.

There are other campsites in our lives, places we arrive at and linger, sometimes with forethought, sometimes by chance. Each of these campsites has names. We may recognize a place, or we may not know its name or the outcome of camping there. Some places are good and fruitful; others, not so. But we stumble on them and stay there for a while.

Perhaps you have camped with me at a few of these sites. Trusting God, I am happy to list first. His Grace and Peace, I also hope to find you there. However, some places are more shady and under the shadow. These places may be called Guilt and Shame, Disappointed with God, Rage and Bitterness, Arguing My Cause, Rejection, or Loneliness. These are places I usually camp alone and often before I realize where I stopped. Sometimes we are so familiar with the terrain that we forget that we can move or find a new camp.

The Israelites camped in the desert, in forty-two different places, before arriving at the promised land. They had many lessons to learn, including release from the victim/slave mentality, idol worship, and challenging God, so they could value obedience and learn to believe and trust in the words given to them by Moses.

As you make your summer plans, look around you. What campsites are you choosing? Are they old and familiar? Are they honoring God and His faithfulness?

It is my prayer that we recognize the campsites of our mind and spirit and that we would pack up and move to higher ground, carefully selecting our sites and camping in community with God's faithful servants.

# A Personal Psalm

You *have hemmed me* in, behind *and before.*

—Psalm 139:5

You have redeemed me from my way of life.
You, O Lord, have lifted me up from the raging sea.
You have hurled stones from heaven and set my life on fire. Your
    presence is overwhelming.
You are a terrifying and an untamable god.
Your saints, O Lord, have camped around me.
They would not let me escape and run for shelter.
They held me in and blocked the path of my youth.
Gracious Father, in Your loving kindness, You have corralled me. You
    watched me buck and thrash in the confines of Your love. You
    waited for my quietness.

You approached me gently, waiting for my glance and interest. You taught and trained me to fall in love with You, to seek Your hand and come under Your traces.

I became useful to You, at Your bidding, and by Your release and guidance. I no longer run in terror and spring to the side at the unknown.

In Your gentle, firm guiding hand, I walk through the valley of death, with the smell of death on both sides.

You prepare abundance for me in the presence of pain, attack, and hardship. You call me Your own and place Your mark on me.

In You I can rest, graze, and be satisfied.

# A Duet

The Lord is my Shepherd. I shall not want.
*Our Father who art in heaven, hallowed be Thy name.*

He makes me lie down in green pastures. He leads me beside still waters. He restores my soul.
*Thy kingdom come, Thy will be done, on earth as it is in heaven.*

Thou doest prepare a table for me in the presence of my enemies.
*Give us this day our daily bread*

Yea though I walk through the valley of the shadow of death,
*And forgive us our trespasses as we forgive those who trespass against us.*

I will fear no evil. Thy rod and thy staff, they comfort me.
*And lead us not into temptation but deliver us from evil.*

Surely, goodness and mercy will follow me
*For Thine is the kingdom and the power and the glory*

All the days of my life.
*Forever and ever. Amen.*

# A Cup of Cold Water

Whoever drinks the water I give him will never thirst.

—John 4:14

Gardening is such a pleasure. It can also be hot and heavy work. The garden beckons me out many times a day. When I am gardening, I sense closeness to God, His creation, joys, and toil to bring beauty out of dry ground.

One time, during a particularly painful period, a friend told me that she had been praying but had run out of words to pray. Instead she went to the gardens. I have done that many times since. It is easy to focus on the Lord in the garden, aware of His constant presence and listening ear.

One of the best moments during gardening is stopping for that cold drink of water! It refreshes the palate and the soul. I am aware that my dependence on water is like my dependence on the Lord. I cannot live without it. There needs to be a frequent connection, much like breathing.

Living in Christ is like this. We are ever mindful of His loving gaze upon us, His interest in what we are doing, saying, thinking. He is attentive to us. Our dependence on Him is also constant, as we breathe and drink, so we need Him. Moment by moment, He offers a cup of cold, living water. All we need to do is drink.

# Absolutely Sure

Pray for us: for we are persuaded that we have a
good conscience desiring to live honorably in all
things.

—Hebrews 13:18 ASV

I don't know about you, but this scripture is a stretch for me. I am
sure I desire to live this way, but I fall so often. Being sure about a
clear conscience is not in my ability. Sometimes I can hardly keep up,
and my soul overtakes my spirit.

We just returned from a trip to the Boundary Waters. It was
a delight to get away from the pressure and duties of everyday life.
One of our favorite places is a waterfall between two lakes that has
a "Jacuzzi" in the middle of the falls. It is so refreshing to sit under
the falls and let it splash all over. It is a deep cleansing in the midst of
camping dirt and outdoor life.

The surety of our clean conscience is based on faith and faith
alone. Not works! The all-sufficient blood of Christ cleanses us
moment by moment. Jesus does not offer us a trickle of forgiveness;
He gives us a waterfall of mercy and cleansing, far more than we will
ever need in our entire lifetime.

Using our own standards of measure, seeking to establish our
own righteousness, the pure and complete work of the cross is not
enough. We need to learn to use the Lord's standards and accept the
righteousness He offers to us freely.

Based on the evidence of the perfect and continual work of the
cross, "we are sure that we have a clear conscience" and that even our
desires can be cleansed "to live honorably in every way." By faith, we
can "calleth the things that are not as though they were" (Romans
4:17b). The mystery of the faith that we participate in is profound,
yet by the help of the Holy Spirit, we not only understand this but
also live it.

# Psalm of Rest

For God gives rest to his loved ones.

—Psalm 127:2 NLT

A dark dawn beckons the day,
The horizon pressing on the sea.
Rain drove down the night.
In the midst, peace fills the spaces.
Joy in the presence of the Creator,
The sun strengthens its rays
And presses glitter on the water.
The darkness remains;
The light glories in strength.
The hard labors of the era retreat,
Complete not to call again.
A finished task does not report for duty.
Rest.

Come to me all you who are weary and burdened,
and I will give you rest. (Matthew 11:28)

I will refresh the weary and satisfy the faint.
(Jeremiah 31:25 NIV)

For I have given rest to the weary and joy to the
sorrowing. (Jeremiah 31:25 NLT)

He gives strength to the weary and increases the
power of the weak. (Isaiah 40:29 NIV)

# Ambiguity

For now we see through a glass, darkly; but then
face to face: now I know in part; but then shall I
know even as also I am known.

—1 Corinthians 13:12

Waiting in the unknown places is especially difficult. Many parts
of our Christian life are dear. We know what sin is and what it is
not. The Holy Spirit can be very dear with us at times when obedience is being asked. There are other times when heaven seems silent.
This silence is at times frightening. Life calls us for a multitude of
decisions a day. We walk, decide, and trust as we carry on with our
responsibilities. There are other times when we just don't know and
the needed answer is not forthcoming. This engages a new level of
faith.

Trusting the Lord in ambiguity, helplessness, fatigue, confusion, perceived judgments, delayed timing, and failure draws us to
a deeper reliance on Jesus. Often, the Lord will deliver us from this
confusion. There are other times He may simply want to sit with us
in our state of not knowing. And so we wait with perhaps a sense of
failure and powerlessness. Allowing Jesus to be with us without fixing
what to us seems uncomfortable is a different kind of trust.

One morning, while sitting with the Lord, this sense of vague
waiting was prevalent. I often like to build a fire on the cool mornings. I had done so but made a poor attempt at a fire. It smoldered
for about thirty minutes. I was noncommittal about restructuring
the wood so the fire would catch. Suddenly, the fire burst into flame,
even burning, picture-perfect! The smoldering was done, the wood
was heated, and the time for the fire had come. It seemed that the
Lord had given me a picture of ambiguity. The unknown becomes
known just when all the needed pieces are present and the time has
arrived. The answer burst into being.

# Belonging

Ephesians 1:3–15

The first chapter of Ephesians tells us that we are adopted, blessed, chosen, forgiven, accepted, and redeemed. I like to remember those in an acronym: the ABCs will take you FAR.

Remembering who we are in Christ does not come naturally. We have an automatic default switch that quickly takes us to enemy camp thinking. We hear that we are different, excluded, unlucky, and unable to achieve.

There is good news. Our identity and our forgiveness were not the only things His blood bought for us. Our membership in the body of His believers is also the result of the cross. You are in! Your dues are paid!

In the battle with the Amalekites, half of David's army stayed behind due to exhaustion. When the battle was won and the plunder was brought into camp, David declared an ordinance, "All will share alike." So it is with us. We share in the plunder of the precious blood of Jesus; we belong to the camp of God.

Our membership in this community is not because of who we are but because of *whose* we are. Our natural inclinations want to earn our way into things. God's way is grace and grace alone. There is a world of caring and commitment of authentic believers in the fellowship of Christ. You already belong.

Our acceptance is not based on good behavior but on the fact that we are in Christ. We cannot earn our forgiveness, nor can we earn our acceptance. Knowing this opens the door for us to receive in full the love that the body of Christ shows to us. If you find yourself in the place of being alone or lonely or in need of help, remember, you are already a member of this community and have full access of the love of Christ being offered to you in real, life-giving terms.

# Book Bindings

Book bindings have short memories. While reading the other day, I dropped my book; it fell down and shut. I knew that if I quickly pick the book up, the binding would "remember" the place where I had been reading. I quickly retrieved it knowing that seconds mattered in this short cycle.

Sure enough, the book opened to the previous place. However, this little process caught my attention. I want my relationship with Jesus to be like that.

As life's circumstances demand and pull, I want to keep my time with Jesus ever present. If I drop my focus, I want to quickly reach back to Him and pick up where I was. I want my relationship to be reaching back to Him no matter what circumstances. Each time I reach back, the relationship deepens. Hallelujah! Our quickly reaching back to Jesus is fruitful; we move forward and read deeper into the character of God.

I want to return many times in a day to Him, like to a frequently used, well-loved book. I want the pages of Jesus to fall open in my life, speaking the ancient—and at the same time fresh—word into my life, relationships, and circumstances. His Word is alive on the page, but seeking is the part we enact. Jesus is the best "book" ever written, and we have the choice to leave it quietly on our lap or bring it into the events of our lives and let it ride the waves and valleys with us. Our circumstances do not get the privilege of giving God His identity. The great I Am stands from before eternity, faithful, true, strong, and victorious!

# But During the Night

Acts 5:19a

The scripture goes on to read, "An angel of the Lord opened the doors of the jail and bought them out" (Acts 5:19).

When we think of times of darkness, unknowing, or difficulty, we sometimes forget how active the refining fire of God's love is during these times. The very things that may have kept us in jail to sin and old habits may be offered deliverance by the darkness. Habits of our nature that fight against change and growth are challenged, and we can choose to call out to the Lord. As we encounter the help of the Lord, joy may be curiously close at hand.

*The angel of the Lord opens doors for us as we trust in Jesus. What was not possible to our old man becomes possible.*

Suddenly, what seemed to be lacking becomes abundant because we are centered on our need for Jesus. Earthly thoughts and shackles no longer serve us in this place of darkness; we walk into freedom. God, in the darkness, is richly present, and we find that we can rejoice beyond what these earthly eyes can see.

The angel of the Lord opens doors for us as we trust in Jesus. What was not possible to our old man becomes possible. I have seen this lived out. There are several in our congregation right now who are walking through their own darkness. Perhaps it is illness or other difficulties. I am so amazed when I see in these saints among us a radiance and peace that does not belong to this world. What a privilege to see Christ in them, their hope of Glory (and ours). May we remember that "during the night," God continues refining His work for our good and His glory!

# Chariots of Fire

"Don't be afraid," the prophet answered, "Those who are with us are more than those who are with them."

Elisha prayed, "Oh Lord, open his eyes so he may see." Then the LORD opened the servant's eyes and he looked and saw the hills full of horses and chariots of fire all around Elisha.

—2 Kings 6:16–17 NIV

As stated in the above scripture, "Greater are those who are with us than those who are against us." What a great way to view the world! And the wonderful part is that it is true. If we have our spiritual eyes open, we can see this fact. So often we forget this and act as if we are not overcomers on a moment-by-moment basis.

The other day, I was praying this scripture for a needed situation. On those hills surrounding Elisha were horses and chariots. I had a sense that I was part of the Lord's army in this situation. It seemed the chariots were the prayers that were being offered. I inadvertently said to the Lord, "I don't feel much like a flaming chariot but more like the horse."

From on high, my Father seemed to speak, "Yes, you are like the horse, earthbound, hardworking, and not aware of the cargo you may be pulling, but you bring the power of prayer to the situation. It is in the arrival of prayers that release chariots of fire from on high to bring the power of God into the situation."

Understanding prayer is a lifelong process. But God has entrusted to us His chariots of fire to bring into the situations we pray about. He arrives behind the horses. He chooses to engage us in the process of redemption of the world. I am glad He gives us what we can accomplish, pray, and speak out. Then behind our prayers, He arrives with chariots of fire!

Greater is he who is in us than he who is in the world. (1 John 4:4)

# Color Guard

My brother, fellow worker and fellow soldier.

—Philippians 2:25

Among some of the best moments of the day at camp is the flag-raising ceremony. It offers a structure to start off the day, brings the camp together, and prepares us for the sweetness of "morning watch."

The color guards do their job with such reverence for the flag and for our country. They take their job very seriously, do it well, practice, and usually have something that makes it unique to their group.

I always felt the respect and honor they offered was more than just for the flag but also to do a job well unto the Lord.

We all are color guards in the kingdom of God. We all seek to bring glory, reverence, and honor to our King. We all offer something unique and special that only we can offer to Him. There is only one of us. Without one of the guards in the morning formation, there would be a hole, a place to be filled by that one individual.

As we recall the morning flag raising, let us be mindful that daily we are flag raisers for the kingdom of God. Our contribution matters. Our place is secure; our hearts give glory to Him as we do well at the job that He has called us to in this season of our life.

# Come with Me

Come with me, by yourselves,
To a quiet place and get some rest.
(Mark 6:31)

He who *dwells*
In the shelter of the Most High
Will *rest* in the shadow of the Almighty.
(Psalm 91:1)

# Empty Jars and Oil

## 2 Kings 4

Being a widow, stories in the Bible about widows catch my attention. I have heard this story many times and always focused on the number of jars she was to collect. It is a reminder to ask big of a big god. That remains important to this story as well as the way God abundantly provides for our needs.

Recently, when I came across this scripture, the empty jars stood out. There are so many empty jars in my life around the loss of my second husband. I started to list them out; there were names of people who are no longer in my life because of his death, people I loved and deeply cared about. Other things like income, being a couple, lost property, the honor in our society of being a family, vacations, and decisions are now made alone. The list went on and on. I was painfully aware of the empty jars around my life.

I believe that I am not alone in having empty jars in my life. The labels on my jars may be very different from yours, but there may also be places of emptiness in your heart and life that need the filling of the Lord. Emptiness is something that creeps into even a very full life.

As I thought about the empty jars in my life, I began to label them with names or circumstances. Then I asked the Lord to fill them with His oil. As the process was prayerfully started, the first two jars filled easily and quickly.

Then I came to the third one and got stuck. I was aware that there was debris in the jar. I had to take some time to take out the junk. Anger, pain, and humiliation were in the pot. (It reminded me of the nearby story of bitterness in the pot [2 Kings 4:38]). The third pot may fill more slowly, but at least it is ready to receive the oil from the Lord. He will be faithful to lead me through this process. He is the one who fills our emptiness; He is not afraid of our needs but desires for us to be "satisfied…with His unfailing love that we may sing for joy and be glad all our days" (Psalm 90:15).

# Even Still

But God demonstrates his own love for us in this:
While we were still sinners, Christ died for us.

—Romans 5:8 NIV

As humans, most of us live with the fear of somehow being found out to be a fraud, a liar, inept, or not the person whom others think us to be. Being exposed for who we are not is a constant fear for all human hearts. It began in the garden with the fig leaf.

There may have been a small incident when we were not our best selves; Satan wants us to live there. Our human nature shrinks down, and often, we do live there, in fear, hurt, or anger.

The *good news truth* is that when we are before God, all is known that can be known about our sinfulness, mistakes, and weaknesses, *and* He still passionately loves us. He does not tolerate sin, but the provision of Jesus is enough that pardon always wins when the heart is sincere. Even still, He loves us. He always looks at us with warmth and love in His heart. Have you ever had a boss or coworker who seemed to always have a critical bent toward you and most likely others as well? Nothing satisfied this person; nothing was enough to make that critical eye happy, relaxed, or acceptant. Did you do your best for him? Or was it the pressure of shame that made you try harder and harder and still feel inadequate? Sometimes we let the image of God be held by sinful man. Let's free ourselves and be open to the truth, realizing that we are always satisfying to God. When we fail, He still loves.

The Lord uses love daily to motivate. Love calls us upward, to be better than we are. He never uses shame as a motivator. We may have grown up in homes where discipline was applied with shame and pressure; that is not at all unusual. That is not the way of the kingdom, and sometimes we need a reboot to realize that is not how the Lord motivates. Weeding out those tentacles in our lives takes thoughtful prayer; not reusing them in our lives is another need for thoughtfulness. Enter Holy Spirit! We have help. He accelerates the process of growth. Our cooperation is needed, but we need not despair or be discouraged. We can rise into all of what Christ has for us; His victory is complete in us!

We are fully known and fully loved—the miracle of the cross!

# Fleas, a Fragrant Sacrifice

> So then, those who suffer according to God's will should commit themselves to their Faithful Creator and continue to do well.
>
> —1 Peter 4:19

Moving to a foreign country, we sometimes encounter foreign pests. We have lived with flea infestation on and off for a year. I have prayed Psalm 91:6 many times. Yet the "pestilence that stalks in darkness" remains. Even in things as small as fleas, God is sovereign. He is completely able to remove those fleas immediately. However, He has not.

Elisabeth Elliot wrote in her book *The Path of Loneliness* that we have two paths for worldly suffering. We can "accept it as God's wise and loving choice for our blessing or resent it as proof of His indifference, carelessness, or weakness." We know that wisdom and love are prime characteristics of the Almighty; therefore, the first choice is the only truthful choice.

Somehow, this reminded me of trying on clothes in a dressing room. Finding something you like and then trying it on and seeing the result does not always match. Choosing to accept the fleas as God's love and wise choice for our blessing did not quite fit my human viewpoint, but it does match the character of God. Likewise, sometimes our friends' choice of an outfit is the one that works out best.

The fragrance of the sacrifice tends to smell like bug spray, but I have chosen *to lift up my suffering to Jesus*. All the cleaning and washing involved in this, the itchy bug bites, the embarrassment of having all these spots are a gift of faith and trust in His wisdom. He has seen all this. I cannot see value in this, but I can see that it gives me an

opportunity to love and trust Him even when I do not understand. I
believe that gift is valuable to my friend and savior, Jesus.
May His presence be real in your trials.

# God's Priorities No
# Matter How It Rolls

All things are permissible but not all things are
profitable.

—1 Corinthians 10:23

Here is the final word. It does not matter which way the roll spins!

It is so easy in life to get caught up in things that really do not
matter. We even get quite attached to those items and want them no
other way. The toilet paper roll is a funny but very true example of
this. We need to learn to set our priorities on what is important to
God even in everyday issues, like which way the roll spins!

We can use this as an opportunity to practice putting our flesh
under the Spirit and very intentionally choosing to let these things
go, even letting them war against our preferences. This offers us a
way to grow up in all things and learn to align ourselves only with
what is important in the kingdom.

Try putting the roll the "other" way and let every visit to the WC
remind you that you are setting your mind on the priorities of God,
not on your own preferences that have no eternal consequence. Make
it a declaration of aligning with the priorities or nonpriorities of God.

Perhaps there is another issue in your life to which you have
attached your opinion or happiness, which might be something that
will never bring you the fulfillment for which you hope. It could be
a bigger issue, something you cannot change but wish you could.
How can allowing God's ways, timing, or priorities take over? In
your human nature, it may even feel like opposition, that internal
war against the soul.

Laying down what we cannot control sometimes requires prying our fingers off that issue one at a time. It is hard on the flesh but good for the spirit and produces eternal qualities of peace and freedom.

Hard times come, and they are good teachers of what is really important. We can practice it now, letting go of what does not matter. We can follow in Paul's footsteps and say:

> I have learned to be content in all circumstances,
> I have learned the secret of being content in any
> and every situation. (Philippians 4:11–12)

No matter which way it rolls!

# Guarding your Heart

The Lord gives many examples of well-guarded cities in the Old Testament. The way to attack a city in biblical times was to breach the wall. A city was unsafe if it did not have walls and gates with bars. People lived within that protection. When the enemy wanted to attack, they would first try to break through the walls at the weak points; if that did not work, they would build a siege ramp. A siege ramp took days or even months to build. It was a slow, deliberate work with the residents inside fending off what seemed to be inevitable—a painful, slow prospect of defeat.

It is the Lord's heart to keep His children safe. Our hearts are His and need tending and building up to remain safe in Him. The world seems to want to break down the bonds of safety, and we often *The siege ramp was made of words, offers, and intimidation. Every tactic used in this book is as relevant for today as it was in biblical times.* inadvertently play a part in our lack of security and peace in Christ.

The book of Nehemiah offers great clarity into how the enemy sought to discourage the Israelites and inhibit the protection they were trying to restore after their return from Babylon. The siege ramp was made of words, offers, and intimidation. Every tactic used in this book is as relevant for today as it was in biblical times. The use of sarcasm and ridicule began the tumult of verbal obstacles; questioning of their motives and ability was next. Creating doubt and discouragement followed, with reminders of their vulnerability, even threats of possible death. The people kept building and holding fast in their confidence and efforts. The enemy came with a new tactic. They engaged other Jews to oppose, embedding the opposition in the group. An illusion of openness and religiosity was followed by an invitation to meet at the temple, each time upping the ante, and then anger and insult began again.

Discouragement was the central focus of Nehemiah's mockers. Similar tactics are also used by the enemy today. If hope is attacked, courage can be undermined and the enemy would have a stronghold. However, the people worked together; they held a weapon in one hand and their tools in the other hand. They worked shoulder to shoulder, and each had a skill and duty to perform. They knew their goal, and it was for their community to be safe and to thrive.

We read in Nehemiah 12 that at the dedication of the wall of Jerusalem, people were gathered to celebrate joyfully, with songs, music, harps, and cymbals. It goes on to say in 12:43, "And on that day they offered great sacrifices, rejoicing because God had given them great joy. The women and children also rejoiced. The sound of rejoicing in Jerusalem could be heard far away."

God wants that same protection and rejoicing in our hearts.

# And When He Was Betrayed... He Took Bread

1 Corinthians 11:23 (paraphrased)

We had communion on Sunday. Communion is so precious as part of our Christian communities. This Sunday, I came to church feeling stung about a situation that came up right before we left for church. Sounds familiar?

It took a while for me to settle into Jesus and be ready for worship and communion. The sermon was on being offended. I needed the Lord to speak to my heart.

The convocation for communion was read. These scriptures have glided over me so many times. Suddenly, they were exquisitely beautiful, heart-moving; tears welled in my eyes. "And when He was betrayed, He took bread."

That is what we can do! Life will betray us, but we have a most beautiful and sure solution—take the bread of life into your very heart. Let Him cause His ways to grow and fill your heart. Let Him knead the ingredients together until it is soft and supple. Jesus, born in the town of Bethlehem (house of bread), offers us living words to change and shape our very insides.

Our mind is the gateway to our heart, soul, and spirit. Giving Jesus free access by keeping the gateway open is essential. If we hold anger or bitterness for wrongs done to us, we keep the gate closed to the free work of the Holy Spirit. Our thought patterns over time affect our attitudes, our friendships, our coping skills, our health, and our personalities. We become a product of what we have focused on.

When those difficult things come, I do not want them to dismantle my spirit and reside there. I want to take bread and eat of Jesus. Without having to figure everything out, we can just open the door to the bread of life and let His life reign in us. An open door is all He asks.

What a wonderful god we serve!

# Here's to Hopin'

And hope does not disappoint, because...

—Romans 5:5

Hope that does not disappoint is one of life's greatest treasures. Some days, disappointment seems like a dog nipping at our heels. We could start living if we could just get past that most recent disappointment. So what is the secret to having a hope that doesn't disappoint?

The partner to hope is trust. Not a trust that we will get our own way but trusting utterly in the only trustable One. Then we can have hope. We can hope in the love of God! That hope will never disappoint. That hope is not dependent on our circumstances, needs, or whims. That hope will always be realized.

Having eternity in our hearts causes us to compare this world to the one where our citizenship has been bought—heaven. As babies in the womb, our first introduction to this world was a perfect one—warm, safe, fed, free, aware of people around us, no needs. We had an innate awareness of perfection. The world does not offer us that perfection, but eternity was born in our heart (Ecclesiastes 3:11). That same perfection is there for us in Christ as we walk though this world, and that perfection waits for us at the end of our final journey when we reach our heavenly home.

Praise be to God for His wonderful gifts to us!

# HSGPS

I will instruct you and teach you the way you should go.

—Psalm 32:8

Just yesterday, I was aware of the way the Lord leads us through the power of His Holy Spirit (HS). We went to a restaurant that I had not been to in a few years. It was in an area with which I am only vaguely familiar. I set out sensing I would know how to get there. As we got closer, I sensed that God would assist this little project.

I have found in my life that the Holy Spirit will lead me if I listen closely. (I would have called for directions if I had remembered the name of the restaurant.) So we began our trip. The sense of direction was clear; I had a few directional pictures in my mind (i.e., a bridge), but I sensed the Lord would guide each needed step of the way. In the end, we drove straight to the restaurant and found a parking place right in front of it! As we were leaving, I sensed a nudge to return a different way; I took a left turn and went straight on the entrance ramp to the freeway we wanted. It was as if the Holy Spirit just wanted to confirm His power and presence in His ability to lead in very specific and understandable ways.

Many times in Israel, this same thing happened. We would set out to go to a place we had heard about. Knowing the general direction and basic description, I would sense the nudge. "Turn here, wait, change lanes, turn off the main road," etc. It was fun and a welcome challenge to be so dependent on listening and trusting those very gentle and often somewhat vague nudges. It also built confidence that I could actually hear Him. Learning to listen in the small and less important ways offers me hope that in the big and crucial things, I can also hear. It has also taught me that often we do not know if we have heard Him or not, but when we obey "the nudge" that may or may not seem right at the moment, we can find ourselves in the midst of God's will.

I am reminded of a woman of God, whose name I cannot remember, who accepted Christ late in her life and grew very rapidly in understanding. When she was asked what was the secret to her rapid growth, she replied, "Mind the checks"—a lifesaving, growth-producing encouragement for all of us.

# In the Whittler's Hand

Olive wood is a beautifully rich, multifaceted wood. The color of the wood varies even within a single branch. The grain may be wide or narrow, dark or light. In the hands of a skilled whittler, a knot, deep below the surface, can emerge in the perfect place. A carving that began quite ordinary suddenly bursts into artistry, wonder, and emotion. The entire piece changed with the shift of focus. The emphasis spoke life into the piece.

Have you ever felt whittled by life? Duties and calls randomly chipping off any energy or dreams that may have once been there? One morning, I could just about see the pile of wood chips around my feet. Life seemed to be whittling at my best efforts and hope.

By God's grace, my focus shifted. I remembered the beautiful olive wood shop near our home in Migdal, Israel. I am aware that we are of the olive wood branch (Romans 11:17–18), that Jesus is the holy root (Revelation 22:19). We are the pieces in the hand of the Master.

It became clear that our heavenly whittler was at work. He and only He can see the knots below the surface of the wood. He knows the life events that will bring beauty and focus from a common piece of wood. What a glorious thing it is to fall into the hands of the living God and to watch Him bring beauty from what would have been ashes (2 Samuel 24:14 and Isaiah 61:3).

# Invited

Come with me by yourselves to a *quiet place* and get some *rest*.

—Mark 6:31

The Lord is aware of our need to be called into rest and quietness. Our world calls us away from that. Busy lives that have great purpose seem to have such a strong pull of value in this everyday world. It is only by a very deliberate act that we can stop and hear the very personal invitation to come by ourselves to a quiet place. We rest so poorly. We use rest as a time to catch up, thinking, *When I get this done, then I can rest.* The enemy knows that the next thing will always call, so he is quick to remind us what the next thing is that will supposedly bring us rest once accomplished. Resting is a discipline of the soul. Quieting our hearts, minds, and activity is a challenge to our spirits. It is a learned skill.

Be *still* and *know* that I am God! (Psalm 46:10)

Being still before the Lord is another unnatural call. To stop moving for a time, to sit in attentiveness to His personhood and presence is a gift to Him and also to us. Even doing this for five minutes deeply rests the heart and mind. He knows how to give us peace, but we need to change what we are doing at times to really engage that stillness. We read in Zechariah 2:13, "Be *still before* the *LORD*, all mankind, because he has roused himself from his holy dwelling." When we are still before Him, we can also begin to see His movement. We can anticipate that He will be there to meet us, to direct our attention to something on His heart.

He who *dwells* in the shelter of the Most High will *abide* in the shadow of the Almighty. (Psalm 91:1)

Being able to take that stillness and rest with us seems to be what our hearts desire. Sometimes we just want the stillness without actually making any changes to our pattern or schedule. To dwell, we have to stay in the quiet, restful place in our hearts and stay under the shelter and shadow of the Almighty. We stay under the covering of Jesus, a place to dwell in stillness and a place to walk and live. As we practice the disciplined, prioritized rest, we do not just expect the tent of God to follow us. Often, we run from task to task and errand to errand, using busyness to fill the void in our hearts created by God for His infilling. Dwelling is waiting for that fullness to come in. Sometimes it takes a lot of time, especially if we arrive empty. Hannah Whitall Smith wrote in the book *A Christian's Secret to a Happy Life* that she would wait until she was happy in Him before she would leave her devotional time. Daily waiting brings us to that place of restful dwelling. There are times when we need to retreat, to dwell, and to rest in a quiet place. I encourage each of us to think about a way/place that we can use for a retreat in Him.

# Just a Few More!

One day I was wondering out loud to the Lord when He would return to earth. At times, the world can feel so despairing and full of trouble. He tarries so long from my earthly perspective. Many nations have come and gone since Jesus promised His return.

As I was asking this question, it seemed the Lord spoke with a longing heart, "Just a few more in, just a few more." The Father's heart desires the salvation of all—a heart that counts each person as valued, wanted, and loved very much. I could sense such a strong longing, almost begging in His heart for "Just a few more in, just a few more." A heart that was unsatisfied, he wanted more in heaven with Him. Once the doors of earth close, the number also closes. He wants His heaven full.

In Matthew 22, Jesus spoke to them in a parable, saying, "The kingdom of heaven is like a king who prepared a wedding banquet for his son. He sent his servants to those who had been invited to the banquet to tell them to come, but they refused to come. Then he sent some more servants and said, 'Tell those who have been invited that

I have prepared my dinner: My oxen and fattened cattle have been butchered, and everything is ready. Come to the wedding banquet.'"

Our Father watches all the painful events of history with the constant thought that if He waits a little longer, there will be more people in heaven with Him. The Lord can take the sadness and tragedies of the world because of the depth of the value He places on "just a few more" into His kingdom, a few more that may enjoy eternity with the King.

It is a sobering thought stated in John 4:2, "Whoever believes in the Son has eternal life, but whoever rejects the Son will not see life." So we wait; we tarry with the Lord, each of us joining the Father's heart to put up with the difficulties of the world, if only all those we love would come to Jesus. The depth of love outweighs the difficulty of waiting. May the Lord help us to have hearts like our Father's.

# Leaning In

> I will celebrate before the Lord; I will become more undignified than this, and I will be humiliated in my own eyes.
>
> —2 Samuel 6:21–22

This was King David's response to his wife who had just publicly humiliated him through sarcasm and insult. Her doing so was on the heels of his own public humiliation in moving the ark in the wrong way that resulted in the death of Uzzah. Despite public, very embarrassing events, David did not hold back his joy in the Lord. In his response to his wife, he *leaned into* the insult and said he would become more undignified than this and in fact be humiliated in his own eyes. What a brave and unwavering response. *Sin or insult could not overcome his zeal to love and worship the Lord.*

This reminds me of another story I recently read. A faithful believer lay dying of cancer in Hong Kong. He eagerly sought to praise the Lord on his deathbed with whoever would come to visit. When asked about this, his reply was, "I will praise the Father for eternity, but I only have a short time to praise him in the midst of pain. So I want to take every opportunity to do that." This is a man who *leaned in.*

A third example came my way in a book I was reading. The speaker was responding to a potential insult but offered an answer to satisfy, even compliment, in the exact areas of the insult. Most of the time, I ignore the rudeness, but this person *leaned in.* The response offered to the person was a sincere compliment in the area of the potential insult.

Anxiety usually is an avoidant reaction, but perhaps leaning in offers us a way to respond with our emotions intact and thus affect our world in a kingdom style as we lean onto the difficulty, insult, or pain and lean on the strength in Jesus.

# Learning Our Vocab Words

In order that Satan might not outwit us. For we are not unaware of his schemes.

—2 Corinthians 2:11

The enemy likes to *pressure* me so that I feel *anxious*, like no matter how hard I try, it is *never enough.* He indicates that *if I was more* disciplined, smart, or organized, it would have all been done much *sooner.* Then he reminds me that I am *less able than others, guilty, and generally not worth much.* How is that for a vocab list?

- Pressured
- Anxious
- Not good enough
- Undisciplined
- Dumb
- Disorganized

- Late
- Guilty
- A failure
- Worthless

Unfortunately, there are probably more you can add. However, we only need to identify these lies so we can recognize them and move on.

The enemy's themes are repetitive, however cunning he may be at applying them. We do not want to be ignorant of the schemes of the enemy.

The truth of who we are in Christ is the list we need to overlay in every area of our life. We do not want any loopholes. The immeasurable gift of God is that He sees us through the lens of Jesus Christ. He loves us at all times, every time, at every turn, even if it is less than our best. When we give our all to Jesus, He takes it, including all the sin and pain.

Love calls us upward.

# Meaningful Beauty

To give unto them beauty for ashes...

—Isaiah 61:3 KJV

We are certainly made in His image when it comes to a love for beauty. The world around us is filled with beauty, color, change, and vibrancy. They are the brush strokes of a creative, inventive, beauty-seeking Savior. There are many days when I find my soul seeking beauty, something that magnifies the Lord in what I see. Beauty makes me feel restful, loved, creative, energized. My heart longs for beauty; beauty is restful to the mind, heart, and spirit.

When I visited a home of a believer in Jerusalem, I found a treasure trove of meaningful beauty. This home was located near the windmill on the west side of the Old City walls, near the Jaffa

Gate. The owner of the home had created the same in his dwelling. Everywhere you looked, you could see a portion of the life of Christ, the temple, and the history of the Jewish people represented in the home's design. It was thoughtful, purposeful, and intriguing. Every movement of the eye caught something of the story of Christ. I found my mind seeking the meaning of what was being expressed through the vignettes around me. It was in everything, from wall color, to dishes, to lighting, to artifacts, to bowls, and to candles. The home caught the intrigue and meaning of beauty right from the Lord's heart.

Being created to worship the Lord, we often have longings the world cannot fulfill. The desire for meaningful beauty may be one of those desires. In Psalm 27:4 KJV, it says, "To behold the beauty of the LORD, and to inquire in his temple." Beholding the beauty of the Lord is the ultimate in *meaningful beauty*. When sought, it fulfills the heart to the deepest measure that can be found on earth.

# Measuring Up

When they compare themselves with themselves,
they are not wise.

—2 Corinthians 10:12

So often the fear of inadequacy plays into our days. Inadequate feelings tell us what we offer is not enough for the job at hand. The wonderful season we have just enjoyed of Holy Week and the resurrection celebration can bring loved ones that need God's touch to the forefront. We may have prayed and shared God's love for years, and still our message is unheard and their salvation waits. That the task is unaccomplished, we use this as evidence for our claim of inadequacy.

As these thoughts mulled in my mind before the Lord, a small section of a fairy tale replayed. As Goldilocks sat in the chair that fit her, we are told, "It was just right." I was reminded that, like Goldilocks, my appointments are "just right" for my ability. A loving

God, like a loving parent, would not assign us a job we could not accomplish.

When the Lord measures us, He says, "That child of mine is just right for the job," and we are hired. He in you and you in Him make an Almighty "I can!" We can do what He has planned even if we cannot see the finish line. The big picture is accomplished through daily obedience. Trying harder does not accomplish the task; resting and trusting does.

There is a lovely saying that states, "Nature never hurries, and yet everything is done right on time." As we look around us at the beautiful spring blooming, we see things that are not yet perfect but are wrapped up in the delight of new life and growth. God never hurries as He forms us into His image, and yet everything is done right on time. We are His perfect selection for the jobs He has given us.

# Mining for Gold

### Allowing His Forgiveness into Our Depths

God is awesome and powerful; He reigns on high and is worthy of fear, but He is kind. He loves you; He watches you with kindness in His eyes. He seeks to draw you deeper in love with Him because then He can fill the new depth with more of His love.

God wants us to be free, not condemned. When we let go of our old ways, we open the door for more of God. We deepen the space for Christ to fill. In underground mining, there is often a small cavern. When the rock is taken out, the cavern becomes larger, and there is room for air. And eventually, water will fill those places. Much like our hearts, as we open up to Jesus, He creates depth and space for His living water. Sin often fills in the places meant for God. When we clean our spiritual house, we deepen our place for God.

God wants to cleanse you from sin. In the process, He wants to bring peace and joy to the depth of your being. He is a good god who has good things for His children. If you are afraid of God, then you have yet to grasp the fullness of His love and your forgiven status. Perhaps you think God is like a parent who may have been harsh or demanding. That is not your heavenly Father. Let Him stand on His own merits. Sins melt in the understanding of God. Holding back a confession holds you back from the depth and joy of who He is and who He wants you to grow into. Seek to clean your house. Seek to let go of that which holds you down.

Once you have invited our mining Lord into your spiritual home, you have the peace of being forgiven and open spaces you can fill with the forgiveness of others. You have taken care of unfinished business. You have let God have His way in your life, and all doors are open to His goodness and faithful hand. Trust is your refuge even when understanding is not complete. Perfection is not the goal; neither is it the complete picture. It is trading anxiety for trust, sin for purity, and eagerness to let the Lord be your guide. His roads may not be all comfort and ease, but they are truth and faith, qualities that will carry you on the long haul in peace and joy.

> Deep calls to deep in the roar of your waterfalls;
> all your waves and breakers have swept over me.
> (Psalm 42:7 NIV)

# Our Invitation to Blessings

The Beatitudes

Matthew 5:3–6

About two years ago, a longtime friend was talking about the Beatitudes. This friend has an anointing that is uncommon; what he says often percolates in me for months and years to come. He shared this at the retreat center's breakfast table in Galilee, where I was working at the time.

In his ministry of church reconciliation, he begins by reading the Beatitudes. They contain what we need to align our hearts with God's purposes. Our own pastor, describes the Beatitudes as "an image of Jesus, a description of kingdom life, and an invitation to living in the fullness of Jesus."

The Beatitudes change us; we move from being world-seeking opportunists to God-seeking pilgrims. Our natural self-reliant independence becomes needful and poverty.

"Blessed are those who realize their poverty of spirit."

Our superficial, pleasure-seeking way of life is changed to a deep, serious, and humble mourning that can relate to others in their difficulties instead of causing them to feel they must hide the truth of their hearts.

"Blessed are the merciful. Those who live in the truth of their difficulties and allow others to do the same."

Self-promotion is sidelined in the face of meekness; we can get off the "me boat" and make it our purpose to seek for humility and tenderness.

"Blessed are the meek."

Our self-will and desire for self-definition becomes an active search for understanding the vast character of the Almighty. Letting busyness define our value ceases.

"Blessed are those who seek and value quietness."

May the Lord live in us as we seek to be more like Him!

# Prayer, Powerful and Effective

The prayer of a righteous man is powerful and effective.

—James 5:16

Do you feel your prayers are powerful and effective? At times, we see amazing things that are clearly the result of prayer. However, in the midst of praying, my prayers most often seem haphazard, brief, random, and distracted.

Praying seems to be a round peg in a square world. It just does not fit this scene. Everything around us seems to point to the physical world. It looks sure and stable. Isn't it strange that the truth is actually the opposite?

Our prayers in Christ are powerful and effective, sure and stable. The physical world that is demanding our attention and efforts is far more fragile. Our prayers are offered up to a faithful, prayer-remembering, prayer-collecting, prayer-answering god.

It is not because of who we are or that we are doing it just right; it is because they join with the power of Jesus, who conquered this earth. Even our random, short prayers are collected, and with His Spirit added, they shoot out into the world as effective, powerful agents of change. I cannot wait for heaven when the veil comes down completely and we can see clearly the reality of the world.

> For now we see through a glass darkly; but then face to face. Now I know in part; but then shall I know even as also I am known. (1 Corinthians 13:12)

# Promised and Not Promised

There are kingdom promises, and there are many. It is good to look at them and hold them in our minds and hearts. Yet there are things that are not promised, to which we can claim no entitlement. We can believe that we are saved based on our profession of faith. That is solid and promised. But there are other things that when we "have done everything to stand," we are not promised they will come to fruition. Christians get ill, get cancer, face tragedies, lose jobs, have plans fail, have difficult marriages, feel the agonies of the loss of loved ones, and even that childbirth is painful.

Sometimes God chooses to heal and respond according to our prayers; sometimes He does not. Sometimes Christians get ill or have a tragedy and go through hard years of pain. It is not because God is fickle or unable or not listening. We are not entitled to having our every prayer answered according to our will. We know God is able. We know sometimes, for reasons unknown to us, He chooses a different course, and our response is to continue to stand in trust and faith.

There are theologies that won't accept this, that put unanswered prayers on the back of the believer and state that this unanswered prayer is due to lack of faith. However, when theology does not match reality, one must check the theology out. God is very engaged in reality. Our response must be to teach our carnal minds not to measure God against our wishes and hopes. The joy comes because we can trust God's genius and supremacy more than we can trust our hopes and wishes. He knows what He is doing and why. And that is far beyond our feeble, earthbound minds to understand. With faith and trust in His goodness, there is joy, and even, at times, we can catch a glimmer of the magnitude of His love, purpose, and eternal kindness even in the difficulties of life.

Be at peace little lambs, hasn't the Father given you the Kingdom? (Luke 12:32)

# Ready Moments

Be ready in season and out of season.

—2 Timothy 4:2

Wondering how many "gospel moments" go by in a day creates a sense of guilt. However, this is a false guilt, one created by the enemy to slow us down and cause an inward rather than outward focus. The best remedy for this guilt is asking for

*While He did ordinary and familiar things, He took the small moments and made them miraculous.*

opportunities to be used and inviting the help of the Holy Spirit daily. Then we can ignore that guilt as if it were a mosquito distracting us from the work of God in our lives.

The Lord never asks us to do things we cannot do. What a wonderful assurance. If it is an impossible strain, the power has not yet arrived, and waiting is signaled. We can be assured that He is able to work through a willing heart and that the time will be right if we wait until the readiness accompanies the appointment.

We are assured in Titus 1:3 that "at the appointed season he brought his word." He will do it again for us. As Jesus lived His life on earth, we observe Him practicing faith every day. He acted faithfully in each situation. It was an ordinary, familiar backdrop, and while He did ordinary and familiar things, He took the small moments and made them miraculous.

We can be ready daily as we commit ourselves for opportunities.

Today I ask for ready moments. I will do my best to notice them. By the power of the Holy Spirit, whom I can trust for awareness and the right words, I will act in the framework of my life.

# Reflective Faith

*Reflective faith* is the faith that can see in hindsight that God *was* there. His wisdom overreached ours. We can see His faithfulness with clarity and recognize that it was different but better than our plan in that situation. Reflective faith but is not limited to hindsight. Reflective faith is one more step than simple hindsight. It understands the wisdom of God in that circumstance. It is born of contemplation, thoughtful prayerfulness of trying to see from the Lord's perspective, from asking, listening, and waiting on Him. Reflective faith moves us off our point of view to another view that may even contradict our own.

Learning to live with *anticipatory faith* is a goal of the Christian walk, using all those answered prayers to remind ourselves that we are only seeing and praying with partial vision. It includes a good dose of humility and confidence born from a history of faith. It tells us in Hebrews 10:35 NIV, "Do not throw away your confidence; it will be richly rewarded." And again in Hebrews 4:16 NIV, "Let us then approach the throne of grace with confidence, so that we may receive mercy and find grace to help us in our time of need." It includes a good dose of humility that may help us "in our time of need, and the faith we have in Christ. It is a reminder that prayer has worked and will again work through the same faithfulness of our Lord's interest in our good and His glory.

As we learn to live in the awareness of the future presence of the Lord, fear and angst must pale. Cultivating reflective faith and moving on to anticipatory faith is the call of our lives. As we remember that not only God was, is, and will be with us. We can live freely in trust and comfort, embracing the yet-to-be-known faithfulness of Jesus.

# Resting in the Storm

As they sailed he fell asleep.

—Luke 8:23 NIV

Jesus had decided to move His location of ministry to go across the lake to minister on the other less populated side. The Sea of Galilee has large cliffs on the eastern side of the lake where they were headed. When the wind from Arabia begins to blow, it gains strength across the flat desert and then drops to the lake that sits three hundred feet below sea level. It has force! This passage reads, "A squall came down on the lake," enough to swamp a boat on usually calm waters. Jesus fisherman friends were not easily afraid of their home fishing grounds, and they knew the strength of this wind.

It was time to change ministry sites, and it was time for the wind to arrive on the lake. Jesus, being both man and God, knew His plan completely. He was offering a chance for His disciples to rest in the storm. Sometimes resting does not come easily. There was such humanity in their fear. Fear cannot rest.

Sometimes in the midst of the storms of life, it seems like Jesus is sleeping. He is so quiet, but He is also so present. He is waiting for the time to act. His timing is perfect, His lessons are valuable, not just a chance to show His power and strength. Being man, He was actually asleep, tired from the busy, pressured days of ministry. As God, He slept, knowing full well His power and the outcome in the lives of His own.

When He arose, He "rebuked the wind and the raging waters." He did not rebuke His disciples. He gave them the lesson of calm. "Where is your faith?" It was a question that they could choose to answer and thereby learn to sleep on a boat in the raging sea.

It is our challenge to rest or give way to fear. In the raging sea, we can curl up next to Jesus and say, "Your ways are perfect. Your guidance, timing, and love are sure." We can offer back to the Lord what He does not possess unless we offer it; our faith and trust in His goodness for "he commands even the winds and the water" (Luke 8:25).

# Sowing for Christ

A man scatters seed on the ground. Night and day, whether he sleeps or gets up, the seed sprouts and grows, *though he does not know how. All by itself* it produces grain, first the stalk, then the head, then the full kernel in the head.

—Mark 4:28 (italics mine)

The above passage is taken from the parable of the growing seed, which is different from the parable of the sower. Jesus is talking about what the kingdom of God is like. It caught my attention because the seed grows in good soil *all by itself, though the sower does not know how.*

This time of year, soil is on the mind of any gardener. In the heat of the summer, it is very important that the soil is good so the plants will keep enough moisture and be able to use the warmth of the sun. The soil becomes either the enemy or the friend of the plant. Good soil is not of a single substance. It's made up of three key elements: sand, clay, and compost.

Our lives are like that soil; they either support or work against the seed of the sower, Jesus. We can tend to the soil of our life with many substances: reading the Word, spending daily time in prayer, frequent fellowship, and pouring out for others from our internal life spring.

When the seed gets planted in this kind of soil, it will grow. We do not need to be concerned with how it grows. It hits the good soil as in the parable and produces "first the stalk, then the grain, and then the full kernel in the head." That is us in Christ as our head.

I am glad I do not have to worry about how it grows. That is not my part; it's the Lord's. I just need to tend the soil of my life and trust that good soil produces good fruit. I can do that and am thankful the Lord is satisfied with my small faithful efforts.

# Stones of Remembrance

Jacob set up a stone pillar at the place where God had talked with him…and called it Bethel.

—Genesis 35:14

The days of summer twirl by, filled with fun, family, food, struggles, and joys. Summer sets itself apart as an active time, yet it can be so furious that we lose the joys, memories, and quiet, reflective moments.

Summer of '07 will always include one memory: the tragic collapse of the Interstate 35W bridge and subsequent death of thirteen people. We will also remember the miracle that not more were lost and the heroic and miraculous rescues that attended the collapse.

However, we are a forgetful people, prone to focus on moments, goals, and chores. We can easily lose the bigger picture. The Lord knows our minds can be like sieves at times. He has given us a remedy.

There are numerous times in the Bible when the Lord has people set up stones or pillars of remembrance. At Bethel, God asked Jacob to set up a pillar of stone to mark the place where he had heard from God. Genesis 35:14 also marks an occasion of God speaking to man. When Joshua crossed the Jordan on dry land, they were instructed to take stones from the riverbed and set up a memorial pile of stones. In Exodus, God asked Moses to set up twelve pillars of stone to mark a place of meeting and worship.

We also read in Deuteronomy 6:4 how to remember what God has done. We are to talk about His goodness and wonderful deeds when we walk, eat, and talk, and we are to tell them to our children. We are to bind what God has spoken to us and write His words on our gates and doorposts.

May we be people of long memories for the goodness of the Lord and His loving-kindness to us. I pray there will be pillars of remembrance in your lives, tangible ways to remind yourself of God and His loving deeds to you and to all of us.

In Malachi 3:16, it says, "Then those who feared the Lord talked with each other, and the Lord listened and heard. A scroll of remembrance was written in his presence concerning those who feared the Lord and honored his name."

May God's victory list be long and remembered well!

# Sarah and Her Children of Promise

I will bless her and will surely give you a son by her. I will bless her so that she will be the mother of nations; kings of peoples will come from her.

—Genesis 17:16

We are reminded in Isaiah 51:2 that it is Sarah who gave us birth. We are not children born of flesh but born of faith. Our parenthood has been decided by faith since we asked Jesus to be Lord of our lives.

Sarah has been remembered for laughing to herself when the angel came to her tent and told Abraham that she would bear a son. That laughter told many tales. She was afraid. Dare she hope again? She had waited through years of pain and loneliness, watched many families start and grow while she waited. That laughter was evidence of hope deferred that makes a heart wounded.

She had borne years of infertility in a society that family defines the very essence of a woman's role. Abraham had remained faithful to her when the culture said he could put her away and select a new, more fertile woman.

Sarah feared that this offer was too good to be true. Faith she did not have was asked of her. She was embarrassed by her infertility, embarrassed by the hope that was once again ignited and had to be quenched by sardonic laughter. Her identity had been barren, incomplete, and unable to fulfill her husband's calling.

Sarah was a woman of faith by many accounts. She married in the central urban core of the Middle East, Ur. Arts were prominent, as were thinking and culture and population. She followed her husband's call to be a nomad, leaving her family and her people. No family of hers came with them on their journey into the unknown, entering a new country among new people, traveling through six hundred miles, some of which was harsh desert. This is a brave and faithful woman, being told to lie to preserve Abraham's life on two occasions—once with Abimelech (Genesis 20) and with the Egyptian pharaoh (Genesis 12). This lie seems most uncomfortable, but I believe there is context we are not clear about. She followed his lead, hedged her bets, and the Lord came through. If she had not lied, chances of Abraham being killed for his wife were great.

Sarah decided to help God with His plan. She knew the calling, and she knew her barrenness. She did the next culturally correct thing—bear a son through her maid. Abraham knew the promise was through Sarah, but he gave in to Sarah's plan and even though it was her own idea, she became jealous of her maid. Sarah attempted to fulfill the call, but God was not satisfied with Sarah's method of becoming the mother of nations. Sarah bitterly regretted taking God's plan into her hands, and her regret moved to bitterness and blame, not an unknown path for many events in any of our lives.

# Standing in Faith

Having done everything to stand, stand therefore.

—Ephesians 6:13

Trusting God is a partnership. He has a part, and so do we. Recently having traveled to Sri Lanka and India, I was poignantly reminded of my part of the partnership. Much prayer went into the trip, things like health, connections with flights and people, a visa that was applied for quite late, and many more things. Each time I was reminded of my part and then His part. As long as I did my part, I could stand still trusting Him for His part. I needed to take malaria pills, use a mosquito net, and apply 100 percent DEET to prevent contracting malaria or, worse yet, dengue fever. I needed to do all I could to make the visa deadline, provide all the documentation, drive to Chicago, prepare to spend the night there, possibly change my travel plans, and then rush like a bandit to the airport once the visa was delivered! These were my efforts, then I could stand back and watch the goodness of God come through in every situation.

Where our ability ends, the blessing and favor of the Lord picks up. We are assured of salvation by accepting the work of Jesus, who did all He could as mortal man and was met by the divine miracle of accomplishing salvation for all who believe. Once we accept this salvation, we have done all we can do to stand, then we stand, trusting fully in faith that the Lord will accomplish His plans in and for us.

We can have peace because He is sovereign and heaven and earth are under His authority.

However, carrying out of that process can be a great challenge, trusting fully that having done everything in my ability, I just need to stand. I needed to teach myself to stand in perfect peace and trust when I had many earthbound reasons to be anxious and worried. The trip was wonderful and full of many challenges that overseas travel offers. It was a learning experience that raised my trust in a sovereign god to a new level of standing in peace.

Praise the Lord! He calls us upward to the heavenly calling of peaceful trust in the face of challenges that are out of our control.

# Surrender

Yet not my will but yours be done.

—Luke 22:42b

My late husband used to say that he could speak German. In truth, the only thing he could say was something he had learned from his father that may or may not actually be German. It is what the American soldiers of WWII said when capturing German troops. "Komme mit deinen hosen in deinen handen." Come here with your pants in your hands. *You can almost feel the old man sloughing off, the new man in Christ taking ground.* Give up, surrender, and bring here what you think you need, what may hide things that could be harmful. It would be humiliating to strip down and surrender.

Surrender is painful, giving up what you have held on to for a long time, something you believe has been right and worth the fight or perhaps like many of the German troops, fighting more out of obligation than of belief.

Can you see where this is going?

We consider what may move us into a deeper walk with Jesus. What He may bring up is something that we thought was valuable, possibly even to Him. We need to capture our will, give up, surrender, and sometimes feel humiliated by the surrender. We did not know we were holding onto what God had not intended for us. It seemed like a good or logical thing. It feels bad to surrender what we thought was right. Yet because we know the goodness of the Lord, His ability to see the big picture going bad in the long run, we can walk toward Him in total surrender. We might not feel a victory except by faith.

Has there been a time for you like that? You can almost feel the old man sloughing off, the new man in Christ taking ground. When we encounter the risen Christ in truth, we usually need to experience something of the cross in our souls. Experiencing the cross is like a trail marker to us. We know we are on the path that leads to Jesus.

# Temple Courts

At day break they entered the temple courts.

—Acts 5:21

This scripture excites the heart. I can see the disciples up early, heading for the temple. Dawn was just shining over the golden-stoned city of Jerusalem. They went there first; they went there anticipating a meeting with the most high King. My guess is that He did not disappoint. As they were just rubbing sleep from their eyes, He was ready and waiting. He was looking forward to the meeting that He had been planning all night. They were His; He had permitted them access to Himself through tearing the temple curtain, top to bottom, and welcoming them into the holy of holies. The blood of Jesus had made them cleansed priests and authorized their access.

"Behold the tabernacle of God is with men." (Revelation 21:3), this verse had not yet been written but they knew in their hearts Jesus was with them. His indwelling was as sure as the death they saw him die and the resurrection they witnessed.

Daily they knew their need; daily they sought the living God with daily hunger. Daily He filled.

Self-sufficiency was not on their agenda. They knew the source, humility, and seeking was the way to be filled. God would be there, and they were coming to collect.

Shame or guilt were not going to be collected. God would call them up to who they are in Him, to replace anything missing because of their past life of sin.

May you find yourself at daybreak entering the temple courts. May you find a holy and loving God waiting to meet you in your need, cleaning, refreshing, restoring, strengthening, assigning, equipping, and accompanying you as you walk out your day in Him.

# The Cost of Freedom

It is for freedom that Christ set you free.

—Galatians 5:1

The God of all the earth who is *maker, creator, builder, designer, abundant, sovereign, eternal,* and *all-powerful,* let go of His creation for the sake of our freedom to choose Him.
Though He created us, He released us.
He no longer possesses our love, worship, hearts, service.
Our relationship with Him does not belong to Him though He has every right to own it.
This release has cost Him untold pain and suffering.
He willingly allowed freedom to not love but to hate, not worship Him but ourselves, freedom to ruin ourselves with self-centered living, wage war, kill others, and be brutal.

All this was released for the price of our freedom to choose Him, or not. We have the ability to apply our God-given freedom in any direction. This is stunning. The price has been so high, and the value to Him must be higher yet.

It not only cost Him seeing His Son on the cross. We cannot conceive the depth of His love for Jesus; therefore, we cannot grasp the depth of the suffering of this moment. It has also cost Him years of waiting for each of us to return to Him. He offers us the choice to suffer with Him, to join Him in prayer and anguish until He restores in His glorious kingdom. What a privilege to intercede at His feet, to be able to offer back to Him what he released so long ago—our hearts, our love, our worship.

The price!
The glory!

# The Dinner Table

John 19:19

We had the pleasure of sitting around a dinner table while in Israel and visiting with some men from Germany who were students of the Hebrew language. They told us the most amazing thing about the words Pilate had directed to be placed on the cross.

In John 19:19, it says, "Jesus of Nazareth, the King of the Jews." Our friends explained that when this is written in Hebrew, the acronym spells the unspoken name of God in Hebrew, Yahweh. It would be like this: Jesus of Nazareth and King of the Jews—J-O-A-J.

We, as Christians, say the name Jehovah. In Judaism, it is unheard of to even speak it aloud. It is that holy. It is no wonder there was such a reaction among the Pharisees and literate of the time. Jesus was crucified because He said He was from God, and then the sign above Him declared that He was God. Amazing!

The dinner table is such a rich store of wisdom and insight. The simplest things in my life seem to produce the most life-altering truths.

Resurrection Day will forever be much richer for me knowing that what was written above Jesus's head was the utter truth. The Lord doesn't miss a beat in His Son's life or in our lives. The more we learn, the deeper He reveals Himself.

# The Great Exchange

## The Enemy's Attacks

Feeling Excluded.

Feeling unimportant to others.

Feeling rejected.

Being criticized.

Feeling ugly.

My dignity attacked.

Feeling controlled by others.

Having difficult relationships.

Being influenced by past injuries and trauma.

Fears and insecurities influencing behavior.

Asking who loves me?

Having unrealized hopes.

Having negative thoughts about myself.

Fearing nightmares or catastrophes.

My grace is sufficient for you!

Feelings of failure.

Feeling empty inside.

Having support withdrawn.

Being accused.

Feeling weak.

Experiencing put-downs.

## The Truth Is

I am adopted by the Father.

The Lord will sing over me with joy.

God has loved me with an everlasting love.

He knows the plans he has for me.

He calls me my darling, my beautiful one.

I will love you so freely.

The Lord is good and does good.

I am the God who heals you.

Even then I shall be confident.

His plans are for my good.

We have hope in the love of Christ.

We are the bride of Christ.

My grace is sufficient.

The love of Christ controls me.

Confess with your mouth and believe in God's protection.

I have been appointed, anointed and redeemed.

Satisfy me with your unfailing love.

I am a part of God's family.

Satan is the accuser, the father of lies.

Those who stumble are armed with His strength.

I will raise you up and seat you with Christ.

| | |
|---|---|
| Feeling inadequate. | I can do all things through Christ. |
| Feeling hopeless and despairing. | Hope in the Lord and the strength of His might. |
| Believing I have wasted my life. | I have appointed you to do good. |
| Believing I have wasted my giftings. | I will reap in due season. |
| Believing I cannot manage. | The love of Christ controls me. |
| Feeling confused. | God gives me a sound mind. |
| Feeling self-doubt. | Be strong in the Lord and the strength of His might. |
| Calling myself names. | I have called you by name, for you are mine. |
| Being closed off or out. | He has broken the barrier of the dividing wall. |
| Experiencing self-loathing. | I have loved you with an everlasting love. |

# The Jail Was Securely Locked

Acts 5:23–25

When the Sanhedrin jailed the apostle Paul, the messengers sent the report, "We found the jail securely locked, with guards standing at the door, but when we opened the door, we found no one inside."

Beloved, that is us! Our jail of sin was securely locked, and we were on the inside. Our selfish motives, errors, and anger kept us in. The guards are Satan's helpers assigned to keep us in jail, guilty and ashamed. The enemy of our souls wants us to stay there, in the dark, cold and alone, with no contact with the kingdom where our citizenship resides.

When the doors of the jail were opened to prove the guilt of the captured, unknown to the guards, no one was inside. Hallelujah! That is us, too! Behind what is seen, God works His marvelous redemption; He does not jail us according to our sins, but within our heart, He frees us. He does not want us to give our authority to the "guards" of the jail. We are free, and we can *walk out*!

Those who were to be in the jail were found in a most miraculous place. "Look, those you put in jail are standing in the temple courts preaching to the people." We also want to be found in this place. They were at the temple preaching and being used by God. What a story! Satan attempted to hold them in jail, but they were found in the midst of doing kingdom work.

I hope that we who deserve jail may be found free of the prison of our sin by the power of Jesus, residing in the temple of God and doing His kingdom work. Let's walk out and walk on!

# The Mother's Heart of God

Can a mother forget the baby at her breast and
have no compassion on the child she has borne?
Though she may forget you, I will not forget you!

—Isaiah 49:15

We often hear about the "Father's heart of love for us" or, on the negative side, "a father's wounding" that may need healing for us to rightfully relate to our loving heavenly Father. This is very central to our relationship to the Father; however, there are times when a wounding from our mothers needs healing as well. The Lord then represents the "mother's heart of God." We are sure that the Lord is prepared to meet this need as evidenced in the above scripture.

I am so thankful that our Lord, who made us in His image, made us male and female (Genesis 1:27). Both mothers and fathers have crucial roles in healthy development; they represent Jesus in the lives of developing children. Finding the loving mother's heart of the Lord is just what our hearts need at times to mend the infractions that come from life, from our imperfect responses to imperfect moms. As mothers, we can think of many times when our responses did not represent the child's need but our lack. Perhaps our need was too great to rise above.

Do you have a "mother's wound"? A need for the mother's heart of the living God to heal you? He will enter into a place that you offer to Him, to rearrange, heal, and fulfill your needs.

> I will heal your wrong ways, I will love you so freely, and you will blossom as the lily, I will be dew to my people, and you will dwell beneath my shadow. (Hosea 14:4–5, paraphrased)

The tender, sensitive, connection-based heart of our Lord and Savior, Jesus, who came to Nazareth to overcome the broken soil of this earth, offers the mother's heart of God not only to heal us but also to complete His redemption in our lives.

# The Vulnerable Heart of God

God misses His children when they are missing from His table. He mourns when they are not connected to Him. His love is vulnerable. We can choose to wound, reject, and mistreat His love.

Being blindsided by His children is painful to Him. He feels rejection, and it hurts Him. His love remains still and strong. He knows there is no intimacy without vulnerability.

He seeks for some of His children with great focus and diligence and yet cannot connect with them. He sees opportunities pass them by with no gratitude from them. God gets publicly sassed, put down, misused, taken apart. His efforts are rejected; His image disrespected.

He set His kingdom up like a family—Father, Son, and Spirit. He wove relationship into His very being. By making himself a parent, He opened wide the door to vulnerability. He sent His Son as a savior who walked out from ill treatment yet stayed in the game, never turning unrighteously angry, bitter, or hurt. Love is not neat and tidy, a feel-good, victorious walk from glory to glory.

We can choose to live superficially self-protected to avoid the pain and heartache but lose love and lose track of our calling to walk in the footsteps of Christ. Christ is the prototype of that courageous love.

> Will their lack of faith nullify God's faithfulness? (Romans 3:3)

May it never be!

# They Hurried Across

> The people hurried over.
>
> —Joshua 4:10

As the children of Israel were preparing to enter the promised land, they waited on the banks of the Jordan River. The ark was to go first, then the priests stepped in, and the waters stopped and formed a "heap" upstream. The riverbed became dry, and the whole group crossed. For some reason, when I read that they hurried across, it strikes me funny. There were about a million people who crossed. God had clearly created a miracle to enable them to cross the river, and they felt they needed to hurry. They had seen many miracles in the wilderness and had been fed by God's faithfulness. Why did they hurry?

The truth is, we are not so different. We have much evidence of God's goodness to us, and yet in the moment, we hurry. Has God not given us the right amount of time to accomplish what He has set for us to do? In the face of His power and His love, we hurry as if He has not planned ahead enough and we have to help Him out.

What is the purpose of our hurry? We forget that God is not only faithful; He is able! Not only is He able, He cares! He not only has the hairs on our heads counted but He also has counted the minutes of the day and knows the amount of energy we have. He has planned for interruptions and has created them to be sweet moments to remember His love for someone in our life.

There is a clue that lies embedded in the event in Joshua. They had received specific instructions from the Lord on how to cross. They listened and then obeyed the instructions. The reason they did not need to hurry—they were obeying. If you have listened and obeyed, please don't hurry. We hurry because we fear God, who is awesome, but we forget He is patient and kind. He is also a good father who plans enough time for His children to do what He has asked. As we listen and obey, we may then walk in rest and peace.

# To Speak or Not to Speak

Psalm 40

Sin seems to come in three forms: action, inaction, or reaction. Recently reading Psalm 39 and 40, I could see David struggling with the action or inaction of sin. To speak or not to speak?

To not speak can cause our emotions to build up within us. "When I was silent, not even saying anything good, my anguish increased" (Psalm 39:2). We need to speak and express even emotions that are uncomfortable. Psalm 40:1 reminds us to "watch our ways and keep our tongue from sin." Yet we run the risk of passivity, not even saying anything good if we are not discerning. That, too, leaves us in a precarious position. We need to speak up. We cannot wallow in self-doubt and insecurity and say nothing. Psalm 40 begins the climb out of the slimy pit to put a new song in our mouth and carries on to encourage us to say, "I proclaim righteousness in my heart. I speak of your faithfulness and salvation. I do not conceal your love and your truth from the great assembly."

We can borrow courage from Jesus and speak out, proclaim the truth of His love and the joy of His kingdom. How small is our piece, and how great is our God! We are a small cog in the big wheel of His kingdom, yet without our well-oiled piece, the work of God in our area of influence is stilted. God is sovereign, but we must act. I recently heard someone say 100 percent God and 100 percent us.

Oh, people of God, speak up and declare His glory and His greatness!

# Trip Wires

Walking in the woods with some friends, we found our feet getting caught in undergrowth we could not see. The path looked clear enough, but that was not the case. There are many times a day we may get caught on things below the surface that cause us to stumble and even sin, at least in our mind.

We may have deep-seated beliefs about ourselves, God, and life that are not readily discerned, but that cause us to fall, even many times a day. Some of those thoughts may be that we are ultimately unlovable, that we are not valued by others, that we don't have a place in this world, that we must earn and prove acceptance and love, or that our value is somehow based in our possessions, jobs, roles, or popularity. Performance, importance, and worth become the measuring stick of our value. These can also become our trip wires.

Thoughts like "I never get it right," "I am not important," or "I am not worthy" interfere with our faith walk in Christ and disrupt our peace and confidence that we have in Him.

When the Lord spoke over Jesus as He was leaving Jordan after His baptism, He said: "This is my beloved son in whom I love, with whom I am well pleased" (Matthew 17:5 NASB). God looks at us through His son. The love He has for Jesus, He also has for us. Each sentence speaks directly to trip wires that are common among us.

*This is my beloved child.* I am worthy to be called His child. He paid a high price for that. The cross brought us into the family of God. We are worthy because of Christ to be called His child.

*Whom I love.* I am important because I am loved by the most high God. He actually loves me.

*With whom I am well pleased.* God, in Christ, is pleased with us. When He looks at us, He smiles. When we make efforts, He appreciates it and does not call us to perfection to be valuable in His sight. He knows we are but dust. He rejoices in our efforts for His kingdom. He is ready to support, praise, care, and strengthen us.

Let the truth of God's love remove the trip wires of our thoughts, emotions, and actions. The truth lies in Isaiah 30:18:

> Yet the LORD longs to be gracious to you; therefore he will rise up to show you compassion.

# Unknown Territory

Recently, I heard about a young woman who was venturing to ride the bus to a lesson rather than get a ride from her parents. She hopped on the bus and began the journey. At first, she knew the surroundings and was sure of the way. Then the bus turned away from the direction she knew she should be going. After a few stops, she did not recognize anything around her and came to the conclusion she should get off the bus. She did so and was in a neighborhood that felt foreign and unsafe to her. The bus had simply gone around a block to pick up a few extra stops. Because it was not what she had expected, she got off the bus and took things into her own hands. A call to her parents brought them to her rescue and a safe arrival to her destination.

I wonder how many times we have hopped off the bus of God's will. We are sure of our direction and plan in the beginning, but when things start to look uncomfortable and foreign, we are unsure of the way, and we abort the trip. When we start a new journey, the excitement of it is fun and challenging, but when time goes on and the thrill and interest die down, it may not take much to cause us to change our plans. Hard work, changes in direction, foreign territory, and lack of support around us may all total up to tell us we were on the wrong bus. In the actual true story above, it is clear what happened. But when we encounter the challenges in real life, stretched over a longer time, it appears less obvious.

We, too, can all our Father. When the Lord is our vision, our dreams and directions have more staying power. Revisiting the original can give all of us the ability to "walk by faith and not by sight." Then we do not prematurely hop off the bus and realize that the struggles are only evidence that we are still on earth. And God is able to meet us with equal strength for the detours we encounter.

> So we fix our eyes not on what is seen, But on what is unseen. For what is seen is temporary, But what is unseen is eternal. (2 Corinthians 4:18)

# Walking in the Valley of the Middle Way

The middle ground is the place in between illness, long-term pain, deep loss, and complete healing. Perhaps it's a partial healing, but there is still the desire of your heart that remains unanswered. It is a holding in a place—the answer is waiting—a place that we continue to long for the complete and fully answered prayer.

It may be necessary to wait in the valley. We can live in angst in the valley, repeating the same prayer over and over, not able to see that God may be orchestrating something different from what we are asking. His goal may be for our faith to increase, our peace to grow in trial, and our maturity in the body of Christ. Whatever it is, it will require long, deep growth.

When we are in that "middle way," it may be a struggle of faith; we may find ourselves constantly angry, begging relentlessly. Or it may be a place of quiet resignation, or best of all, trustful rest in faith that we have been heard.

John 11:41 states, "Jesus looked up and said, 'Father, I thank you that you hear me, that you always hear me.'"

We have the same listening Father. He hears; He bends down to listen.

When we are in the middle way, it is not because we have a father who didn't hear, who is unconcerned, or who is slow to respond. The middle way must have a purpose. We know we can rest in the middle way when we can say, "I wouldn't have had it any other way. What I learned has been so valuable. I would not give it up." Other times, we may see the growth and be hard-pressed to agree it had value. The journey had been so hard; the pain, excruciating. And our faith has not yet caught up.

The middle way is the place of learning and of leaning. It is waiting on God while continuing to trust Him to know exactly what He is doing. The middle way is between trusting prayer and asking prayer. It can be a place of bitterness or faith. We can grow in grace and love for others who share this middle way with us. Something in our heart is being worked on. The temptation to choose bitterness and faithlessness is palpable. We are left in the valley to make many choices. The Lord trusts you for those choices. There is a great cloud of witnesses cheering for us in heaven. Look up. Wait for the dawning.

# We Needed a Rugged Cross

Obedient to death, even death on a cross!

—Philippians 2:8

The cross is one of the worst ways to die. In fact, the entire crucifixion is a terrible, rough, ugly, confusing, and shocking death for the Prince of glory. The death of Jesus was not understood by those who witnessed it whether prior to it, during it, or after the fact. It did not look like a complete plan of God. It did not look like the penalty payment for man's sin through all eternity.

*Oh, the joy we get from knowing that Jesus is enough, that the cross was rugged enough.*

We needed that rugged cross. The world does not look like a tidy place. People die in awful circumstances. Children die way too young. Life is hard, messy, unpredictable, and scary at times. So was the cross. Jesus's death needed to be severe to pave the path for us in an imperfect world. Only a rugged, very rugged, cross would do.

The confusion the cross presented at the time of Jesus's death is a confusion we can relate to in our lives. The answers to *why* do not seem forthcoming. The future is obscure and shifting. Imperfection and confusion were part of the scene as the hoped-for King hung dying.

However, He did it! Jesus accomplished the will of the Father. He completed the law, redeemed Adam's fall, and finished the work.

The cross, rugged and mean, is sufficient to carry us through our earthly journey and into glory.

We need a mighty savior who has overcome this world, has mercy for us, and abundant love.

Oh, the joy we get from knowing that Jesus is enough, that the cross was rugged enough. The way is cleared for us to walk on and walk strong, with the strength of the cross carrying and supporting us though our lifetime and into eternity.

D. L. Moody said that "a broken vessel only remains full if it stays under running water." The running water that first flowed down from the side of Jesus on the cross is that water for us. Lord, we receive the blood that cleanses and the water that flows from the heart of God.

# There Is Purpose

Very rarely will anyone die for a righteous man, though for a good man someone might possibly dare to die. But God demonstrated his own love for us in this: While we were still sinners, Christ died for us.

—Romans 5:7–8

Independence Day is a joyful time: fireworks, picnics, parades, food, friends, and family. Along with the joy is the awareness and appreciation for those who have given their life and health for us to have the freedom we celebrate.

There is a stoic feeling in my heart when I watch the veterans march in the parades, knowing they represent only a portion of those who fought. They are people with the courage to face death, people who believe in their cause enough to be willing to die for it. These people had a view that was greater than themselves. These soldiers are much like Christ in that while our nation is imperfect and our path sometimes unclear, they were still willing to fight to attain freedom to the best of our understanding and ability.

Sometimes there are deaths that do not seem to have a purpose. No one seems to benefit from it, and from every angle, it looks like a loss. It takes an extra amount of faith to believe that these lives and deaths also counted. I wonder if this is how the family members of the soldiers also feel. When someone near to us dies, we usually are not able to see the big picture, at least not with our natural eyes.

Yet there is a bigger picture. It transcends patriotism and gratitude for our troops. It is a picture of a loving God calling someone home—a death timed by the Creator for His purposes and plans. We understand the fight for freedom on the earth, and it is much harder to grasp the eternal freedom gained by one precious death and offered for all people who believe—the Lord Jesus Christ who died to set us free.

# Score!

During the hot weather of August, I vacillated between having the air-conditioning on and off. One particular day, I had opened my windows in the morning before work to cool the house and accidently left them open all day while I was at work. Upon arriving home after work, the heat was pouring in and the air-conditioning pouring out. The waste of it was distressing.

As I shut the windows, I inadvertently said out loud to the Lord, "I am sorry for wasting your money today!" At the time, a friend's son was staying with me and overheard my comment to the Lord. Including him in this conversation, I said, "I wonder if the cross even covers wasted air-conditioning." (I technically knew the answer but was being silly at the moment.)

Silently spoken into my consciousness was the word *score*. It made me laugh out loud. The Lord is really funny and met me in my silliness and guilt. The cross does "score" for all our errors, large and small, serious and not. As I shared this word with my friend's son, it was especially poignant to him as an athlete and a guy. I think the Lord wanted to not only forgive me and make me laugh but also to minister His goodness to this young athlete.

2 Timothy 4:2 says, "Preach the Word: be prepared in season and out of season." I was perhaps out of season with my AC on and windows open, but God gave me a word that is always in season. His cross covers all the needs of our lives. That is worth preaching.

# Your Agenda or Mine?

I wrote a devotional on resting and asked a rhetorical question: Why is it a sacrifice to rest? After some thought, I want to investigate that question. Resting when it is on our list of things to do today is easy. It is when we are asked to superimpose God's agenda that it becomes more difficult. Dropping our plans and list of jobs for the purpose of simple obedience with no seeming purpose is difficult. It comes down to letting go of control and trusting. Now that is a theme we are all engaged in.

We treat time as one of our possessions. It is the great equalizer. Everyone on the face of the earth has twenty-four hours in a day, seven days a week. What we do with that 24-7 changes our lives and potentially those around us in concentric circles of impact. Thinking that we own time is logical on one front, but in truth, we need to let go of that possession in submission to Jesus, the true owner of time. *Control* is almost a dirty word. We don't want to be controlling, and yet we are called to it on some levels. Being under submission to the Lord keeps us from acting in pride or fear and moves us to act in ways that are trusting of God's character and His goodness.

What is our response? Applying God's agenda to our days allows Him to whittle us into the image of His design. Resting does not become law but a preference to follow the Lord's priorities and allow His agenda to supersede ours. The Pharisees were great at keeping the Sabbath, but their hearts were far from Him. As we rest and follow Him, controlling, anxiety, fear, and rigidity become less and His imprint becomes evident in our lives. When we offer Him the sacrifice of rest, we suspend our to-do list for the peace of God.

Want to sign up? I do.

# Sweet Forgiveness

So then God has granted even the Gentiles repentance unto life.

—Acts 11:18b

As our humility goes, so goes our forgiveness. I often find myself struggling to forgive. I say the obedient "I forgive them, Lord," and then I add, "Lord, I have not yet arrived at that place in my heart. Please help me to completely forgive."

Complete forgiveness is a wonderful place of freedom. My goal is to have a very short forgiveness list. Daily life often interferes, and something small creeps in or a past wound opens up, and I need to tend the garden of forgiveness again.

Lack of humility is usually the weed that is holding on: A very honest look at myself *will produce enough humility to forgive* even in the tough situations.

Honesty equals humility, and we can then move forward. Another difficulty of forgiveness is that we think we would never offend the way we were offended.

Even as I write this, my pride cries out, "Oh, but I wouldn't do this or that."

If I let the Spirit of Jesus speak to me, I begin to see that I am fully capable of sin of any sort. Except for the life of Christ in me, who, moment by moment, delivers me from myself, I am like any other human.

I remember a time I was in a cabin on the shores of Lake Superior; I was crying out to the Lord my deep need for comfort. I was reading Isaiah 57, and there I found the secret for comfort—humility. "I live in a high and holy place, but also with him who is contrite and lowly in spirit" (Isaiah 57:15). This understanding of God's access to our hearts created a joyous time of praise in that beautiful setting, one I will never forget.

Truth equals trust, and the truth of Jesus is what gives us the ability to trust Him. When you are told the truth, no matter how difficult it may be, your spirit rests and feels as if it has landed on a solid foundation. Sweet forgiveness equals reckless humility on the bedrock of truth. I am so glad the Lord gives us solid ground to walk on.

# Waiting for Contentment

But godliness with contentment is great gain.

—1 Timothy 6:6

A lesson I never stop learning is that contentment is a state of mind, not a condition of life.

My internal voice says, "When this or that happens, then I will be content with life."

I hope on this topic that you are a faster learner. Contentment is far more about our outlook and thought life than our external life.

There was a time in my life that was excruciatingly difficult. As I was pouring my heart out to Jesus, He said to me, "Practice contentment." Contentment was the farthest thing from what seemed possible. My husband was dying of cancer; I would soon be a single mother to my three-year-old. Contentment was not on my to-do list.

The idea of practicing contentment was a new thought. Contentment is a skill we can learn, not a condition to meet. It is within our reach. Watching the Summer Olympics is a keen lesson on skill training. Each of the Olympians were not born with their skills. Their proficiency was hard-won after many hours and years of training. Like the heavenly skill of contentment, it takes practice and focus to learn.

Recently, I had another trial era, and once again, irritations and frustrations seemed to be pouring into my life. I remembered the Lord's words to me about practicing contentment. This kingdom skill changes our lives, hearts, and relationships. We can have hope for the future, and circumstances may improve. The reality in the future is, if we are still on earth, there will also be trials. Contentment today is a honed skill of trust in Jesus, but once we press in, the gain is great for us and for those around us. Let the games begin!

# Autumn

# The Word of God Speaks

For the Lord is our judge, the Lord is our lawgiver,
The Lord is our king, it is he who will save us.

—Isaiah 33:22

After my second marriage, my daughter and I maintained a great relationship with my first husband's family. We had been especially close to his second cousin and his wife. They were staying with us while visiting from out of town. Having daily quiet times is part of my regular routine. I love that time of *"Cannot I do what I want with what* day to think, read the *is my own?" (Matthew 20:15)* Word, and pray. I try to remember to listen every day, but it is easy to forget. One of the mornings, I heard from heaven very clearly, "Do not set yourself up as judge of the living God." Hearing from the Lord so clearly is not common. I was stunned, and the words I heard terrified me. Immediately I began repenting. I had no idea what I had done. Since that time, I have come to realize that this is a strong tendency for all of us. We decide what a just god should and should not do. We have little regard for His grand and sovereign position when we are spouting opinions about what we think is right and what is not.

However, back to the morning quiet time. I asked the Lord if He would show me when I had done this. I heard nothing. I decided to ask the wife of the couple who was staying with us. She is a discerning woman and hears clearly from Jesus. She said she could not see it in my life but would ask the Lord. A few days later, she came to me and said, "It is not for now." Less than a week later, my second husband died unexpectedly. I believe the Lord was preparing me for this. I felt I had many reasons to be offended by what had just happened. I know that God holds our life and our death dates. I knew that He had known and tried to prepare me. He did not want me to fall into anger and blame Him, but to respect His right to His own. "Cannot I do what I want with what is my own?" (Matthew 20:15).

My reasons for offense continued to race through my mind. This was the second time in eight years that I was a widow. My eleven-year-old daughter had lost two fathers. She could not remember her own dad but loved and was loved by her second dad. Also, the two men had died only a day apart, July 28 and July 29. That felt like an affront. We had made room in our hearts and home for my second husband's four daughters who lived with him. Now their biological mother who had moved out of state was telling them they had to come and live with her. Life was rugged.

When I asked the Lord why the two husbands died only one day apart, I heard, "So that you may know it was my hand." The harshness of the two dates never again were an offense but a point of trust in His sovereignty.

Angrily, I told the Lord I was not going to ask why I had lost two husbands. Maybe I didn't want to know. It is easy to feel that I was somehow deficient in my personality and needed this kind of treatment from the Lord to bring me up to speed with everyone else. Though I did not believe it, I often returned to that thought. Also, I didn't want to fall into the despair and entitlement of that question. Asking why is not really a question; it is an opposition to what happened. I choose to accept and trust to the best of my ability. There were hours and sometimes days that were a huge struggle.

# Running Home

About three years after my second husband's death, I needed a break. I love the land and people of Israel. I have had the privilege of living there for four years and touring there another five times with various groups and friends.

My first time in Israel, I went to spend a year (that turned into three) with a Christian discipleship group that lived on a kibbutz for a year at a time. A kibbutz is a shared community built in 1948–52 for farming and defense of the newly formed county. About 50–150 families live and work together in a rural setting.

This group was based on Navigator principles of study and Bible memorization, prayer, and worship. It was led by wonderfully mature and godly people. It was a foundation for me in the development of my new faith. We could not share the gospel, but we could live it and answer questions that came our way. It was a wonderful relationship with the people I lived among. I worked primarily in the babies and children's homes as a childcare worker.

Upon my first arrival in Israel, I heard my spirit say "I'm home" as the plane touched down. I did not expect to have that thought, nor did I anticipate the sense of home that I eventually felt. It is just a fact.

You may be familiar with Twila Paris's song "The Warrior is a Child." There are words in the song that say, "They don't know that I go running home when I fall down. They don't know who picks me up when no one is around." All my heart wanted to do was to "run home." So I began to plan and walk in that direction. My daughter and I had toured the previous year with a beloved pastor and his wife on a tour group. I asked her if she wanted to live in Israel. She said she wanted to wait till her ninth-grade year.

So as it approached, we began making preparations. It was amazing what fell into place—someone to house-sit our home with great love and care and her school agreed that they would count her education in Israel if she passed her classes.

So I ran home, to Israel, a place where not everyone knew of my losses and I would not have to confront the conversations many times a day. I worked at a Christian guesthouse and told only the staff of the guesthouse about my situation. The guests were just friendly and wonderful. It was a relief, a great shift of focus!

> Consequently, you are no longer foreigners and
> strangers, but fellow citizens with God's people and
> also members of his household. (Ephesians 2:19)

# September 11

Fear or Grace?

The date 9/11 is etched in this generation's memory. It is a watershed of our vulnerability to an enemy desiring our destruction.

This is not a new concept to believers. We also have an enemy desiring our destruction. But we have a warrior on our side who has already won the battle. As we tread on earth, our goal is to walk in the territory that God has given us to possess. This is the challenge of our Christian life on this side of heaven.

Fear is one of the enemy's main objectives. There are many fears that we may walk in. Often, we do not recognize the fear until it has caused us to react in some way. We are told in 1 Peter 3:6b, "Not to be frightened by any fear." That is a tall order! Anything that we worry about is a fear we have not surrendered to the cross of Jesus.

Isaiah 1:18 says, "Come let us reason together." We are privileged to have a god who wants to reason with us. He does not leave us in our vulnerabilities. He will work with us, as we work with Him. When we find ourselves in the grip of fear, remember to walk straight into it with Jesus at our side.

Running and hiding from our fears is exactly what the enemy wants us to do. As we investigate our fears, name them and challenge them, we can begin to transfer the ownership of the fear to the One who has already spoken into it and provided deliverance.

We know the end of the story. Brother Yun reminded us of this when he shared at North Heights last winter, "The whole earth is filled with the glory of the Lord" (Isaiah 6:3). Nothing less than this will be the end of the story.

We need not fear for future generations because God is the same then as He is now, able and willing to show His love, power, and strength. The enemy roars, but God conquers.

# Tabernacle in the Wilderness

> For we know that if the earthly tent which is our
> house is torn down, we have a building from
> God, a house not made with hands, [but] eternal
> in the heavens.

> —2 Corinthians 5:1 NASB

We are a privileged people. We have a god who not only has
described Himself to us but has also allowed us to live in the era of
His Son's offer of redemption. God Himself is our tabernacle in the
wilderness of an unredeemed world. We are near the season of the
Jewish High Holy Days of the Bible: the First of the Year, the Festival
of the Trumpets, the Day of Atonement from sin, and the celebration
of the tabernacle in the wilderness.

We can draw aside from the hurry and pressure of life and come
into the holy tabernacle of God, Christ Himself. The wilderness
calls back to us, demanding we work harder, faster, and be on guard
against poverty, trouble, and persecution. The call to strife at times
seems louder and stronger than the call to rest and listen. We are
fickle people to even entertain this temptation.

Being called to listen is our heritage as believers. Being of Christ
and also of this world, we can often feel the tug of busyness and
avoid that call to the side of our Savior. Once we do draw aside,
we continue to feel the press between the world and our Savior. We
understand that it can be an awkward thing to hear the Word of
God. It pits us against the world and requires obedience from a pure
heart, something that exceeds the ability of our natural self. But God
makes us able to hear, listen, obey, and delight in His Word. What an
Awesome God we serve.

Hear and fear the Word of the Lord, remembering Hosea 2:14,
"I will draw her into the wilderness and there I will speak tenderly to
her" (paraphrased). We are assured of the tenderness of our Lord and
Savior. We are a privileged people.

# Cloudy November

I will give you hidden treasures, riches stored in secret places, so that you may know that I am the LORD, the God of Israel, who summons you by name.

—Isaiah 45:3 NIV

Oh, cloudy November, gathering strength for the cold. Clouds that bring slumber, slumber that brings safety and endurance to the grass, plants, trees, and even our souls.

The quietness of winter is beginning to set in, reminding us of tasks to close down, telling fragile birds it's time to move on to warmer climes.

November clouds direct us, prepare us, tell us that life doesn't always move at the same pace; it slows, it quiets, it dulls.

In the quiet, the rest, the bland, the voice of the Lord rings clear, pure, and undistracted.

In the leafless trees and brown grass, the life of the Lord shines brightly.

As our world goes to sleep, let our hearts awaken anew and let the presence and rest of the living God shine brightly on our hearts, our gatherings, our families, and the coming Advent.

Shine, O Lord, pure, strong, and solo. Summon us to search out the riches stored in hidden places. Bring strength to our roots in You, unseen but deep and enduring.

# The Trumpet's Call

Praise him with the sounding of the trumpet...

—Psalm 150:3a

In the biblical year, the Festival of Trumpets "incidentally" corresponded with our united worship season at North Heights. That holiday caught my attention this year, and I decided to research the purpose of the blowing of the trumpet or shofar.

The shofar would blow for a number of reasons in the Old Testament. Here are just a few: to call a sacred assembly, to gather the people to praise, as a battle cry, or to gather warriors to fight the battle before them. It is a call to alarm, a call of warning; it was to announce the Lord's presence or to announce an anointing over a leader. It was blown before the ark of the covenant. It is a reminder that "our God will fight for us." It is a call for rejoicing over victory and a signal of triumph and celebration.

How amazing to have the Festival of Trumpets just at a time when we were seeking the Lord's face for unity, anointing, and to call us together to praise Him and listen to His directions for us.

Now seven weeks later, the season of united services is ending. I pray that what was on the Lord's heart for this time has at least begun and that we would be a people who continue to listen and heed His call in a fresh, new way.

As I sought understanding from the Lord about the Festival of Trumpets, it was very touching to see His use of the trumpet call historically and currently to all of us who seek His face.

It was as if He was saying:

> Be awed by Me,
> Notice My careful hand,
> Know your call to My people, Israel, you and
> your offspring,
> Retreat to My presence and listen to My
> announcements,

Be awed by the holiness of My covenant,
Be anointed by My blood,
Assemble with My people,
Take up arms against the enemy,
Praise Me among the assembly,
Heed My warnings,
Fight for the King,
See My deliverance.
(Leviticus 23, 25; Numbers 10, 29; Judges 3, 7; 1 Samuel 13; 1 Kings 1; 1 Chronicles 2; 2 Chronicles 7, 13, 20; Nehemiah 4; Job 39; Isaiah 27; Jeremiah 4, 19, 51; Ezekiel 7, 33; Joshua 6; Zechariah 9; Revelation 8)

For the trumpet will sound and the dead will be raised imperishable and the mortal with immortality. But thanks be to God! He gives us victory though our Lord Jesus Christ. (1 Cor. 15:52, 57)

# Awake, North Wind!

Awake, north wind, and come south wind! Blow on my garden, that its fragrance may spread abroad.

—Song of Solomon 4:16

As fall is turning colder and it is time to put our gardens to bed for the winter, this scripture comes to mind. The cold north wind blows on our gardens and reminds the plants to strengthen their roots. This strong wind is not out of order; it is a process of life. Challenge and difficulty are also a process to us. Though

*Deep within are places you cannot find, Safe and warm places that will warm and still your currents.*

hard to understand, they are not out of order but are ordered for this time in our life. We sang a chorus in church a few weeks back. One little phrase has stayed in my mind: "It's all right." It may mean "It's okay," but my heart heard, "It is all as it should be and perfectly right just as it is." There is such peace in accepting what the Lord allows to come as right, timely, and perfect for our growth and His glory. I will never hear "It's all right" the same again.

I wrote a poem during a difficult time in my life that I would like to share with you. It is about the north winds that blow in our lives.

The north wind blows cold and hard.
It burdens every crack with its force.
It brings frost and leaves coming from faraway places
To my doorstep.
Eagerly it seeks entrance to the softer, warmer places of my life.
It comes to the hearth and blows down to extinguish
the flames dancing with warmth.
Sending forces from behind and beneath and above,
Cast this way with relentless foreboding.
Oh, north wind, don't dance with folly.
You are a mere agent of usefulness.
You puff yourself up as if you are the sender.
Your fury is not your own.
We see your hand move, yet you cannot move yourself.
You cause the traveler to turn and seek shelter, but you are kept out.
Though you knock and clang, you cannot enter the heart.
Deep within are places you cannot find,
Safe and warm places that will warm and still your currents.
Boast not, north wind, for you, too,
Are not your own.

The south wind will come and will spread its beautiful fragrance to many places. But the seeds of that fragrance come from knowing whom to trust and placing our heart safely under the shelter of His hand, letting our roots go deep because we need Him and He satisfies.

# A Land Flowing with Milk and Honey

Exodus 3:8

Did you know that honey is a food that will last forever? A discovery in an Egyptian tomb revealed honey buried with the person some one thousand years prior was tested and was still safe and edible. Apparently, honey has its own bacteria that keeps it clean and edible forever. Milk, on the other hand, can spoil in just hours.

When the Lord invited the Hebrews to enter "the land flowing with milk and honey," perhaps it was more than just a land. Israel does have the land that supports abundant milk and honey production. Yet, we can see a longer-range view.

Our relationship with the Lord is like this. We need daily sustenance, as in milk. We need to keep our connection with Him fresh. We need to go daily to our source, and He will give our supply for that day. Sometimes if feels like what He gives is not as abundant as we need. He promises to be sufficient with His grace. He did not say abundant. If He gave more than necessary, we would not have to go back to Him and reconnect to get more. I would love to be self-sufficient and be enough in myself. That is not the Lord's goal for us. If we try to live on yesterday's relationship, things begin to go sour. We can get off course.

This is also like our prayer life. We may pray and ask for many things and then quickly forget what was once a diligent request. God appears to balance the detail of His answers with our faithful attention to what He is doing. The more we notice His hand at work, the more He continues to attend to the detail. Once again, we find a relational god who seeks moment-by-moment connection with His children.

He promises us substance for eternity, our honey, and sufficiency for the day, our milk. What a god we serve! Let us remember to walk in the land flowing with milk and honey.

> Your words are like honey on my lips. (Psalm 119:103)

# A Willing God

Take up your sleeping mat and start walking [and keep on walking] that you may know beyond a doubt that Jesus has the right, authority and power to forgive sins.

—Mark 2:9b–10 AMP

Traveling around India and Sri Lanka, I encountered many stone gods. Temples were filled with idols, candles, incense, and worshippers prostrated before the stone images. With all their hearts, worshippers were seeking help and deliverance. I found much faith in their hearts, sincere desires to worship, reverently praying, seeking a stone god. They were seeking power from a source that ultimately destroys and nullifies the person. Their beautiful faces full of sadness, confusion, and anger at times.

I am so glad that we serve a willing god. Jesus is His name. He is the One who opens our blind eyes and deaf ears so we may have a heart to understand and be delivered from darkness, a Lord who supports and directs our steps. He speaks faith into our lives by the authority of the name of Jesus, His earthly authority purchased by His shed blood on the earth.

The earth was cleansed and delivered by the blood of the Son of God that dripped on the dirt below the whipping post and at the foot of the cross, a costly deliverance. It was blood that was freely given to reverse the effects of the curse of Eden, and this freedom is made available to us by faith in Him who paid the price.

Family of Christ, "Take up your sleeping mat and start walking, and keep on walking, that you may know beyond a doubt that Jesus has the right, authority, and power to forgive sins and deliver you safely into His everlasting kingdom."

# Be Ye Holy as I Am Holy

Leviticus 11:45

The Holy Spirit Conference was dynamic this year. The atmosphere in there was as rich as the teachings. There seemed to be a magnet on my car drawing me there when I had a spare moment during the four days of the conference.

One evening, I came late, tired from work and the responsibilities of the day but eager in my spirit to be near the presence of God. During the uplifting worship, a very quiet voice of the Holy Spirit spoke to me about something I had in my purse. At work, I had played a game with some patients that involved dice, an innocent game of drawing a bug named Cooty. I had left with the dice in my pocket and moved them to my purse to assure I would remember to return them to the game in the morning.

The Holy Spirit gave me unrest about the dice in His presence. One of the speakers had spoken of things above the line and things below the line. Much of our life is lived with things below the line, normal, earthly, natural. The dice were in that category, and the Lord did not want to hinder the presence of a holy god. This is not about the dice; this is about the utter holiness of God and obedience to His Word. The impression I had was that His presence would be compromised if I did not remove the dice from the sanctuary.

It shocked me. I began to reason and then stopped and brought them out to my car. Leviticus 10:10 tells us to be able to distinguish between the holy and the common. The Lord was giving me practice.

It has taught me once again that His presence is holy; He wants us to know the difference between the holy and the unholy and live as much as possible "above the line."

It reminds me of a Moravian story about an offering of a lamb for a ceremonial dinner. The Holy Spirit spoke to one of the elders that it was a blemished lamb they slaughtered. He addressed the provider of the lamb, and he agreed. What we think should pass does not always pass.

God loves our praise and worship, but He also wants our holiness and obedience, even in things we do not think matter that much. May we all seek His holiness.

# Betrayal

The friend in whom I trusted, with whom I shared my bread, has lifted up his heel against me.

—Psalm 41:9

This is a showstopper in my life if ever there was one. It can cut to my core faster than any other situation. Trusting and then being betrayed by that trust is something we all can relate to. Jesus found the same situation in this world. As I look at my life, I see instances of betrayal that are still in the process of being healed and restored. I wonder if you can relate.

Years ago, I lived in a kibbutz in Israel, with a Christian discipleship program. It was a fabulous experience. When they were assigning roommates, I specifically prayed that I would be with anyone but this one woman. You guessed it, I was put with her. We could not have been more different. I liked to move; she liked to sit. I liked quiet; she liked constant radio. And so it went. We learned to like and love each other and are friends to this day. However, there was a time that we were at odds to the point of not speaking for a while. (That is tough in a ten-by-ten-foot room!) I thought our friendship included talking out problems. She refused, and I felt betrayed.

There have been other betrayals over the years. A staff I supervised went to the administration with complaints I had not heard and then she quit before any changes could take place. No chance of reconciliation there! Another deep betrayal was that when my second husband died, his outdated will made no provision for me. After his death, his children quickly left our home and distanced their lives. Loving and trusting people certainly has its risks!

The pain of betrayal nips at my heels every day. We need to lift these things up to Jesus daily. The pain is too much for us to bear alone. Learning to trust His love and care is the key. I have learned that the only one I can fully trust is the Lord Jesus. His love is faithful and full every day. If I lift up my pain, He takes it. Sometimes I need to give it to Him many times a day. It would be easy to slide back into thinking, *What have I done to deserve this?* This seems to be one of Satan's most repeated taunts. At times, and in ways, we are culpable. The fingerprint of Satan is that the pain and guilt go on and on, regardless of our honesty before the Lord. Offering one honest confession for what we may have contributed to the situation is all that needs to happen. Then we need to step away from Satan's target practice and move on into the plans of the Lord. Rebuilding trust is the job of the offender. If that is not possible, then we must leave that too and move on, building trust in the Lord and allowing Him to heal our broken hearts.

> Trust only in the Lord, with all, all of your heart,
> Lean not on your own, weak and short sighted
> understanding and He will deliver you, save you,
> keep you safe, renew, redeem, revive, and restore
> you. The Lord straightens out our crooked paths
> and brings us safely home to His heart. (Proverbs
> 3:5–6 AMP)

Pain and trouble are not necessarily signs of sin, but they are always signs that we are in the world.

# Broken or Bitter?

A broken and a contrite heart, O God, You will
not despise.

—Psalm 51:17

When the unexpected happens, we get shocked. What we do
with this shock has vast and far-reaching effects for our lives and
the lives of those around us. As we walk through our grief and
stay close to God, we are safe. Press into God long enough for
Him to mend you. Keep the wound clean daily so the healing can
come from the inside out. We need to let God transform our desire
from what we wanted to acceptance of what is. An interruption
in that process is when the red flags begin to fly and our peace is
disturbed.

It is always when our expectations are highest that our disappointments are deepest. This is true when loved ones disappoint
us. We want to believe that these people in our lives will hold up
the expectation that we have placed on them. Sadly and frequently,
this is not true. Church wounds, just as family wounds, run deep
and so often last way too long. Wounds seem to collect wounds so
that any small offense turns into "more of the same." When brokenness morphs into bitterness, infection has set in and healing is long
delayed.

Bitterness may begin to wear victimhood as though it is a badge
of courage. When this happens, it should also be a warning. Being
a victim is powerful and sends a strong message of "Stay away,"
"Watch out," or "Treat me as special." Once we are in this place,
we are unaware that we are actually cutting off the very relationships we need, closing the mouths of those who could be helpful to
us. Bitterness is somehow easier than the quiet patience needed to
allow the broken pieces to heal. "See to it that no one fails to obtain
the grace of God: That no root of bitterness springs up and causes
trouble, and by it many become defiled" (Hebrews 12:15). Troubles

come, but we are promised company along the path—Jesus and the fellowship of the saints.

> See I have set before you a way of life and a way of death. Therefore choose life. (Deuteronomy 30:15)

# Calling Us Beyond

To make the riches of his glory known.

—Romans 9:23

Have you ever been in a situation that is too hard for you? You may have found yourself saying, "I wish God did not trust me so much to give me this to face." We know well the scripture that God does not give us more than we can handle, yet often, it seems too hard for us to get through.

That is exactly the plan. It is too hard for us to get through. We are being asked to give beyond our capacity. The Lord always calls us to more than we are, to more than we have, to more than we can give so that He will be our supply. He wants us to reach our end so we will call on Him.

He calls us beyond ourselves, beyond our understanding, beyond our strength so our hearts will move off our self-sufficient, personal, success-oriented, natural pride. He calls us beyond so He becomes our sufficiency, our success, and will get the glory that is so easily His.

Then we can see His very personal interest in the affairs of mankind. We can see His loving character. We can see His big heart that beats for His people.

Our eyes are lifted off our small world with all its challenges and look toward heaven from where our strength, ability, and fruitfulness comes (Psalm 121:1, paraphrased).

# Climbing to Our Fortress

You are my strong tower.

—Proverbs 18:10

There is a mountain fortress in southern Israel called Masada. Herod built it in 37 BC as a palace for the protection and beauty offered by a mountaintop. In the time of the Roman overthrow of Israel (AD 73), the Jewish people gathered on this mountain as their last place of resistance. They were together seeking refuge from the army that had surrounded them. The Roman army waited them out and then built a siege ramp and broke into their community. The outcome was grim.

*With our eyes fixed on our goal, we manage the rocks at our feet, the twisted trail, and keep climbing.*

On the recent NHLC trip to Israel, we visited Masada. There were a few of us who chose to climb the twisted path to the top instead of riding the cable car. It took us about thirty minutes to climb up the narrow path. As we climbed, we realized what a deliberate choice it is to come to a fortress for defense. It does not just happen.

When we come to the Lord for our protection, it is also deliberate. We seek it, help one another on the way, but we climb. If there are those who are tired, weak, or sick, we keep them near as we journey upward. With our eyes fixed on our goal, we manage the rocks at our feet, the twisted trail, and keep climbing. Finding our refuge in Jesus, we are safe, the outcome is good, but it does not happen by chance. We run to the strong tower, and we are saved.

# Comfort and Rest

I live in a high and holy place,
But also with the one who is contrite and lowly in spirit,
To revive the spirit of the lowly
To revive the heart of the contrite.
I have seen their ways, but I will heal them;
I will guide them and restore comfort…

—Isaiah 57:15, 18

Recently, I found myself engaging in a pastime I love. I draw floor plans of small cabins. These are places I would love to go to at the end of a long day—a place to rest, find comfort and peace to soothe and help in sorting out the events of the day. We all have an inborn need for comfort and rest. Yet our souls wrestle against these blessings. Our actions at times oppose the very rest we long for. On one hand, we long for the quiet peace of rest, but we seem to act in a way that is opposite to seeking that peace. We seem to think that we will happen upon comfort and rest after all our duties are finished. Yet that day comes only once—at the end of our earthly journey.

Being busy can fool us into thinking it is equated with being important. Resting may suggest that we must be unimportant. Having many things to do and many people to contact is valuable but is not the real measure of our value. Rest embraces a place of humility; we trust that family or work responsibilities can carry on without us. We can enter His rest with a contrite heart, one that can rest and know that rest offers us what we need; comfort is ours. Our hearts are in the place of trust and humility; there is no safer place on earth.

# Enemy Possession

It has amazed me when I have visited the sites of Jesus in the land of Israel. Often, the sites most precious to believers have fallen into disrepair or have a palpable darkness around them. Yet other sites that have been recreated by a faithful group of saints have the light shining around them and a sense of easy access to the Lord Himself. It is as if the enemy has wanted to possess ground that was precious. Surprised? Maybe not. Yet the clarity of it does surprise me.

Bethlehem has become almost inaccessible since it was given to the Palestinian Authority. It is not safe to travel there. Even when it was, the church built on the traditional spot is dark and cold; the atmosphere seems preoccupied with protocol. Bethlehem Square used to be the sight of beautiful Christmas Eve celebrations, not anymore.

It is written that the enemy is the prince of this world (John 16:11). Wayward princes seek power. Remember, Absalom, David's son, was working to take power away from his father and was fairly successful to a point. We know there is a similar enemy seeking to take power from his creator.

As we approach Christmas this year, let's be very aware of what the enemy is trying to possess—a place in our heart, our joy of the celebration, the meaning, or a healing? Does the Lord want to do a precious work in your heart this Christmas? We can be sure that He is.

Ask Him what it is; ask Him what it will look like and how you can cooperate. He never gives us hard tasks that weigh us down. He gives us things that bring joy, freedom, and peace. Be aware of how the enemy will want to take possession of the very things that give life and salvation. Above all things, guard your heart; it is the wellspring of life (Proverbs 4:23). Dig your well deeper, let Jesus cleanse the waters, and drink deeply from the wellspring of life. You will be refreshed and able to offer cleansing water to those you meet.

# Exchanged

For they exchanged the truth of God for a lie.

—Romans 1:25a

I needed some new shoes for an upcoming wedding. Really, I did! I ended up purchasing two pairs, hoping one would fit the bill. Neither did, so on Saturday I had to exchange them for something that would work.

On Saturday, another exchange occurred. I went to a women's event at church. The evidence of prayerful preparation by the leadership was clear. There was time to be with the Lord during which the Lord spoke to me about some exchanges He wanted to make in my heart.

As I considered areas in my life that needed a touch from Jesus, some themes developed. I was feeling powerless, invisible, unheard, alone, put down, afraid, embarrassed on the outside, and like honesty does not win. As I prayed, I gave the Lord the reasons I had for all these areas. I needed an exchange of much greater importance than the wrong shoes. I realized that I had exchanged the truth of God for lies and supported them with life experiences. The shoes were returned and new ones selected, but better yet, here are the exchanges I made for some of those difficult situations and emotions attached to them:

> The truth is that God is for us, and so are His people.
> There is power in the blood; I just need to stay there.
> Sometimes we are the voice in the wilderness at work, at home, and the nation. I can be brave.
> The Lord will never forget us; He loves us completely as we are today.
> He sees our best efforts and credits us for the attitudes of our heart.
> Even if our "gentleness is not evident to all" (Philippians 4:5), He will stand in the gap.

Hallelujah! I cannot do all the exchanges every moment, but God will stay with me throughout my life and into eternity. Praise the Lord for the great exchange Jesus made for us on the cross and the exchange He offers us every day to live more fully in Him.

> And we stand because God is able to make us stand. (Romans 14:4)

# Facing Jerusalem

> Hear Oh Israel, the Lord your God is one God. Praise His most holy name, His kingdom is forever.
>
> —Deuteronomy 6:4

This is a prayer that is recited by Jewish people. It is called the shema, which means "hear, listen, and respond." They face toward Jerusalem, recite this prayer, and remember the character of our God.

Life is full of distractions; our focus on the Lord is in competition with the ruminating worries of everyday life. We get caught in the internal distractions of practicing conversations with many people and for many distressing situations. White noise is all around us, trying to distract. The enemy uses any voices that may get your attention, and he supplies you with every good reason to get off course.

Face Jerusalem, face your God, and look full in His wonderful face. Let your eyes and heart rest on Him.

Here is what is sure: God loves you dearly; He is able to do all things. You can do all things in Him who strengthens you. In Him you are strong and pure. You have a birthright in Jesus, and your kingdom inheritance is for today as well as to come.

Stand, beautiful one, in the heavenly light that shines on your life. Stand quietly, still, strong, and joyously.

Shema: listen, hear, and respond.

It is all yours in Christ as you look full in His wonderful face.

# Forgiven Is My Name

A line in the hymn "Come Home" has always stood out to me. It says, "Calling, O sinner, come home." It is so endearing to be known as sinner. I can do that; I can be that! He really knows me, and yet the Lord lovingly calls me to Himself. Knowing my penchant for sin and my need for a savior is crucial to realize my daily need for Him. Yet there is a place to grow further.

To accept the change in my identity from sinner to fully and utterly pardoned is when Forgiven becomes my name. That name embraces my need for forgiveness and goes beyond to who I am in Christ, fully forgiven, all the time, every day, and every moment. Not a speck of time passes when the finished work of the cross is not active in my life.

What an identity we have waiting for us to embrace! We must leave the old bedfellows of shame, guilt, and regret. We will receive a name change in heaven, but here on earth, I am delighted to know that I am called Forgiven by the Most High! What a miracle. What an honor. And what a choice we have to fully embrace His work on the cross. All who call on the name of Jesus can rightfully declare, "Forgiven is my name!" Hallelujah!

# Godfullness

> Whose delight is in the law of the LORD, and
> who meditates on his law day and night.
>
> —Psalm 1:2

There is a practice that is being used in many places, even in public schools. It is the skill of "mindfulness." Being mindful is to be present to the moment and focused on the now. It is the skill that often translates to different types of meditation.

I would like to direct our thoughts to the Word of God. Meditation is a skill that dates to the very early writing of David.

We are reminded to meditate on the Word day and night. We are being asked to be in the moment, turning our awareness toward the one and only. I like to call it Godfullness. That is how we as believers want to live. Our daily tasks become illuminated by the awareness and presence of the Lord. We keep before us *our moment-by-moment need* of Him and at the same time *His moment-by-moment supply*. This Godfullness is available to us as we live in the clarity of His loving gaze upon us.

With Godfullness as a mindset, our mistakes are instantly lifted. At times we make a tug-of-war out of sin and hold onto shame and embarrassment as a form of payment. As we lay hold of Godfullness, we understand that neither sin or self-payment can outweigh the blood of Jesus. Love held Him to the cross, not the nails. He is the rightful owner of our sin.

We can choose to live in the same joy of Godfullness that Adam and Eve experienced. They rested with their Maker on their first day, enjoying His presence and absorbing the identity of rest and trust as foundation stones of human kind. That is our inheritance in Christ. May we grow in the moment-to-moment supply of Jesus and His love.

# Healing

Jeremiah takes healing very seriously.

In Jeremiah 8:11 NIV, he writes, "They dress the wound of my people as though it were not serious… They have healed the wound of my people lightly, saying, 'Peace, peace,' when there is no peace." We come to understand that healing is not a quick fix but more often a process of seeking God, His Word, and the support and prayer of others. Jeremiah does not want superficial peace that comes from superficial healing. Neither does the Lord.

Jeremiah goes on to say in 8:22 NIV, "Is there no balm in Gilead? Is there no physician there? Why then is not the health of the daughter of my people restored?" The balm of Gilead is an example of our part of healing. Gilead is a certain place. To get that balm, one must take action and go to that place. Pursue it, and use it. The balm is not helpful closed in a book or set on a shelf. Jesus is our Gilead; we can go to Him for the real healing. Often, the seeking for the balm of Gilead was not a solitary process. It involved others. Communion is the coming together of others in one.

The balm needs to be applied. Having Jesus is not our only response. We must apply Him to our life. It has been said that emotions last for only twelve seconds; after that, it is what we do with our feelings that continues to affect us. If we refuse to embrace the full forgiveness of Christ into our life, we get stuck in shame and remorse. If we refuse to see as the Lord sees, we can get stuck in unforgiveness or offense. It says in Galatians 5:15 that when we bite and devour one another, we destroy ourselves (paraphrased).

Once again, in Jeremiah 15:18–19 AMP, Jeremiah discusses healing and asks, "Why is my wound refusing to be healed? Will you…be to me like a deceitful brook, like waters that fail and are uncertain?" And the Lord graciously answers him, "If you return [and give up the mistaken tone of distrust and despair], then I will give you again a settled place of quiet and safety… [Then] you shall be My mouthpiece."

Not only does the Lord desire to heal us, He wants to give us quiet and safety and to use us as His mouthpiece. Now that is the complete healing that we seek.

# Hidden Manna and a White Stone

> I will give some of the hidden manna. I will also give that person a white stone with a new name written on it, known only to the one who receives it.
>
> —Revelations 2:17 NIV

We are told in this verse that God will give us some of the hidden manna, from supplies in heaven that we do not know about. During the traditional Passover meal, there is a piece of the flat bread or matzo that is broken and then hidden for the children to find. They search all over the house to find this hidden matzo. There is a prize for the first *It is He who writes a name that is known only between Him and each of us.* to find it. This hidden supply is mentioned in the book of Revelation. To some, the manna is still hidden, and according to the scriptures, their salvation is yet to come. We are told that the full revelation of Jesus as the Messiah is yet awaiting Israel and is linked to the "fullness of Gentiles" coming to faith as spoken of in Romans 9. There is also a meaning for us right now: we have a supply in heaven that cannot be seen—a supply that is waiting for us, to call, ask, and search for. Then it becomes ours; the prize is the very presence of Jesus Himself.

We also receive a white stone with a new name written on it, known only to the one who receives it. This picture is stunning. Jesus is our white stone, and we in Him, purified and strong. Jesus, our solid rock on whom we stand, is the One who has sealed our purity for all time. It is He who writes a name that is known only between Him and each of us. This name will be revealed to us in a time to come. He is an utterly personal god who speaks to us one personal time after another. The conversation is only between us. The name—how He sees us—is private between Him and us. It is not a comparison to another; it is a name born from His love and in His heart, to and for only us.

As parents give their children names, so does "our Father who is in heaven." He has named us—a name that is personal, growth-producing, deep, secure, purposeful, and settled for all time. Our name is spoken only by the One who knows and loves us best. What a heritage we have in Him! Hidden manna and a white stone with our heavenly name. God is a god of mystery, intrigue, and love.

# Humility and Authority

Be completely humble and gentle.

—Ephesians 4:2

Pride is such a constant condition of the soul. My heart longs for the fulfillment of the above verse, complete humility, and gentleness. Then pride rushes in. It exaggerates problems to look beyond God's reach. It says "Yes, but" a hundred times a day, even to godly solutions and answers. Pride is impatient because its precious time is wasted; it fears, worries, rages, defends, and reacts. Sometimes I am jealous of Moses; he was the most humble man on earth. His relationship with the Lord was so close.

Humility simply trusts at each turn. It listens for the voice that knows. Moses, who conversed with the Lord, also kept his word and passion through long periods of heaven's silence. Perhaps humility is born and fed during these times. Moses knew his source and his need. Based on this, he had great authority in God. He had boundless courage before Pharaoh and others in following the Word of the Lord.

Humility is not low self-value, passive living, and giving way to others. It does not defend ourselves or boast. Humility shines the light off us and onto the Lord. *It is not our relationship to others; it is our relationship to God and His power.*

Humility is bold. It trusts God, even in our pride and our sins. It discerns truth and gently addresses the world around us with this truth. When "self" is under God's power, we can move in peace and boldness for kingdom purposes.

Lord, help us walk in Your humility so we may hear Your voice and bring Your purposes to our world.

# Is Your Soul at Rest?

Having a soul at rest seems to be such a challenge. Worries about kids, friendship, abilities, the endless to-do lists are all pressures that tug on my potential serenity. It is potential because sometimes it doesn't get any further than worry.

Reading Matthew 11:28 gave me a key. I know the yoke is supposed to be easy and the burden light, but so often it doesn't feel that way. "Learn of me," Jesus says, "for I am gentle and humble of heart." Here, it is becoming "gentle and humble of heart." A gentle, humble heart is a safe heart. It is not our natural state of being. We have to ask Jesus for a heart like that. An unassuming heart is one that takes time for the tender things of the day. This heart enables us to find peace in the crowd and even in the pressure. "O Lord, please make me a good student of Yours. What You offer me is life and living water in a parched land."

Is your yoke too heavy? Set down the heavy yoke. Discuss with the Lord if it is yours to carry. Perhaps you weren't allowing Him to carry His portion. Perhaps you shouldn't be the one carrying that yoke.

Seek Him for that gentle, humble heart. Let Him bring you the help He offers.

Take time to unload now; rest and lean onto Him. You need never be ashamed. He is love at every turn. He is the Lord of Hosts, the God of the universe, and He is gentle and humble of heart. He knows how to give you safety and rest. Blessed be His name!

# Joshua

Joshua 1:3 tells the story of the Israelites' entrance into the promised land—a promise to Israel and principle of partnership to us. There are times when God clearly leads us. He acts as the front-runner and clears the path. We stumble upon it and realize the bushwhacking He has already done. Those are sweet times, grace times, praise times, bask-in-His-goodness times. Our eyes are open, and we can see, even list, His preparations for us.

I recently heard a couple's story that reflected how God had orchestrated their relationship with little more from them than accepting His goodness. He is able, and He acts in this way.

For most of life, it seems that God is after a partnership. His promise to Israel came with a partnership principle. "Where *you* set *your* foot… I will give." God wants to give us what we desire and are willing to go after. Like a parent listening to the child's birthday wish, He listens to our heart's desire, but just giving it to us may lessen our partnership. *He follows our lead*. Isn't that amazing? The God of the universe following our lead? We enact; God acts.

When we prayerfully initiate, God joins in and partners. He is asking us to take action in trust, to want something that He can give. But He wants us to act, pray, reach, stretch, and grow our dreams *with* Him.

I remember praying for something I wanted to see happen. I heard Him speak to me, "Walk in that direction." I was to faithfully begin to put into place the path to my prayer.

He was faithful to bless my time, work, and efforts. We were a partnership in the answer. I love surprise gifts, but I believe it more often the case that God is after the partnership with Him. He will do anything to spend time with us! Let's prayerfully "set our foot" on the ground we want.

I will give you every place you set your foot.
(Joshua 1:3)

# Rebooting Our Lives

Then a great and powerful wind tore the mountains apart and shattered the rocks...then an earthquake...then fire. And after the fire came a gentle whisper.

—1 Kings 19:11–12

We often find ourselves at a place we did not intend to be. We had thoughts, goals, dreams, and hopes of how our lives would pan out. Then we find ourselves in a completely different place; the surroundings, relationships, and events took a turn somewhere along the road. Perhaps in tragedy, but more often, just a slow turn off the course we had set in our mind.

It is time to reboot. That is a technical term to go back to the original settings, the neutral place to build from once again. When events turn for us, we may have emotions both on the surface and deep within that may be shouting "This is not right or fair!" "How did I get here?" or even "Why am I all alone in this?" We must answer the questions with the same depth that the primordial compass needs.

The great and powerful wind, earthquake, or fire has knocked our lives off-kilter.

We are alone, and intellect or the natural realm does not give the answers.

Gratefully, the Lord is in the depths and in the answers. Sometimes our internal world is so loud that when the gentle whisper comes, it seems far too quiet to reach into what our souls are craving. If we can quiet our souls and ask the questions, the Lord can meet us in the calm with a gentle voice. "I have a plan. Your path is secure. This, too, will be redeemed and used for My glory and your good."

What peaceful knowledge that no wind, earthquake, or fire in any realm can oust the redemption of the One who loves our very soul.

# Just as He Was

Leaving the crowd behind, they took him along,
just as he was, in the boat. There were also other
boats with him.

—Mark 4:36 NIV

During this portion of Jesus's ministry, we can tell from just this sentence that it was busy and it was full of people. It must have been hard for Him to get away and think, pray, or even sleep. Once He was in the boat, He fell asleep and slept through the terrifying squall that He quieted. Coming along with the disciples, His overreaching travel planners, He did not have a chance to prepare for the trip. In the International Standard Version of the Bible, it reads, "Without making special preparations." He left the crowd and went onto the next event, not even preparing a sermon, taking clean clothes or a shave kit. He was ready to move to the next place of ministry.

He was available and willing. He could see there was more to do, more waves to still, more people to deliver, and more sermons needed. He left one ministry to do the next ministry. There seemed to be no personal focus. He could see there were needs He left untended, but it was time to move on. He did not check His to-do list; He was available for whatever was next. He was available, attentive, and willing. He stepped into the unknown of the next thing with what appears to be great peace and trust that God would be just as present in the unknown as He was in the known.

We are so apt to think we cannot go to the next thing because we are not sufficiently prepared. We have many things that should or must get done, and the next ministry chance may be completely missed. Jesus went, just as He was, not specially dressed, not greatly prepared, just available and willing, trusting in the bigger plan that was not at all evident as He stepped into the boat. Then He went to sleep, deeply, trusting that God would prepare Him and His next step.

He was used "just as He was," available, willing, trusting completely. Lord, help us be like Him!

# Leaning into the Wind

A furious squall came up, and the waves broke
over the boat, so that it was nearly swamped.

—Mark 4:37

When difficulty comes, our natural response is to move away from it. When that is possible, it is nice. So often we are unable to escape, and yet we try to flee. Flight comes in many forms, from addiction to denial. What if when the harsh winds come, we lean into them? What if we remember that Jesus has authority on earth and has promised to never leave us? The winds take on new form and meaning. They are the winds of possibility, shaping us to be more like Jesus, increasing our faith and our testimony. These winds carve into hard surfaces, causing a sweeping, softer design. In nature, even the rocks submit to the invisible, strong wind.

We can't see the source of the wind, but we can see its effect. Water ripples, leaves quake, branches bend. What if when trials come, we do not turn our backs on the winds but face them with Jesus at our side? What if with God-given courage, we say, "Yes, the winds are blowing hard, and I don't know how this will turn out, but I do know that nothing, nothing escapes the notice of my Savior. And I will lean into the wind."

Once we fully credit Jesus with His power on earth, we can say, "I will face the winds, even lean into the winds," allowing lessons and shaping of those very winds to carve into our lives. We know that before the disciples' boat was swamped, Jesus powerfully said, "Quiet, be still!" Even the winds and the waves obey Him (Mark 4:40)! He is the same Almighty God and will do the same for us.

# Little Foxes

Catch for us the little foxes, the little foxes that ruin our vineyards, our vineyards that are in blossom.

—Song of Solomon 2:15

When Samson wanted to destroy the grain field of the Philistines, he set the tails of foxes on fire and let them run loose in the harvest (Judges 15:4). Samson is an odd character in the Bible. He does things that rarely seem to have *We are to watch for the little foxes that can enter the vineyard of our life.* the blessing of God, and then God blesses the outcome. In this incident, he was intent on destroying the harvest of his enemies.

Someone else is seeking to destroy the harvest of his enemies. Satan wants to destroy the harvest of God. We are part of that harvest, the vineyards of God.

We are to watch for the little foxes that can enter the vineyard of our life. These little innocuous areas of sin do not appear harmful. Yet used by the enemy, they can set fire to a field and do much damage to the harvest.

Often, the little foxes of our lives are silent and illusive, much like a fox in the wild. Yet they can be very damaging. They are the "little" sins in our life, thoughts, patterns, a hard heart, superior attitude, or impatience at the person in front of us. God wants to touch these things with His forgiveness and cleansing.

There is nothing that refreshes a life like repentance. We are in the season of the Jewish Holy Day of Atonement. It is a good day to listen quietly. As you come before the Lord, ask Him to reveal where the little foxes are in your life. Expect Him to meet you, never with condemnation or criticism but with hope and the joy of cleansing refreshment in Him.

Please, Lord, catch for us the little foxes, the little foxes that ruin the vineyard.

# Mount Sinai

Have you ever felt like the Lord just told you to take another lap around Mount Sinai? Has the same problem or frustrating situation shown up again and again? The repetition is its own point of frustration!

The children of Israel wandered for forty years in their slave clothing, repeating the lesson of trust, and belief. Unfortunately, our heart is cut from the same cloth of earthly sin and worldly perspective. The knowledge of God and the understanding of His ways are often as slippery to hold onto as a desert skink. Without knowing it, we can pit our reason and logic against the knowledge and ways of God. This battle ends in defeat of our mind and heart. Our reasoning can become so ingrown that it tangles the pipeline to God. He wants to speak into our hearts, but the message is scrambled.

In the example of Job, God's heavy hand was upon him, but the battle was not against sin. Job was righteous and devoted to God. The Lord was using Job's faithfulness as a staging ground for winning a heavenly battle with Satan. It was not about Job at all; it was for heavenly purposes in the heavenly realms.

The spoils of the battle was Job's faithfulness; he was the evidence of God's victory.

Let that be true in your battles as well. Let your trust in the love and goodness of God be spoken of you in heaven. Let your declaration of faith be the foundation stones in building heavenly temples of praise.

Job never saw the purpose of his trials. However, he left us a prototype of understanding. When the next difficult situation comes along, once sin is ruled out, the answer may be, "This is for My kingdom's sake in the heavenly realms. Will you bring in the victory in My Son?"

> You have not come to a mountain…that is burning with fire, but to Mount Zion,…to thousands of angels in joyful assembly. (Hebrews 12:18–22)

He will see us through.

# Overcoming Shame

Guard my life and rescue me; let me not be put
to shame, for I take refuge in you. May integrity
and uprightness protect me because my hope is
in you.

—Psalm 25:20–21

Shame is a strong tool of the enemy. From the garden of Eden when Adam and Eve first felt the sting of sin, it was shame. They responded by covering their nakedness. They defended themselves from the exposed humiliation of shame. Guilt says, "I have done wrong." Shame tells us, "I am bad and must hide."

King David repeats many times in the Psalms, "Let me not be put to shame." He asks nine times specifically, and there are many other related references. Shame is a fierce enemy. It binds us and keeps us in a defensive and protective mode. It keeps us from serving freely and looking outward.

Jesus's first miracle was at Cana. His goal? To protect the bridegroom from being embarrassed that he had run out of wine before the wedding celebration had ended. Jesus wanted to protect the groom from the shame of poor planning or insufficient money. How kind Jesus was! He could have let the natural consequence of an error happen, but He stepped in.

The fear of exposure that Adam and Eve felt in the garden, the fear of humiliation that the groom may have felt at Cana, and David's repeated plea, are all examples that tell us of the formidable and paralyzing enemy that shame can be. From the garden to the first miracle of Jesus, we know God addresses our shame. And the enemy uses this very basic human emotion of being found out to be lacking.

We have a Savior who scorned the shame of the cross, the ultimate in exposure (Hebrews 12:2). I have heard that those who were crucified were often naked. We don't know if that was true for Jesus, but the public humiliation of the cross is huge. The scorning of shame was accomplished on the cross. The public disgrace faced squarely, the undoing of Adam and Eve's shame-filled covering, the refusal to submit to shame but to overcome shame publicly, once for all mankind, are the works of the cross of Jesus.

When we disengage from shame, we can be free to make errors and then be free to step out in the world to make an impact for Christ. It allows us to be about leading people to Christ and strengthening their faith, not dwelling inwardly and afraid but facing outward in trust. Jesus has our backs. Shame is not our enemy. It has been overcome on the cross. Let us join with Jesus, scorn shame, and walk confidently for the sake of the kingdom.

# Present Tense God

Jeremiah 31:33

There are so many promises in the Bible. Many are for a time yet to come. They offer us hope and a glimpse of God's goodness in the permanent future.

We serve a god of the past, present, and future. We can build our hope not only on a waiting hope but on a living, present tense hope of God's activity and help in the moment of the very day. We serve the great I Am; He is here now as much as He will be in the future.

We know of the scripture in Proverbs 13:12 NIV, "Hope deferred makes the heart sick, but a longing fulfilled is a tree of life." Being only forward-focused causes us to lose the moment. We hope for change in the future and forget to be content and accepting of God's current choices for us now.

We have a god who meets us in the day, in the moment, not a god who is only waiting for us out there in the future. We want to live in the actual hope of the current God. Hindsight can make our view of the Lord's hand more accurate. But faith is in the moment and trusts in His goodness in that same moment. Our understanding of His goodness is the only understanding we need. It is sure and true.

# Resting

God Blessed the Day and Made it Holy.

Genesis 2:3

The Lord is very concerned with our rest. We, on the other hand, seem more concerned with our effectiveness, activity, striving, and production. Very early in the Bible, we find a god who rests, who stops His labor and rests in the pleasure of His creation.

Sabbath rest is not reserved for the Jew. Long before God called out the people of Israel, He instituted rest for mankind. Genesis 2:2 says that God rested from all His work. Abraham does not come on the scene until Genesis 12. Resting from our labor was instituted for all people. Hebrews 4:1 begins by saying, "Therefore, since the promise of entering his rest still stands, let us be careful that none of you be found to have fallen short of it."

Why is it so very difficult for us to rest? Do we really think our labors are of more value than the call of God to stop once a week for a whole day and rest? I remember Saturdays (the Jewish Sabbath) in Israel. It took so much effort to stop working and rest. It is natural for us to go and go. Stopping is a discipline; sometimes I can feel the war in my flesh to stop and rest. I miss that focus here in the US. We sort of kind of stop, go to church, and maybe socialize for the early afternoon. Then we carry on. Resting for a whole day is like a tithe of time. Instead of one-tenth of our money, it is one-seventh of the week returned back to the Lord. Isn't it strange that it feels like a sacrifice to rest?

The first thing the Lord made holy on earth was a time for resting. Genesis 2:3 tells us that "God blessed the seventh day and made it holy." Part of growing in Him seems to be rooted in learning to stop and rest—really rest. May we come to understand this concept more deeply and begin to practice the discipline of resting. My guess is that by resting, we will increase our effectiveness in Christ.

# Seek His Face Always

1 Chronicles 16:11

Our eyes see so many things in a day, from lovely to ugly. Beauty is a restful place, things in order, arranged to look balanced or strikingly asymmetrical, a house cleaned, a dinner done, children happy and at play, a fire at the restful close of the day. Our eyes continually scan our lives, seeking providence or problems.

*Our eyes continually scan our lives, seeking providence or problems.*

I love the scripture in Psalm 32:8–10 NASB, "I will instruct you and teach you in the way which you should go; I will counsel you with my eye upon you. Do not be as the horse or as the mule, which have no understanding, whose trappings include bit and bridle to hold them in check." We can see that the Lord wants to instruct us, guide us, and lead us. He loves the gentle approach whenever possible.

He is our wonderful counselor, seeking our good every step of the way in this life and beyond. He does not want to tug on us, block us, or thwart us, ever. In Psalm 32, we read that He counsels us with His eye upon us.

For our part, we need to have our eyes on Him. When we are looking into His face, into His eyes, we can be easily guided. If we look to Him, a glance of His eye can lead us in the path or still our searching hearts to wait. Then we don't need the external traces to constrain and control us.

When we make up the rules and ask the Lord to tell us which one to use, sometimes we miss the mark completely. We have limited God's say in our lives, asking Him to choose between our methods. Then He must use the more directive, exterior way to lead us.

It is my prayer to be one who is directed by the Lord through the glance of His eye. That I would "look to the Lord and His strength, seek His face."

# Standing in God

God is jealous to be our identity. He wants us to believe Him, not the world, in how we view ourselves. In Christ, you are blessed, belonging, loved, esteemed, defended, protected, valuable, brave, secure, faithful, able, forgiven, alive, awake, self-controlled, and redeemed. Sometimes I find myself walking in less than who I am in Christ. I have a hunch I am not alone. Our mistakes, history, family roles, and jobs may all try to define us. Let us remember that God's definition of us is the truest.

> If anyone is in Christ he is a new creation, the old has passed away, the new has come. (2 Corinthians 5:17)

> We are destroying speculation and ever lofty thing raised up against the knowledge of God, and we are taking every thought captive to the obedience of Christ. (2 Corinthians 10:5 NASB)

Ask the Lord to cleanse and heal you from an untruthful view of yourself. Do you feel unconnected? Like a target for criticism? Angry? Out of control? Superior? Impatient? Guilty? Unloved or disregarded? Pinpoint these things and bring them under Christ's identify for you. Your Father loves you; in the amplified version of the Aaronic blessing, it says, "He watches you with an approving gaze." Remember, God looks at you constantly, lovingly, and approvingly. Not that He winks at sin, ever, but He longs for your full redemption and sees you that way.

Walk in the full redemption of Christ. You are beautiful in Him.

# The Bride and Her Groom

Hallelujah!… The bride has made herself ready.

—Revelation 19:6–7

Weddings and brides hold a dear place in all cultures. They represent innocence, beauty, love, promises, and all the potential of the joy of long-lasting wedded love. Life can tear at those pictures as real life sets in and can bring disillusionment, disappointment, betrayal, and separations. Yet there is another love story happening in the heavens.

God is the ultimate romantic; He never gets off this theme. The whole Bible is about a marriage covenant from Genesis to Revelation. He desires for His Son to marry His church. It begins with "bone of my bones and flesh of my flesh" in the creation of women, and then the two are one flesh again. God's loving call for intimacy ends with God dwelling with man, perfectly united in the New Jerusalem. There are many calls from on high to His beloved.

We have the old covenant and the new covenant. Both contain promises God makes to man so that man can dwell in fullness with Him. Just as God took woman from the side of Adam, so Christ's side was pierced as His sacrifice made a way for the church to be brought to her groom a clean and forgiven bride. We know the end of the story as prophesied in Revelation 19:6–8, "Hallelujah! For the Lord God Almighty reigns. Let us rejoice and be glad and give him glory! For the wedding of the Lamb has come and his bride has made herself ready, dressed in linen, bright and clean."

> Let us be ones who trim our lamps and make ourselves ready for the Groom when He comes from His pavilion to take His bride the Church. (Psalm 19:5)

Maranatha!

# The Cross of Completeness

Jesus knows exactly what it takes for our hearts to be happy, complete, and whole. It is the love of God that leads us to the cross of completeness. The refiner's fire burns and then purifies. He gave us hearts shaped for eternity to live in a temporal world; He also gave us the keys to live in the presence of His loving care here on earth.

Pastor John Piper wrote in his book *Pierced by the Word*, "Love labors and suffers to enthrall us with what is infinitely and eternally satisfying… God. Therefore God's love labors and suffers to break our bondage to the idol of self, and to focus our attention on the treasures of God."

Our hearts are safe as we live the surrendered and crucified life. That is the wisdom of the cross, the treasure in the dark moments of history. The key to this protection begins as we give unconditional ownership rights of our hearts to Jesus. The more we turn our hearts and life over to Jesus, the more we find peace, hope, and joy. We can live in this temporal world in peace and joy. That is great news. It came at a price to God, and it comes at a price to us.

Oh, sweet, sweet surrender,
I found my place of rest.
The loving hand of Jesus,
Knows how to make me blessed.
It is not from wane or wanting,
Nor things I may possess.
It is not from all things perfect,
That gives my soul its rest.
The compassion of our Calvary,
Is our heart placed in His.
Not seeking from all others,
What is only His to give.
Oh, sweet, sweet surrender,
I place my hope in Thee.

# The Faith of a Humble Woman

"Yes Lord," she replied, "but even the dogs under
the table eat the children's crumbs."

—Mark 7:28

This scripture bothers me. It appeared harsh for Jesus to answer a mother's request to expel the demon from her daughter with such a brisk dismissal. He said to her, "It is not right to take the children's bread and toss it to their dogs." At this point in His ministry, miracles had been done in Israel. Now He was entering the territory of the Gentiles. Granted there were many cultural things in play. Jesus was in the current country of Lebanon, speaking to a Greek/Syrian/Phoenician woman. People were openly—and still are—opposed to the Jewish people. However, something seems amiss with this statement. Knowing the Lord's invitation in Isaiah 1:18, "Come let us reason together," I decided to take the Lord up on His offer and reason with Him.

The Lord did not defend His words but drew my attention to the faith of the woman. In our lives, there are things said that may sting, things we do not understand, or may be out of context. Yet our reply to these words is key and perhaps one of the important lessons of this scripture. She knew Jesus was Lord and allowed Him to say even something seemingly difficult, yet she stayed true to His nature and replied in great strength of faith and humility. There are circumstances in our lives too that are very distressing and beyond our understanding. Believing that God is sovereign causes us to see even the difficult and confusing things through the lens of faith. God knows our circumstances, and He is good, all the time.

It is my prayer to be like the Syrophoenician woman. Whatever comes from the Lord, I want to face with strength of faith and great humility. Remember, He said to John the Baptist's disciples, "Blessed is he who is not offended in me" (Luke 7:23 NASB).

# The Head and Not the Tail

The Lord will make you the head, not the tail...

—Deuteronomy 23:13

I often need to remind myself of this truth. You as well are destined by the Lord to have an impact on this world. There are many things every day to fulfill in the heart of God. People's lives await a touch; words need to be spoken. Our lives are not a collection of random or vague circumstances. For example, God has not called someone else to your work or position. He calls you by name. The saying "You can make a difference" is not true. You do make a difference!

Your very life is part of God's master plan. We don't need to stress about "how to live every day," because a trusting, obedient heart always makes a difference.

In Jesus, we have authority, leadership (sometimes known as parenthood), and recognition. These are ours in Christ! We walk in them all the time. The issue at hand is that we keep our hearts and minds aligned with the truth and seek to glorify the Lord in all things. The enemy strives to fool us with counterfeit characteristics. For instance, he may try to substitute superiority for authority or replace leadership with dominance and recognition with boasting. The key is to keep our eyes on Christ and allow the Holy Spirit to lead.

You are the head and not the tail. If the enemy has you feeling like the tail, sit a spell in the lovely presence of Jesus. Let Him minister truth and love to your heart. Then rise to your appointments, speak out, create, trust, love, and make the difference only you in all time can make. You are not replaceable; you are unique and uniquely called.

Remember, He has said, "I have loved you with an everlasting love; I have drawn you with loving-kindness. I will build you up again and you will be rebuilt..." (Jeremiah 31:3).

So arise!

# The Lord Knew

I will be glad and rejoice in your love, for you saw
my affliction and knew the anguish of my soul.

—Psalm 31:7

Recently, a situation came up that left me feeling jilted. We had made mutual vacation plans months ago, and suddenly, a significant group backed out. I had to carry out the plans alone and with added responsibility.

*We set up our own standards of righteousness and become offended by God for not working on our stage.*

My comfort came from the above scripture. The Lord knew this would happen, and He was well able to support me and cause good to come from the change. And to His glory He did.

The Lord has known circumstances that throw us since the beginning of time. Just as He allowed sin to enter the world, He knew free choice would potentially be disastrous, hurtful, painful, and deter His ultimate plans for humanity. His broad shoulders and sovereignty do not flinch at our erroneous ways. He gets to victory and ultimately wins!

We set up our own standards of righteousness and become offended by God for not working on our stage. In truth, our offenses, unforgiveness, and anger are really against God, because He knew and allowed the challenging situation. We become offended because He did not meet our expectations of how He should be strong, sovereign, and kind. Pain and anger bubble up quickly and can be quite raw.

Through all of life's disappointment, it is worth the effort to bring each one before His throne and let Him minister His life into the heart of the difficulty.

When John the Baptist was in prison, he sent his disciples to ask Jesus if He was the Messiah. Jesus's response is stunning; it seems so off track. "Blessed is he who is not offended in me" (Matthew 11:6). He knew what was coming, that His lordship would not fulfill the expectations of the current Jewish people. They could have taken offense at Jesus. So can we.

We need to keep His Lordship ever before us, trusting and casting all our burdens upon Him, for He knows our affliction, and we will stand safe if our standards are His and His alone. "Blessed is he who is not offended in Me."

# The Parenthesis of Time

Man's days are determined; you have decreed the number of his months and have set limits he cannot exceed.

—Job 14:5

Among other things, most of us struggle with two regular challenges: time and money. Having just finished a particularly busy season in life, I began to appreciate time in a new light. I began to appreciate it as being my protector. Time was the first created thing that the Lord blessed: "And then God blessed the seventh day and made it holy" (Genesis 2:3). Time offers us a sense of safety and security. It contains the moment we are in; the next thing has not yet arrived, and the last thing is not there. We have the choice to be anxious about the unknown and regret the past, or we can stand in the protection of the parenthesis of the time we are living in.

Time parenthesis offers us focus; it can become our friend in the moment. We can trust time to move forward at a precisely metered cadence. Time is predictable. It offers us space to enjoy and trust the current offering of God. Nothing can accelerate the moment; we are guarded from the front and the rear. What a point of rest we are offered with time. We do not control it, God does, and He wants to bless the moment we are in. As I wrote the word *parenthesis*, I noticed the word *parent* in it. Our parents are set up to be our protection, our boundary setters, our shields. And we are offered that moment by moment by living within the first thing the Lord blessed.

Time, by its very nature, offers us the rest it was blessed for, and with that comes the holy presence of God in each moment. Seeing time as a friend rather than a foe that presses on us, we are able to enter the peace in the presence of God in a new and sacred way. May you be blessed as you live within the parenthesis offered to you by your creator for this moment.

# The Patience of Seven-Layer Jell-O

> The LORD is gracious and compassionate, slow to anger and rich in love. The LORD is good to all: he has compassion on all he has made.
>
> —Psalm 145:8–9

Do you remember seven-layer Jell-O? Perhaps you called it rainbow Jell-O or another name.

In my family, it was made for special occasions not because it was expensive but because it was time-intensive. For anyone who is not familiar with this treat, you would choose the order of the colors and then proceed to make one layer at a time, waiting until each was completely set before adding the next.

The entire process would take a day, but the end result was worth it. Shimmering squares of multiple colors were loved by young and old.

God has that kind of patience with us. He so cares about each portion of our lives. He has carefully chosen which experiences He wants us to have and the order in which they should happen. Sometimes outside influences (like sweetened condensed milk in the Jell-O) change the color, texture, and setting time, but God knows and waits patiently. He also knows when our faith is strong enough to add the next layer. The world sees the beauty, but God values the process.

> But the plans of the LORD stand firm forever,
> the purposes of his heart through all generations.
> (Psalm 33:11)

# The Restfulness of Belief

As we prepare for winter, we button down our homes, protect what we can from the cold and blowing winter that is to come. We rake the leaves, the beauty of the bygone summer, and gather them together so the grass can breathe freely of the cold and the warmth that is to come again.

*Trusting that He has done all that was needed to forgive us completely, and responding to the finished work of Jesus on the cross, we can rest and rest fully.*

We want to rest knowing we have done all we can to prepare. We read in Hebrews 3:19 that the Israelites in Sinai were not able to enter (God's rest) because of their unbelief. He called them to action, and they did not respond. They did not believe, so they were not able to enter His rest. When we act according to the call and the need, we can rest. When we believe that we are forgiven, we can rest. If we don't, we continually strive to do all that we think needs to happen.

Trusting that He has done all that was needed to forgive us completely, and responding to the finished work of Jesus on the cross, we can rest and rest fully. When we finish our fall tasks and prepare for winter, we can rest knowing that our work is complete.

"And yet His work has been finished since the creation of the world...and on the seventh day God rested from all his work" (Hebrews 4:3–4). It continues in verses 9–11, "There remains, then, a Sabbath-rest for the people of God; for anyone who enters God's rest also rests from his work, just as God did from his. Let us, therefore, make every effort to enter that rest." Our rest in Christ is because of our belief that His work was finished, we are utterly forgiven, and there is no sin greater than the power of His blood to forgive.

That is rest!

May you rest well in faith.

# The Sacrifice of Hope

Their hope is in his unfailing love.

—Psalm 147:11

Hope is often the sign of life, joyful living that has hope in all kinds of things. Hope is a wonderful component to life; however, we can get our life of faith derailed by hopes that are not rooted in God.

All our hopes need to remain on the altar of God, or we may begin to make an idol of the good things we hope for. We need to sacrifice our hopes and dreams to God. Even the good ones that we hold onto and possibly insist are what we should have. We need to release these to God's right to choose their fulfillment. We need to trade our hopes in for the faithful and attentive love of God.

This is a protection to our hearts. We read in Proverbs 13:15, "Hope deferred makes a heart sick." This has always been a difficult scripture for me. In my work as a therapist, I peddle hope. Hope is important. But we learn that hoping in anything but the love of God can disappoint, and we often can get derailed by disappointments of life, which sometimes translate into disappointment in God.

What does hope deferred look like? It may be holding onto a hope of our own, repeating the same prayer requests day after day without trusting, and releasing those requests to the altar of the love of God. He then can choose to fulfill our hope or not. When hope is deferred, our hearts can get sick. We have turned our hopes into idols; the hope becomes our focus and not the love of God. What we begin to notice is that our hope is not fulfilled rather than the focus of God's unfailing love. The second half of the Proverbs is, "A desire fulfilled is a tree of life." Our desire becomes God, and He is the tree of life.

Paul might have understood this when he only prayed three times for the thorn to be removed. He could have prayed daily, moment by moment, as the thorn bothered him. He prayed and then rested securely in being heard and God's full ability to act. He left his hope and his prayer on the altar and went about his daily business.

We know we can ask God for our heart's desire; we know He tells us to ask and keep on asking, like the widow who kept asking the unrighteous judge for a decision. We know all authority has been given to us in Christ. Where is the key to asking? It's having inquired of the Lord regarding this prayer focus. Are we to keep asking, rest in His unfailing love, let others prayer for you? Watch and rest.

Let's look at the repeated story of success and defeat in the Old Testament. Time and again, when they lost the battle, it was because of sin that they had not addressed or they did not inquire of the Lord (2 Chronicles 18:4), and many other times, we read about the need to inquire of the Lord.

Inquiring of the Lord is key. That is His way with man; God does not want to be a Santa Claus of our wishes. He wants a living and active relationship between ourselves and Him. He listens and wants us to do the same with Him.

# There Is Always Time

There is a time for everything...

—Ecclesiastes 3:1

You have enough time today to do everything the Lord thinks is important. It may not feel like it; however, based on who He is, it must be true. He does not assign us a pressured, anxious, impossible list. Satan does; he is not kind, realistic, evenhanded, or complimentary.

*Should* may be one of the enemy's favorite words. Anything that will produce guilt, shame, feelings of inadequacy, or hopelessness are hallmarks of his earthly "outreach." Messages we believe are very important because they tell us the source. When we hear or sense "Do more, do many things at once" (which is difficult, if not frustrating and stressing) or self-put-downs, we can recognize the source is not our loving Savior. These tactical negative messages are whispered into the spiritual atmosphere around us. At times, it is difficult to tell our thought from the enemy's. He may try to refute our love for Jesus, criticize our love for others, or remind us of mistakes that we have no ability to repair. This is how we are kept from walking in the peace and joy that the Lord sets before us.

We want to be kingdom thinkers, able to recognize the destructive and despair-producing voice of the enemy. Instead we must tune our ears to what Jesus says to us through His Word and His Spirit.

There is always time for everything that is part of His plan for you. You are equipped by Him for His purposes, and the Lord never expects more of you than you are capable of giving. Loving parents know the skill of their child and, with a little challenge, assist them to succeed. Our Father in heaven is the template for that design.

Let His peace and comfort sink in as you begin to trust Him that "there is always time" for the children of God.

# Top Down

That in all things He might have the preeminence.

—Colossians 1:18 ASV

Recently, on a backwoods retreat, I attempted a new fire-building technique, completely opposite of what I had grown up with. Rather than building the fire from the bottom up, the fire is ignited from the top down. The large foundational logs are close together, and next comes a perpendicular layer of medium-sized sticks, then the kindling, and then the ignition (birch bark, paper, or a fire starter). It worked amazingly well.

Sitting around a fire is a great place for thoughts to drift to Jesus. I saw the hot smaller sticks fall inward to ignite the medium ones and then the larger base logs. The fire burned downward. I thought, so it is with us. Jesus is the top layer, a flame with love and energy. His passion overflows and filters to us and we to others, creating a long, slow burn.

Jesus often works in a way that is counterintuitive and not the norm, just like lighting this fire. I recognized the effectiveness of this as I sat before the fire. As we keep ourselves under Jesus's lordship, His overflow ignites us. It is not by force or effort; we just stay in the waiting position, and He does the igniting. Our own strength is less important than our position. His ways are often new to us, not according to worldly patterns. We can respond to the newness of our eternal Creator and find His ways effective and fruitful.

Let His love ignite you as you flow out to others.

# Used by God

Being used by the Lord is what every Christian wants for their life. It offers us a piece of heaven here on earth: purpose, guidance, fruitfulness, and the blessings of obedience. Our lives become more meaningful. Being used by Him requires us to be in a relationship with the Almighty. It has a glow to it.

But sometimes being used by God is exactly what does not feel good to the flesh. It may not make sense in our mind, it may have invisible returns, or it may require us to dig in areas that we simply don't much care for. Sometimes being used by God hurts. We get bruised, dirty, and our hearts feel dry. We experience betrayal, loss, fear, and anxiety. The bigger picture of the kingdom is hidden from our eyes. The fruit looks so meager we struggle to trust it is worth calling fruit. These times, the word *used* feels more earthly than heavenly.

The amplitude that we began with has shrunk to survival of our faith. We have struggled to hold onto what we once understood. We grasp at the threads we hold tight, waiting to see the glory, wanting a glimpse of His Majesty. We hold. We stand. We wait.

What if that is just the time to let go, to fall back, and to release what we understand so that we may drop into the loving arms of Jesus? David said to God, "I am in deep distress. Let me fall into the hands of the LORD, for his mercy is great; but do not let me fall into human hands" (2 Samuel 24:14). We may have been holding onto our understanding of faith or effort or security, but we needed to let go of our efforts and enter that soft place of God's own heart.

When our expectations drop away, may the closeness of God's Spirit enfold us in the gentleness of a father's care for his little one. There, we find rest for our weary hearts, our striving minds, and our endless seeking. We enter into a place of being with God. My dear reading friends, let us help one another to stay in that place long enough to have courage again, strength for the day, and comrades to help us.

# Walking on High Places

He makes my feet like hinds' feet, And sets me upon my high places.

—Psalm 18:33

The LORD God is my strength, and he will make my feet like hinds' feet, and he will make me to walk upon mine high places...

—Habakkuk 3:19

He makes my feet like hinds' feet, And sets me on my high places...

—2 Samuel 22:34

Sometimes I feel more like a lowland gorilla than a mountain sheep that scales the heights. Our base nature is like this; simple and safe is the motto. It is only with Christ that we even have the motivation, let alone courage, to reach and try for things beyond us. Almost daily I need to remind myself that in Christ, all things are possible. It seems so much easier to be that lowland gorilla.

Our confidence, not our ability, rests in Jesus. If He can save the world from sin, it can't be that hard for Him to give me courage to once again believe and rise. Once the Spirit of Christ dwells in our hearts, we are changed. We have a vision and a sense of the impossible. Our eyes are raised from the turf below us to the heights and skies above. We can move, however shaky, with the knowledge that He sees us, loves us, and believes in His power in us.

Our path is formed from before our birth. Plans for our lives to bless Him and others are made and set in motion for us to walk in. "He knows the way we take," we are told in Psalm 142:3 and Job 23:10. And Job goes a step further, "When he has tried us, we WILL come forth as gold." We are told that God "sets us on our high places." Not just on any high place. We are not crawling, gasping as we go to find somewhere to stop. He knows our struggles and wants to give us victory on the very issues of our struggles. He *sets* us on our high places, and we *will* come forth as gold! These are part of the plans set in place before we are born. He is a victorious god and loves His victory won through us tearful, fearful, lowland gorillas.

# When Sins Collide

Hold on to that which is good.

—1 Thessalonians 5:21 NASB

Have you ever been caught off guard by your reaction to something? Often, when we are not prepared, our sinful nature is exposed. Our sins, our negative thoughts, our earthly reactions, or our lack of trust and belief in who God has made us to be suddenly enter the scene. The result is often hurt feelings, embarrassment, or anger.

When we move away from the situation, we can begin to see that our sin, on whatever level, collided with someone else's weakness. I wonder if that is how God sees it. He sees the flawed reactions and perceptions stand in the way of our relationships or our peace. At this point, we need to decide what we want to focus on. We need to recognize what is valuable and what is distracting us from who God is and how He wants us to see ourselves and others. We need to hold to that which is good and recognize rubbish for what it is.

As we focus our eyes on Jesus, we can stop turning the rubbish over and over in our minds. We can then begin to watch for inspired interruptions that refocus us on that which is good. We set ourselves up to hear from heaven. We accept the forgiveness of our sin, which makes pardon of others more readily available in our hearts.

Life can be messy, but the Lord is ever present in our midst. Hallelujah!

# Winner's Circle

> Thanks be to God who leads us in triumphal procession.
>
> —2 Corinthians 2:14

I do not always remember that God wins. The things of earth cause me to look down, trying not to stumble. I forget to look up and remember that the victory is sealed by the one who overcame the world.

A recent large event at my home, with some difficult relationships, came just after the death anniversaries of my two husbands. This combination of events challenged my compass of trusting in God. That is usually how tailspins start—stress, sadness, pressure and worry, and a dim view of the future. I am sure that we all have our details under each one of those headings.

When I was seeking the Lord, He brought to mind a childhood poem my parents taught me. I would like to share it with you.

> They drew a circle that shut me out,
> Pain and anger, hatred and doubt.
> But Love and I had a wit to win,
> We drew a circle and included them in.

There are many circles in life and sometimes people who shut us out. The good news is, we know there is the next page. Love wins! And by His power, we win with Him.

> Thanks be to God for His indescribable gift, Christ in us the Hope of Glory. (2 Corinthians 9:15, Col 1:27)

# Kingdom Commodities

> Remove the obstacles out of the way of my people. I live in a high and holy place, but also with him who is contrite and lowly, I will guide him and restore comfort to him.
>
> —Isaiah 57:14–18

Emptiness is not part of our salvation plan, neither is striving or fear. Learning to live by what counts is the key to our fulfillment and peace. Not in a theoretical sense but in the actual sense of being content and complete in Christ.

In making an assessment of value in the kingdom, I have found a few things in high regard and that have top rating on the satisfaction scale:

*Face down* before Jesus is our ultimate place of safety and a joy that is unworldly. It is our right position before the throne. It is comforting to know our position of security before our King. He loves us and does not demand us to be face down. It is a soul realizing how great He is and how safe we are when we are rightly related to His greatness.

*On our knees* is our place of conversation. God has everything at His command, as His children can ask for anything. He only wants our faith and trust in His way and timing. Asking for His plan and waiting for Him has "cash value" in the kingdom commodities.

*A contrite and lowly heart* is another way to cash in on contentment and satisfaction here on earth. The Lord wants to be able to comfort us, but He cannot offer kingdom-shaped comfort to an earth-shaped heart. The hymn "Come Thou Fount of Every Blessing" includes the phrase "Tune my heart to sing thy praise." It reminds us that our hearts need a heavenly shape or tuning to enter into the commodities the Lord offers to us.

*In the heart of fellowship* is another net to catch all that Jesus has to offer. Our need to belong and be loved is answered once in Christ and a second time in the heart of godly fellowship. We are not left without love and care here on earth. We just need to position ourselves under the flow. Humility enables us to allow any shortcomings to be washed away in acceptance and understanding.

Lord, please help us steward Your kingdom commodities.

# Walls of Jericho

## Joshua 6:1–20

When we think of Jericho, we usually remember the seventh march around when the walls fell down. What about the other six? When it comes to prayer and prayers answered, the other six times around may be more similar to our lives. God is faithful to answer prayers. We have all seen many wonderful answers, and the more we look, the more we see. However, there are areas of prayer that seem to carry on throughout our lives. Perhaps we are praying for the salvation of a parent, a child, or a redeemed life for one who is lost. Our prayers may include praying for a conception during years of infertility or praying for healing in the face of a life-threatening disease. These are both longing and searching prayers, prayers that may last for years. These are the marches around Jericho.

Six times the whole crew got together and paraded around Jericho, blowing trumpets as they carried the ark of God and their weapons. They were encouraged by their leaders to march in faith. They saw no results, only felt the taunts of their enemies. Those six marches must have been difficult, humiliating, and seemingly point-less. I'm sure there was grumbling in some of the homes on the six evenings before the walls fell.

Philippians 4:6 tells us to "pray about everything." So we pray, sometimes with visible fruit, sometimes with faith, and sometimes with fear and a weary heart. When the Lord tells us to pray about everything, we can be sure that everything we pray for, He can touch. He is not a god who wastes our time doing things that have no value for the kingdom. Based on His character, everything is within His grasp. We know this to be true.

In Galatians 6:9, we are told, "We will reap if we do not grow weary." That is a promise illustrated by the seventh time around Jericho. Six times they marched with no result. Yet they got out there every day, a mass of people who marched amid scoffs from within and without. Growing weary is a part of a long prayer, yet we can take courage because the seventh time around, God brought the walls down so they could possess what was promised.

As we press into long prayer, let us take heart from Jericho. The Lord hears, and the Lord acts.

May you have eyes to see the daily answers of prayer so you can have faith to know we serve a god who sees and acts for our good and His glory.

# Clueless

They did not know what He was talking about.

—Luke 18:34

Jesus had just told His disciples that He would be flogged, beaten, and killed and then rise on the third day. His disciples "did not know what He was talking about." Somehow, with our twenty-twenty hindsight, it seems impossible that they did not have a clue what this meant. Perhaps they were to used to parables to understand that He really meant this.

Such blindness we have all walked in. Those around us who see may wonder how it is possible for us to not see. Distance and time make things much clearer. God is good; He is totally in control and fully trustable. Yet how often we think and pray and live like these are not true. We walk in darkness, waiting for it to be spelled out to us again and again. I don't know if you can relate to this, but I sure can. I don't mean to be this way. I drift here.

*He never stops creating in you the beauty of His Son.*

We engage in worry, fretting prayer, or anxious thoughts. We may complain about our circumstances, our husbands, our children, our lack of money, or the personalities of those around us. All this is fretting. It could easily be said of me, "She didn't know what she was talking about. She does not yet understand that *God's plan is in effect now!* She still doesn't see that God is for her in every circumstance, that He loves her dearly, has helped her enormously, and will do so again."

It remains unclear to us that these "momentary afflictions" are the prescribed medication to bring us health and wholeness and to create for Himself His bride. Bringing these issues to Him one by one gives us understanding item by item. He wants to speak to us. At times He may be quiet on an issue, but He will still bring us peace and rest on that issue. He never stops creating in you the beauty of His Son.

May you find trust and rest waiting for you at every juncture today.

# Zipporah's Intercession

Exodus 4:24–28

The story of Zipporah's anger at Moses is a one-of-a-kind event in the Bible. I have never cared much for it; words like "bridegroom of blood," "a foreskin at Moses's feet," and "circumcision" are not in my interest range (a sign of health perhaps). However, after recently reading the account, the Lord opened a completely new understanding of the circumstances that reveal the powerful and faithful actions Zipporah took on that day.

Zipporah, Moses's wife, was an intercessor for Moses, and her actions demonstrated deep faith in the One who had called her husband to a monumental task. God had spoken to Moses from the burning bush and shown His power through the staff that became a snake and the leprous hand that was made whole. God had offered help through Moses's brother when Moses was afraid to carry out the calling alone. At this point, Moses's father-in-law, Jethro, had released Moses to take his family to Egypt to carry out the calling.

In Exodus 4:24, we find Moses about to kill himself. His wife knew action was needed now and dramatic. She could see the powerful calling on her fearful and passive husband who was ready to give up on the whole thing. She interceded and called forth the covenant that God had established—circumcision. Moses should have done this on the eighth day after his son's birth. Apparently, his passive nature was a pattern. She performed the sign of the covenant; she also knew that blood sacrifice was an act of intercession. She placed the sacrifice at Moses's feet (a foreshadow of another Son who would offer an even deeper sacrifice), and by bringing the blood sacrifice to Moses's feet, she elevated Moses to meet the calling of his life. In doing this, she proved her willingness to pay the price of his calling.

Zipporah understood the covenant and calling of God. She acted to remind Moses of who he was called to be and acted on behalf of the calling. She committed herself to stay at his side even if the road was going to be difficult.

Moses talked with his brother (when his brother came to him) and responded to the call of the covenant between God and the Israelites. We read the result in verse 28. Moses and Aaron brought together the elders and the people and told them everything the Lord had spoken:

> And when they [the people] heard that the Lord
> was concerned about them
> and had seen their misery, they bowed down and
> worshipped.

# Wired to Worship

Wired to worship was a powerful concept that was presented at church a few years ago by a representative of Campus Crusade for Christ. It was titled "Dog and Cat Theology." It was offered as a central idea to obtaining a heavenly mindset. We all know the pet joke that "dogs have masters and cats have servants." This "theology" expands on that idea. Cats are self-centered; dogs are master-centered.

We need to focus our mind around the idea that the Bible and salvation are about God and secondly about us. As we ask ourselves what was the point of Jesus's death, the understanding that needs to come is more for God's glory than our salvation. We were offered salvation, but our forgiveness was for God's glory. In Colossians 1:16, it is written, "All things created are *for Him.*"

God is perfect truth. He is not egocentric or a glory seeker as we can easily believe. The truth is that God is the only thing worth praising and giving glory to; therefore, on that truth, He seeks for our hearts to walk in truth and glorify Him. God lives to radiate His glory, and that truth brings light and joy to this dark earth.

It is so easy to focus on and ask for God's blessing. However good that is, it is not the best. We are wired to worship. As we seek blessing and favor from God, we can easily slip into becoming the primary and God being the secondary. As we ask for comfort, relationships, control, and a hassle-free life, we are asking Him to serve us. This is the reverse of what molds a heart to be like His. If our goal is to bring glory to God and to make His name famous, we are beginning to tap into a free and exuberant life.

We are saved in order to worship the King of the universe. By doing this, we bring the truth of God into this world. Our reason for not going to hell needs to be that there would be one less person to praise and glorify God. We often think it is so we won't suffer. I remember a line from the "Cat and Dog Theology" talk. It is, "Cats walk away from hell. Dogs walk toward love." One is self-preservation; the other is pure-hearted love and reverence. I want to be in the dog camp. Instead of asking "What would Jesus do?" (WWJD), the speaker encouraged us to ask "What does God get?" (WDGG).

Let Habakkuk 2:14 be the goal of our lives: "For the earth will be filled with the knowledge of the glory of the Lord, as the waters cover the sea." I believe that a life focused on God is the happiest and most fulfilling life we can live.

# Winter

# The Word of God Speaks

My Grace is Sufficient for…her.

—2 Corinthians 12:9

After the death of my husband, as a mom, I not only grieved for myself but also for my daughter. She had lost her father at age three. She would never know him past this age. I was careful to write down her memories as she told them to me, but I knew that all those transitions in life will not be attended by her father.

Statistics are not friendly to fatherless children. I could bear the loss, but growing up without a father has impact that I could not intercept. My father was with me until I was fifty-nine, a wonderful, kind, quiet, gentle man. He was there and was supportive in hundreds of ways my daughter would never know. I was whining to the Lord about all these things. Then I heard Him quote a scripture to me but changed the last word from *you* to *her*. He wanted me to increase my faith to fit the circumstance.

His grace would be with her all the days of her life; He would cover the transitions, ease the pain, or walk her through it. He was aware of her, her loss, and the statistics that show the profound loss of a parent on a child. He was not worried. He was able. My part was to be who He wanted me to be to the best of my ability. I was not in any way a perfect parent. She would have to bear my weakness and sins, without the mediating presence of a loving father. In all this, He was asking me to trust Him to be the God that my daughter would need. It has not been easy. He has been faithful. Little did I know at the time, this would not be the only father she would lose.

# Treasures in Darkness

I will give you treasures of darkness, riches stored
in secret places, so that you may know…

—Isaiah 45:3

This time of year is so dark here in Minnesota. Winter is coming; daylight saving time has not yet begun. Growth has ceased for the season. For some reason, this time of year is one of my favorites. It is time to stay home, read, make fires, have cocoa, and do things in small groups.

*Treasures that come from darkness work deep in our heart.*

These are some of the treasures of darkness. Often, other types of darkness carry treasures. At times, darkness shadows our sight. We need our night vision improved. These treasures happen by faith, in faith, or perhaps hidden from our faith. The heroes in Hebrews 11 had many treasures in darkness. They held their faith, though they did not see what was promised.

There are times in life when we see all kinds of wonderful promises of God—eras full of sunshine, friends, comfort, joy, and thankfulness. There are other times when the only promise we have is that He is faithful and always at work. It is those times that the line "When you can't trace His hand, trust His heart" is the only explanation we have.

Beautiful stones are made in darkness, pressed hard by the earth, found only by those who work in darkness, digging through a lot of hard dirt and rock before finding the brilliant stones. These stones represent our struggles, treasures that come from darkness work deep in our heart. We read in Revelations that the streets, walls, and gates of heaven are made of precious and beautiful stones. I wonder if some of our pain and difficulties are pressed into utter brilliance and used to line those beautiful streets.

Dear reader, will you trust the Lord with me in your dark places? Places of minimal understanding, long-suffering, yet-to-be-answered prayer, disappointments, unresolved conflict, unhealed wounds? He will not leave you; He will bring wonderful moments of sunshine, perhaps from another direction, but it will be there. He sits with you in your grief and hardship; often, He is quiet but nevertheless there. The pressing in for the length of time will produce diamonds in your heart, even when you cannot see them. The Lord only allows things for a purpose; that is His nature. When He begins a good work in you, He will, by His power and awesome ability, complete it (Philippians 1:6, paraphrased).

In Joel 2:18, the Lord answers to the calamity he had sent. "I am sending you grain, new wine and oil, enough to satisfy you fully." The Lord will give you substance, new joy, and anointing as you wait on Him. What He gives satisfies us fully. There is such joy in the promise of God.

# The Manger

I want to be the manger to hold the little babe,
I want to be His backdrop to see His glory made.

I want to be so humble, nestled in the straw and hay,
Where lambs are not afraid and kings are drawn to stay.

Holding forth my risen Savior for all the world to see,
That power rests in little things and His I'll always be.

She wrapped Him in cloth and laid Him in a manger. (Luke 2:7b)

# Writing Our Own Habakkuk

Though the fig tree does not bud
And there are no grapes on the vines,
Though the olive crop fails
And the fields produce no food,
Though there are no sheep in the pen
And no cattle in the stalls,
Yet I will rejoice in the Lord,
I will be joyful in God my Savior.

—Habakkuk 3:17–18 NIV

This time of year, the darkness is increasing, and life can feel like it is pressing us on every side. The responsibilities of the fall, school obligations, and political campaigns filled with stress that even the weather can set a tone of duress. Habakkuk seemed to reflect on the sense that things are going wrong at times, *but God* is still in the picture and just as powerful as the day He created this world. One day, while feeling hard-pressed, I wrote my own Habakkuk. I would like to encourage you to write your story and include the *but God* as part of your verse.

> Though the recession presses us;
> Though hard work and long hours seem to
> evaporate into invisible products;
> Though visions, hopes, and dreams remain unseen;
> Though our eyes blur the deeds that have been accomplished,
> *But God…*
> Yet we trust in Jesus who triumphs in our
> hearts and slays enemies unseen.
> Our faith and love in Him is the laurel wreath He wears.
> He is blessed by our hearts and our efforts.
> The fruit is His to see; faith is ours to give.

# Christmas Joy

It is easy to miss the wonder of Christmas in the busyness, yet it is a most amazing time of year. The week before Christmas is my favorite time of year. It is the royal anticipation of an event that we have thought about for months. Only at this time of year do we receive gifts in remembrance of Jesus's gift to us. I love the darkness; it gives a backdrop for the beautiful lights that adorn even the

*There is no celebration big enough to commemorate the introduction of God to this earth.*

smallest tree. Lights remind us that "the true light that gives light to every man was coming into the world" (John 1:9).

I love the trees, evergreens to remind us of our eternal life.

People love to celebrate. Even people who do not believe in the salvation of Jesus celebrate His birth this time of year. I often remember the verse that says, "He who is not against us is for us" (Mark 9:40). Drive down the street and look how many people are for us. Remember, "He who began a good work is faithful to complete it" (Philippians 1:6). God will be faithful to those who do not turn their backs. As you see the lights and decorations, rejoice! The world is acknowledging Jesus, who changed the calendar, the course of history, and the eternity of you and me.

There is no celebration big enough to commemorate the introduction of God to this earth. Celebrations are full of decorations, lights, gifts, food, friends, and family. There are many celebrations in the Bible that include these very things. God laid out celebrations to help us remember to stop and rejoice. This time of year, we have it all. If fireworks went off every night, it still would not be big enough and loud enough to celebrate the miracle of Emmanuel—God with us!

It is a miracle that God released His treasured Son who was in complete unity with Him into enemy territory. It would be like setting your only child in the middle of the enemy camp in Iraq. Yet our Father asked the question, "What if I gave all?" And He did. He took the chance and released the greatest gift into the enemy's domain. He is a courageous, faithful god who gave all to win back what was lost in the fall of mankind. Praise His name! Jesus accomplished what He came for, and we gained an inheritance in heaven.

Merry Christmas! Rejoice!

# Christmas Alive

Brightly You shine,
Holy, divine.

God came to earth,
Natural birth.
Pure, righteous life,
Ridden with strife.

Sins placed upon,
Risen and gone.

Your Spirit returns,
Our love for You burns.

# Tidings of Comfort and Joy

This is a wonderful time of the year. Believers and nonbelievers alike are celebrating the One who changed all history, Jesus. We see the peacefulness of the new snow and the celebration in the beautiful lights. The scene makes us want to snuggle into a comfy, warm home with family and friends.

Other times, comfort and joy seem to be slim, if not lacking, as we carry out the daily duties of life. Our hearts seek things that are perfect, ample, and full, but we rarely find that here on earth. There are days when God's grace is just sufficient for our need (2 Corinthians 12:9), not abundant. We also know that He promised an abundant life (Matthew 13:12). Why the gap?

Perhaps we can learn to find comfort and joy in small bits, at least on this side of heaven. We are created for eternity; no wonder this earth does not quite fit the bill. If we absorb the comfort and joy in the small doses this life offers, we may be able to discover the secret of abundance. It is called synergy, when the final product is greater than the sum total of its parts.

This season, let us check the moments for comfort and joy and absorb them into our hearts. Be comfort and joy magnets. There are many gifts of God offered in our life and days once we take the moment to notice them.

As we practice the synergy of grace, I believe we will find 1 Timothy 1:14 fully revealed: "The grace of our Lord was poured out on me abundantly, along with the faith and love that are Christ Jesus."

Glad tidings of comfort and joy!

# The King of the Universe in a Feed Trough

The Lord turns what is tough and barren into wonderful places of His presence. He loves to show His ability and splendor in the worst and most unlikely ways.

It was the year after the most horrendous losses of my life. It felt like Job had nothing on me. I had lost my second husband. My source of income for both now and the years to come was gone, a completed but unsigned will lay on his desk. I had lost four stepchildren from my home, whom I had come to love with a mother's love. They had hired a lawyer to get "all they could" from their father's estate that was only represented by a will that predated our marriage. My neighbors were suing me for land they wanted from me. Despair was a frequent stopping spot during my days. My life felt like a feed trough, rough and barren.

*It was precisely the most barren, cold, and dark places that Jesus entered into the world.*

Yet the Lord was pouring His love into my heart with His Christmas message. It was precisely the most barren, cold, and dark place that Jesus entered into the world. In the hills of Bethlehem, there are caves all around. It is thought that the stable was a cave. Most of the caves in this area are below the surface of the ground.

Does it surprise you that God would send His Son to the poor, uneducated, lowly shepherds to be born below the surface of the earth, in a dark and cold cave? Talk about a tough and barren place. Using an animal trough as a cradle is so very humble, and yet that was what God chose for His Son. He knew how to get the attention of those who would listen. The pompous and proud would not even notice.

I hadn't meant to be pompous or proud, but when life was relatively carefree, I wasn't paying attention. This year was different, and the Lord reached to me in a deep and very present way. My times with Him were long and sweet. I simply could not face my days without spending enough time with Him that I was strong enough to move on.

Each of us has our "feed trough" days. They won't look like anyone else's; they are unique to you. Jesus wants to be your star in the darkness, your savior in the cold night. He is gentle and lowly of heart. A smoldering reed He will not put out. He longs to save you not from what the world has given you but to save you unto Himself. Join Him today in those places that are hard for you. He loves to show His ability and splendor in the tough and barren places. Our Lord and Savior, King of the universe, used a feed trough as a cradle. His gentle arms will cradle you.

# That the King of Glory May Come In

Lift up your head oh you gates…that the King of Glory may come in.

—Psalm 24:7

We sing this song of joyful triumph about the birth of the Lord, Jesus of Nazareth, whom we celebrate in this season. It is amazing to know that He occupied a town that still exists and sits on Galilee's hillside even today.

The God of Abraham, Isaac, and Jacob comes to earth as God Incarnate. This thought stretches the human mind so much that many people cannot believe that it all happened. I am thankful for the gift of faith that allows me to see the miracle, the wonder of magnificence in humble form.

The other miracle that happened is that after Jesus died, He did it again! God Incarnate came to dwell with us through the indwelling of His Holy Spirit.

The curtain was torn, and the tongues of fire left the holy of holies and came to dwell in every believer's heart. Once again, the Lord God Almighty takes on an incarnate form in us! Only a god who is not afraid of having His reputation ruined would do something so bold. To trust frail, sinful people to hold the treasure of the presence of God on earth in their feeble hearts is another miracle of incarnation.

As we gather to celebrate His birth this Christmas season, let us also remember the treasure He has put in our hearts, God with us through the power of the indwelling Holy Spirit. The presence that once dwelled in the holy temple has come to dwell with us. We are only worthy through the power of the blood that was shed by that grown-up babe on Calvary. What a story; what a fact.

# Christmas and Beyond

I am coming and I will live among you. Many nations will be joined with the Lord in that day and will become my people. I will live among you and you will know that the Lord Almighty has sent me to you.

—Zechariah 2:10

We were promised the Lord's indwelling thousands of years ago and in many ways. Emmanuel would be our inheritance. Christmas Day was the proof of the predicted. Emmanuel was the beginning of the miracle we are living at this present time. As written in the scripture, that would change everything. Many nations would be joined to the Lord and become His people.

That is His birthright and our re-birthright.

The truth is, we have a hard time, even today, believing it. When we utter, "Please be with me, Jesus," truth is, He is there already. We are not uttering with eyes of faith. "Thank you, Jesus, that You are with me, in me, and on my side of every moment of every day." That is closer to the truth of Christmas.

To live the truth of Christmas and the truth of Easter is a life-long journey of learning the intimate closeness of the Father and our shared victory in Him. Practicing His presence at every moment is more real than asking Him to be with us. Thanking Him for His victory in every circumstance is closer to His Word than begging Him for victory. The problem is, we live by sight, by feeling, by circumstance; we let those things be the light to our path and forget that His presence in us and His victory in us is truer than the circumstance.

"How do we live this?", becomes our question. How do we live in the space provided for us rather than the shack we so quickly return to? Moment by moment, living in "Thank You for Your presence," moment by moment, faith that thanks Him for the victory even if the fog of the present obscures our goal. At times, the chasm seems too wide. To be in touch with the strain of the moment and to live in utter faith and peace is the challenge of faith in Christ.

Oh yes, enter, Holy Spirit! Hallelujah! We have a helper, our cheerleader, and the Father's biggest fan. Come, Holy Spirit, help us have the eyes to see and remember and live in the truth.

# A Season of the Soul

It was winter, and Jesus was in the temple area walking in Solomon's Colonnade.

—John 10:22–23 NIV

This is a beautiful little scripture. I love being told that it was winter. In the above scripture, we know it was cold outside because it goes on to say that it was during the Festival of Lights or, as we know it, Hanukkah. Perhaps Jesus was in the temple for shelter or protection, or He was there because of a soul need. He went to the temple for protection from the outside elements, a good place to go. Run to the temple of the Lord and stay close to His heartbeat. Soak your heart, soul, and body in the presence of the Lord. Let's remember that. Run toward Him in the times that we need warmth and protection. Stay long while we get filled. Move about in His shelter.

A season of the soul is a deep longing for the warm attendance of God in a certain area. It is a position of the heart; when flowers are blooming and the warm sun is pouring on the body, we can still feel the chill of our need for the Lord's warm touch.

Jesus was walking in Solomon's Colonnade. Just a location, or is there more? When we think of Solomon, we think of wisdom. What a lovely picture, to stroll among the pillars of wisdom. This is a rich reminder to us. Stay near and among the wisdom and covering of God when we are in a winter of our soul, a place where we are safe. Pillars are built strong to support the covering of the temple. Wisdom protects us; it does not come naturally, and we must apply ourselves to the wisdom of the Lord. We have a narrow view and are by nature self-serving even when we are focused on doing the will of the Lord. We need to stay in among His words of wisdom and use them to build the protective shield of Jesus over our lives.

Our simple choice is to stay near God's heart in times of winter, need, cold, rain, or just general drear. This builds the covering of protection over our lives. Not that we cannot or will not sin, step out from the wisdom, or leave the temple area. But we know where home is. It is in the temple area, walking among the pillars of wisdom that God has built into our faith.

# Bittersweet

The New Year has come. We greet it with joy and anticipation, yet new brings changes unseen. We leave the old behind and embrace the yet to come. Fear at times lingers in anticipation of changes we are seeing around us, changes that may not be welcome. We all have a relationship with change; it is a promised constant in life.

We live with the bittersweet; every change is a loss and a gain. This is what makes change so difficult. The tangible loss seems to outweigh the potential gain. The stress of the bitter can linger, and the presence of the sweet seems fleeting, as anticipated bitter moves in and can undermine the moment. Our joy in life seems to be in the ability to hold the sweet with the bitter, to rejoice in who reigns and not fear what is to come. Martin Luther said, "You have as much laughter as you have faith."

Somehow, our protection mode kicks into the belief that anticipation is our shield. Anticipation never protected us from the future. Our hope needs to be in trust that the God of the unknown is known. Our return point needs to be the faithful presence and work of the Lord. We return to Him, the One whose predictable presence ever nurtures and delights in His children.

Fear demands our service, often disguising itself as protection. We, as children of the Most High, need to boldly name our fears and answer every one with a call to trust. We stand in power, we stand in position, and we stand in victory. How quickly we concede ground when faced with change and the unknown.

We read in Daniel 10:18–19, "Again the one who looked like a man touched me and gave me strength. 'Don't be afraid,' he said, 'for you are very precious to God. Peace! Be encouraged! Be strong!'"

Oh, my wandering, mourning soul, still yourself in Christ. Settle into His calm, presiding power and love.

> Let them give thanks to the Lord for his unfailing love and his wonderful deeds for mankind, for he satisfies the thirsty and fills the hungry with good things. (Psalm 107:8–9)

> He stilled the storm to a whisper; the waves of the sea were hushed. They were glad when it grew calm, and he guided them to their desired haven. (Psalm 107:29–30)

# Repairing

But we have this treasure in earthen vessels, so
that the surpassing greatness of the power will be
of God and not of ourselves.

—2 Corinthians 4:7 NASB

The holidays are over. Many people, places, and opportunities were visited; many were missed. Some hopes may have been met; other ones long to be fulfilled. Gifts of all kinds were given and appreciated; long-awaited salvation may have not been received by family or friends. In British literature, the term *to repair* is used differently than how we commonly use it. A person may "repair to the sitting room after a long day." It seems to indicate sitting alone or with a supportive person and talking about the events of the day or season. Sometimes that is the very invitation the Lord offers to us. When we look back on the holiday season, we see people we love, others we missed, opportunities taken up, and others we would like a chance to redo. We see a world that mingles the sweet and the sting of events, of others, and of ourselves. The golden moments are quickly mixed with the murkiness of sin and trial. It is time to repair, to draw away, and to sort out our acceptance of the fallen with the golden.

When we think of the word *repair*, we think about fixing something. God is, by nature, a fixer. The Lord is the best fixer there is and waits for us to call on Him. What is broken that needs to be fixed? The Lord not only excels at fixing; He possesses the ability to quietly listen as we wade through events, as our hearts desperately wait to be heard. Lamentations 2:19 NIV tells us, "Pour out your heart like water in the presence of the Lord." Let your words be heard; take your needs to the cross. Both fixing and listening are valuable. Both are from the Lord, and both He does exquisitely! *Repairing*, in both meanings, is what we may need. Time to sit together with our Father and someone to fix the things that are broken.

Do you need time to "repair" to the sitting room of the Lord's sweet presence? Let Him fix what's broken, and pour out your heart out to the greatest listener and lover of your soul.

# Heart Cleaning

The holidays are over; life is settling back to a more normal pace and schedule. As we look back, we have joys, fulfillments, strains, and sin. It is time for house cleaning and perhaps also "heart cleaning." We had many hopes, efforts, and plans. Our heart was to serve Jesus and represent Him to family and friends. At times, it is hard to see if that is what came through. It is comforting to realize that what we have in our hearts, our intentions matter before the Lord.

In 2 Chronicles 6:8, we read, "The LORD said to my father David, 'Because it was in your heart to build a temple for my Name, you did well to have this in your heart.'" We have a God who honors our intentions. With David, the Lord did not allow him to fulfill his intentions, and still the Lord honored the intentions of his heart.

Difficulties arise and can be rather painful. It is a hard mix to have the joy of the holidays and the pain of disappointment. The Lord allows difficulties. He has plans for these difficulties. As we read in Isaiah 41:10 AMP, "Fear not [there is nothing to fear], for I am with you; do not look around you in terror and be dismayed, for I am your God. I will strengthen and harden you to difficulties, yes, I will help you; yes, I will hold you up and retain you with My [victorious] right hand of rightness and justice."

In Zechariah 8:13, we read the same message, "Fear not, but let your hands be strong and hardened." Difficulties and disappointments come with a purpose—to strengthen us and cause us durability in trials. Becoming durable for Jesus opens many other doors in which to serve Him. So often disappointments can cause us to have hard hearts, but the Lord wants us to have soft hearts and a thickened outer layer. The way of the world is to be overly sensitive and with a calloused heart. We are called to be different.

As you are doing your "heart cleaning," pay attention to offenses that may need to be identified and released to Jesus's care. Offense needs justice.

We can let go of the court of law that we may carry in our head or our heart and let God, the wise judge, take it over. He is kind, but He is wise and just. We don't want to drag our sack of offenses over from one year to another. Go through His gates and leave behind those things He is most capable of dealing with. Walk through clean, clear, and free, pure-hearted, strong of spirit, and free of baggage.

# Only One Resolution

Romans 12:1 tell us, "In view of God's mercy...offer yourself as a living sacrifice; this is the logical [Greek translation] act of worship." Logical because it is in view of God's mercy and kindness that you relinquish all and trust Him fully.

The happiest people I know are those most surrendered to Christ. Their faces seem to shine with love and warmth; they are less likely to get frazzled, angry, or offended. They rarely speak ill of anyone.

A truly surrendered life is a rare treasure.

Total surrender to Christ often comes at a cost. The cost seems to be built on points of great difficulty in life. Suffering and surrender seem to be linked in our hearts. A life totally surrendered to Christ is born from many deliberate acts of the will during times of trouble. The total picture looks so daunting. I love the quote "Success is many small steps in the same direction." I can do the small steps.

The nearness of Jesus is so present during difficulty. At the end of a hard season, a question has come to mind, I wonder, would I be willing to go through the pain again in order to have the nearness of Jesus? His nearness is so precious, but when the pressure lifts, so does the sense of His extraordinary nearness. We find ourselves walking instead of being carried. Trusting His ability to carry us gives us confidence to surrender all and continue walking.

Abraham is an example of a person who gave up all to follow a promise-keeping god. He left his country, possessions, family, reputation, business, and dreams; He was even willing to sacrifice his son using his own hands! God's record is good; He is a trustable, loving god. Surrendering all to Him is not only logical, based on His character, but it produces great freedom and beauty in our lives and hearts.

# Ski Tracks

A snow blanket for the world, crisp and quiet.
Action, rhythm, conversation.

Hard, scary, exhilarating.
Communion with God, bright blue sky.

Awe of creation, propelled by the body.
Apart, alone, relief.

Sadness comes like snow at my feet.
Sparkles in the snow, centered, gentle, held.

His beauty, His sparkle, centered, electric, gentle.
He holds the heart; He holds the hand.

Maps and trails tracked and untracked.
Emmanuel is with us.

# God as the Author of Romance

Valentine's Day actually began as a day to honor a man in prison for his faith. Valentine faithfully wrote letters from his cell expressing the love of Christ to many. His letters led to the salvation of a young blind girl to whom he wrote on the day before he was martyred. This young new believer wanted to keep his memory of love and kindness alive, thus began this holiday.

The Lord rejoices in our expressions of love to one another. This is a day of rejoicing in the love He created. He gave us a heart not only for love but also for romance. He himself is the perfect fulfilling of that desire. God's love for us is not only full and complete; He is also romantic in His affection for us.

Zephaniah 3:17 says, "He will take great delight in you, he will quiet you with his love, he will rejoice over you with singing."

How amazing that God, the Creator of heaven and earth, sings over each of us with rejoicing! This gift exceeds any earthly gift we may receive today. I hope that each of us will tune our ear to heaven, listen for the song God sings over us, and be filled.

When we fill our cup with Jesus, everything else is in abundance.

Psalm 90:14 says, "Satisfy us in the morning with your unfailing love that we may sing for joy and be glad all our days."

As we tuck into the joy set before us, all our days will be overflowing with the satisfaction and contentment of the Lord. When our cup is under the spout of His flowing love, we will have enough for ourselves and some to share. May your day be filled with the abundance of Jesus Himself.

# Post-Valentines, Present Love

> Let the beloved of the Lord rest secure in him, for
> he shields him all day long, and the one the Lord
> loves rests between his shoulders.
>
> —Deuteronomy 33:12

Valentine's Day is a poignant reminder that love is a universal need. Only God Himself can satisfy that need.

The story of Valentine's Day is a triumph of the love of Jesus. A Roman Christian was in prison for his faith. The jailer saw his character and asked Valentinus to disciple his blind daughter, Julius. He led her to faith in Jesus, her sight restored with a flash of white light in the prison cell. His death sentence was carried out on February 14. His parting letter to Julius was signed "From your Valentine." Valentine's Day is about Jesus, His love and healing power. It is about faith, courage, and martyrdom for the love of Christ.

The day after Valentines, our need for love continues. Perhaps on some front our hopes are disappointed. Hope in people is fragile, but hope in the love of God is a rock! We can rest secure in Him. His love shields us all day long. Satisfaction found in Him does not disappoint. Refreshment comes every morning, and His love letters abound in the Word. When we tuck into what He offers, we can find rest, security, protection, and strength to love others anew.

As the disciple John laid his head on Jesus's breast at the Last Supper table, I wonder if he thought of the above scripture. Resting between Jesus's shoulders, in the center of His love, over His heart, and between His mighty arms is our safe home. At a particularly difficult time in my life, the Lord told me to just lay my head on His chest and go ahead and pound out my angry heart to Him. It was clear to me that He could bear all I had to give, but what would have broken His heart was for me to walk away. Beloved, lay your head, like John, on His breast, and let His love sort out your needs. Your love honors the King.

# First Miracle

> Nearby stood six stone jars, the kind used by the Jews for ceremonial washing. Each jar holding from twenty to thirty gallons.
>
> —John 2:6

On the recent North Heights Tour of Israel, our group had a chance to visit Cana. During the visit, one of our beloved couples renewed their wedding vows after 10 years of marriage.

What a sweet place to remember Jesus' first miracle.

A wedding, the beginning of a lifelong covenant between man and woman, reflects the loving and eternal covenant the Lord makes with us. It was the beginning of Jesus' ministry, and symbolically entering into the covenant of his enduring relationship with us.

How perfect that the jars he used to make the wine were jars normally used for ceremonial washing. We are familiar with the washing of his blood to take away our sin, and that wine is what he used to symbolize his blood.

Marriage, like any daily relationship, is one that requires frequent washings; we need his blood to cleanse our hearts, minds and souls as we live through the grinds of life.

It's amazing that in his first miracle Jesus symbolically tied together our need for ceremonial cleansing (baptism), and the cleansing of his blood that is symbolized by wine as in communion. These elements are physical signs here on earth of his covenant love, salvation and forgiveness.

What a first Miracle!

As we approach Valentine's Day, let's remember with thanksgiving that Jesus' first miracle honored the strength and vulnerability of loving relationships. May you receive the washing of that beautiful red blood of Jesus every day.

> "This is the one who came by water and blood Jesus Christ. He did not come by water only, but by water and blood. ... For there are three that testify: the spirit the water and the blood:—1 John 5:6–8

# A Leader and the Cross

My work involves leadership, and over the years, a reality has become crystal clear. Decisions aren't made by picking a good way over a bad way or doing wonderful things instead of terrible things. Often, decisions are between two good situations and having to choose one and not the other. Or it might be choosing one way among many when several have merit and supporters. People's lives can be changed. Most times, it is impractical to share all that is considered in finally making a choice. This leaves room for those with partial information to quickly judge leaders as foolish or wrong.

The only way to stand amidst this is to know that everything has been carefully weighed and that the Lord's counsel was sought and received. When all around there is tumult because of a decision, having the internal sense that it is the best one keeps you going.

There has never been a leader who has not walked through this. Jesus Christ made some difficult calls (He chose only twelve). He had people who judged Him wrongly. Obviously, the Pharisees, but so did His friend Judas. Nonetheless, He deeply understood the direction He needed to go and knew He pleased His Father in all things. He always appeared sure and internally intact.

Until the cross.

It struck me anew as I read of His death on the cross that He became sin. When He cried out because His Father had forsaken Him, when He took all our rebellion as His own, there was no longer any internal compass He could cling to. He was sin; He didn't just carry it. While He was still righteous, He entered the foreign and truly forsaken experience of not being right. I imagine for that moment He couldn't take comfort in knowing He was doing the best thing. The horror of being separated from the Father—all that is right and good—became a new reality. As a leader, He literally lost everything.

The Bible describes it this way, "For our sake, God made him to be sin who knew no sin, so that in him we might become the righteousness of God" (2 Corinthians 5:21).

As a leader, I stand in awe of His willingness. The weight of it humbles me beyond words.

# A Safe Place

"Hide in the Cherith Ravine, east of Jordan, and stay there." The ravens brought him bread and meat in the morning and bread and meat in the evening, and he drank from the brook.

—1 Kings 17:5–6

Camp is a place where we feel cared for by the staff, friends, and especially the Lord.

The namesake of Camp Cherith was a place where a man who was very dear to the Lord's heart was also protected and cared for. It was a camp by the stream Cherith, an actual location. We know that God called him there to move away from usual life. Is that sounding familiar? We also know that he was well-fed, meat in the morning and the evening. We sure can relate to that at camp. We just sit at the table, and food, good food, is set in front of us. Thankfully, they also include lunch!

Elijah also found water to drink; it was from a brook, which meant it was running and therefore clean and clear. This was during a drought in other parts of the country. At camp, we drink from a living stream of water, Jesus. Clean and clear, running freely for everyone to drink.

In the Middle East, where I have lived for a total of four years, a ravine is slightly different from what we think of. It is a dry riverbed for about half the year; it only flows during the rainy season. When the Lord called Elijah to his hiding place, He knew there would be water flowing for him. You, too, can know that the Lord has the refreshment that Jesus wants to give you, flowing just for you when you come to camp.

The name Cherith puzzled me while I was volunteering there for a week this last summer. I know some Hebrew but could not figure this out. When I got home, I dug around a bit and found out it meant "cushion or pillow." I had used the word hundreds of times while I worked in a children's house in a kibbutz in Israel. It is pronounced *kar-rit* in Hebrew. The ravine that God called Elijah to must have had a squishy streambed, a soft area around where the water flowed. Perhaps a stream flowed beneath the surface, as well as on top. When God called him, He called him to a soft, comfortable, probably cool place in a dry, hot desert.

Once again, we see the kindness of the Lord, supplying food, water, protection, and a soft place for him to rest and lie down. Camp is that kind of place, a rest away, a hiding place from the usual things of life. The Lord goes before us and gives us what we need. Praise His name.

# A Scepter and a Sword

Rightly dividing the word of truth.

—2 Timothy 2:15 NASB

Taking our position in Christ is a lifelong journey. We may never be fully successful at this quest while still on earth. The authority of Christ in us is a complete authority over darkness in our lives and the world around us.

Continually moving into our position in our everyday life is a challenge. You have a scepter—"You are...a royal priesthood" (1 Peter 2:9)— and a sword is in your hand. We reign with Him. What a blessing and joy. How *We take our full authority—sword and scepter—and apply the word of truth and the finished work of Christ to our need and our world* astounding and beyond our capacity to comprehend. We have the sword of the "Spirit, which is the word of God" (Ephesians 6:17b), that wields truth in all areas of our daily life.

I want to take my full authority in Christ. I do not want to be malleable and convenient to the world. I want to say no to wrongdoing within the crevasses of my mind, to my world, and to where the enemy wants to gain entrance.

Using the word of truth, I can make corrections to call others or myself up and out of sin. There is a call that invites us to rise to integrity and authority. It is a call that says, "Rise up, oh man of high esteem and stand upright" (Daniel 10:11). "Practicing sin does not do justice to who you are in Me."

There are times when our sin is not the problem; the problem is the harassment of the enemy. The enemy wants to trick us into thinking our sin is the problem and we are to fix it. This causes us to focus on ourselves and our shame (the sin of self-centered introspection). Then we are in charge of the remedy. The truth is to apply the blood of Jesus to the thought or situation. Then we take our full authority—sword and scepter—and apply the word of truth and the finished work of Christ to our need and our world.

# Becoming the Beatitudes

Matthew 5:7–10

The beauty, simplicity, and depth of the Beatitudes are rapturing. The concepts are so grand the stretching of the mind is almost visceral. Yet they read like poetry.

*Blessed are the merciful.* Mercy invites us to be free from self-thought. It moves us into the other-centered world where God lives. We are soft and vulnerable. Efficiency is not our goal; the love of others is central. We craft our lives to be available, leaving gaps in our busyness to change course and reach out.

*Blessed are the pure.* When we are pure, we are aware of our sin, yet more aware of the awesome cleansing that is ours in Jesus. Sin is easily washed off, our own or the sin of others that can so easily stick to our hearts. We have a single motive: Jesus and His glory. Self-promotion, defensiveness, and justification pale in the presence of God Himself. Our eyes are clear so we can *see God*.

*Blessed are the peacemakers.* What would it feel like to stop all the mental conversations that are conflicting, argumentative, and defensive? What peace we could live in. Self-interest is laid aside, and God's interest is taken up. In this political climate, we hear so much about peace. We see many claims of being peacemakers, yet it is only in grasping hold of Jesus that we can we know peace, no matter what the storm.

*Blessed are the persecuted.* When we look too much like Jesus, we can look very vulnerable in this world. Standing in His righteousness is safe and dangerous at the same time. Laying down our self-protection takes much faith and trusting moment by moment. The attacks may come, but when we stay in His cloak, the smell of smoke does not come on us.

This is kingdom living. This is our home.

# Broken Pieces

And they picked up the broken pieces.

—Mark 8:8

This sentence is repeated in each of the gospels after the feeding of the four and five thousand. It is then again said twice more in the references made to those events. Whenever something is repeated in the Bible, we do well to pay attention.

These broken pieces were partially eaten pieces of bread and fish. They were left for the dogs to eat, refused in the mind of the picnickers. Yet the Lord instructed His disciples to pick these up and collect them. I doubt they were making stuffing. Something else is here for us.

What looks broken and unusable to us seems to be an object lesson of what is valuable to Him. Those left over, refused, cast aside, He sent His disciples out to collect. We are not told why or what was done with the leftovers. It seems that is not the point for us.

It is a reminder that not only does He collect our tears; He also collects what is broken and left over. He values every portion of our life, keeps it, watches over it, and cares for it. The mere collection of the broken pieces were evidence to the disciples that a miracle had happened, but I believe there was another meaning to be found in the collection.

Let Him collect the broken pieces of your days, your lives, your losses, your disappointments. He values them. He sees, and He cares. He even collects them and uses them for unknown purposes in your life and the lives of others. As we see as He sees, the mystery is mixed with the miracle. We learn that by faith, nothing is refused.

I long for the day when my faith will be sight, all the broken pieces put together like a piece of pottery, collected, redeemed, and beautiful to the eyes of faith.

As we learn to value those broken and difficult pieces of our lives, we learn to see as the Lord sees. You have a God who sees, knows, cares, and redeems!

# Thick Darkness

Moses approached the thick darkness where God was.

—Exodus 20:21

This sounds terrifying: to approach a thick darkness in faith that Moses would be preserved and even spoken to by the living God. This is amazing faith. He knew and believed God was fully reliable. It seems we can live in a thick darkness when circumstances press in. It is in that darkness that we can honor God with our faith and approach Him, even when we cannot see or understand what is going on.

Recently, it came to mind that I did not have enough faith for the situation I was in. I was afraid, fretting, feeling a heavy weight because of my sense of helplessness to make the change I wanted to see happen. I had lost track of His goodness in the midst of the needs around me. I needed to call on the Lord, asking to please give me faith to fit my circumstances. I can tell when my faith is not big enough. I feel despair, fear, disappointment, even dread. Yet lately, when I asked for enough faith, the Lord, as He does, delivered. Hope and peace returned.

I needed a new growth of faith, faith that would rise and trust even in the unknown. Faith in the midst of darkness must be very pleasing to Jesus. I started praying, and I could see bit by bit my discouragement and despair being pushed back.

Peace and joy were coming in as I rested quietly but firmly in His love. Seeds of joy and peace came in, restoring His love. It is the cornerstone of my life.

Amy Carmichael wrote a poem that has been inspiring me. It ends in

O love of God, do this for me,
maintain a constant victory.

Perhaps this is a prayer to the God of my life.

# The Love of God

We love Him because He first loved us

—John 4:19

Communion is the point of contact to the physical evidence of Jesus's life here on earth. It is the only institution He gave us.

Communion is the physical testimony of our oneness with Christ. We take in and *Communion: a community in union* take on His love for us and for others. We can rely on and know His love. Communion is the evidence that Jesus gave us.

When Jesus said this is the new covenant, He was quoting from the bridal covenant in the Jewish culture. We at that point became His bride, and He entered into a new relationship with us. As the two become one in marriage, so we become one with Christ in the new bridal covenant of communion. He wants us also to become one with Him in His desire for the redemption and transformation of the body of Christ.

> And so we know and rely on the love God has for us, God is love, whoever lives in love lives in God and God in him. (1 John 4:16)

> There is no fear in love, but perfect loves drives out fear because fear has to do with punishment. The one who fears is not made perfect in love. (1 John 4:18)

Communion is the point of contact with the atonement of Christ. At the offering of communion, Jesus takes on the punishment that should have been ours. The broken bread and poured-out wine demonstrated that we now have no need to fear, because we will not be punished as we should have been. We can receive His atonement and receive His perfect love for us, a love without any fear.

This is the verdict. Light has come into the world, but men loved darkness. Everyone who does evil hates the light and will not come into the light for fear that his deeds will be exposed. Whoever lives by the truth comes into the light, so that it may be seen plainly that what he has done has been done through God (John 3:19).

"Communion offers us a point of courage." We can go forward with tangible evidence of Christ with us. It lets us rest on the truth and not on our fears; it is courage based solely on the work of Christ and the strength of His blood. At the moment, God may convict us of sin. He simultaneously redeems that sin and draws us to Himself in love.

> For God did not send his son into the world to condemn the world, but to save the world through him. (John 3:17)

# Walking in the Truth of Christ

## 2 Cor. 10:4–5 NAS

"Casting down imaginations, and every high thing that exalts itself against the knowledge of God and bringing into captivity every thought to the obedience of Christ."

There are times when we are brought down by circumstances and can begin to believe the lies of the enemy about ourselves. We each have a set of lies that we are more prone to believe. It is worthwhile to know our points of vulnerability. Feeling unimportant is one of my areas to work on. I wrote a letter of truth to this area. Please think about writing a similar letter to one of your points of vulnerability.

Dear Devalued,

You have influenced me since my birth. You have tried to tell me that my presence in my family was unwanted and that I was in the way of what would have otherwise been a perfect situation. You have convinced me that I am tolerated in every situation, but not of value and importance. You have told me that I am different, less than those around me. You have been brutal and accumulated evidence against me over the years. You have told me that I am ignored and insulted because of who I am. You have interpreted actions of others as pejorative toward me.

I have learned from you to be quiet, to keep my thoughts, opinions, and conflicts to myself. I have been taught that what I say is not important and is seen as a disruption and a bother. You have directed me to be superficial with information about myself and to engage in what others have to say to keep the light off myself. You seem to indicate that it is all about everyone else but me. I have been a student of that and rarely am comfortable sharing about myself. When I do, you have convinced me to feel guilty and selfish. When I offer my opinions that may conflict with others, you make me feel guilty. Like I am being selfish, you often win on this issue.

I challenge you, Devalued. I have parties at my home, and my home is called the "center of the family." You don't get to be boss anymore. You still wedge your way in. I stay busy and not engage in lives and conversations of my guest on an equal level. Somehow, you have said that my value is in offering and serving others. That is not true.

I am learning that you do not have my best interest in mind. There is not a need for me to respond to you in relationships. I get to have a say. I get to have power. I do not need to believe you; you lie. There are people who think I have value and listen to what I have to say. So long, Devalued. You have not been a friend. I am breaking off this partnership.

Signed:
Date:

For we are God's masterpiece. He has created us anew in Christ Jesus so we can do the good things he planned for us long ago.

—Ephesians 2:10 NLT

# Entrusting Ourselves and Others

When they hurled their insults at him, he did not retaliate: when he suffered, he made no threats. Instead, he entrusted himself to him who judges justly.

—1 Peter 2:23

Jesus offers us a perfect example. He kept His divinity in the depths of humanity. Because He was able to live the sinless life, we are able to come to a victorious Savior. Sometimes walking in that victory is the challenge.

A few months ago, when determining to walk in forgiveness, I spoke with my mother-in-law who walks closely with the Lord. She offered some spontaneous thoughts that have been life-changing for me. There have been instances in my life when forgiveness has been a repeated process with little ground maintained. I have had to go back to Jesus many times even in a single day to find the forgiveness I desired for another, myself, and even for the Lord.

Finally, a breakthrough came as I put into practice what she shared with me. The steps of forgiveness became very clear. I find it most effective when I am able to speak this aloud. First, forgive those who have offended you. Next, ask the Lord to reveal any judgments you may be holding over them, then release all of them to Him. This may take some time and thoughtful soul-searching. Often, our judgments are correct, but holding them does no good. The next thing is to release the person to Jesus completely. Then let Jesus deal with the situation as you stay out of it. And lastly, bless them.

Jesus entrusted Himself to Him who judges justly. May you find much freedom in this simple yet cleansing process.

Our path to freedom, 1-2-3-4-5: Forgive. Drop all judgments. Release them to Christ. Hold nothing against them. Bless them.

I pray this will bring you much peace.

# God as Central

He is before all things, and in Him all things hold together.

—Colossians 1:17 NASB

There are so many things that pull our focus off the Lord. Many of them are good things: children, family, friends, errands, and the list goes on. These good things can quickly turn to worries, fears, and distractions. They can even become modern-day idols at times. When we turn from these points of focus to face the Lord full on and sitting on His throne, we can find rest for our weary hearts and minds. We let the many features of life remain on our right and on our left, in our line of vision, but not central to our focus. Resting in His presence, we are allured by His love and peace; we find an atmosphere free from judgment, fears of failure, or anxiety. It is a resting place of acceptance. Fear has no place before the throne of God.

Another view of God as central has a much different look. Have you ever been to Grand Central Station? It is a bustling hub of purposeful chaos and activity with people coming and going, only to return again. Lives lived large and small return to the hub. Complexity, busyness, pressure, and waiting are a part of these lives. Still, the return to the hub, the core, the "check-in" is always ready. It is as if the going out and coming in form a type of petal that is connected and loops back to the center of a flower.

Living with the Lord as central to our busy lives means deliberately, quietly sitting before Him, leaving the world in our periphery and, at other times, living the busy, full hustle of life with an intentional return to the throne many small times a day. Living with God as central keeps us aligned with His character and purposes.

# God's Glory on Earth

We have seen His glory, the glory of the One and Only.

—John 1:14b

Magnificent changes began when Jesus was born. His fulfillment of the prophecy was obscure to the eyes around Him. Only after His death did the apostles begin to put together all they had witnessed.

God came to dwell among men, having to be "received as a little child."

In Matthew 18:4, Jesus told His disciples, "Whoever humbles himself like this child is the greatest in the kingdom of heaven. And whoever welcomes a little child like this in my name welcomes me." I wonder if He was telling them who He was and how to respond to Him.

God broke through the heavens to live among us. He later told us He wants to dwell in us. Our battles are not only understood from on high but also felt by God on the soil of the earth. How God honored us to care in such a sacrificial way.

Each of our hearts replaced that magnificent temple on Mount Moriah. The temple curtain was physically torn at the time of Jesus's death to demonstrate that the holy of holies, God's presence, was open to us. God's nearness, which began at Bethlehem, became an invitation for us to enter the holy place of His dwelling. The sending of the Holy Spirit became God's indwelling presence to each who would receive it.

The Shekinah glory of God, which shone on Bethlehem, also came to dwell in our hearts. Only the powerful cleansing blood of Jesus can make our hearts habitable for the living God.

> He has given us this command, whoever loves
> God must also love his brother. (1 John 4:21)

Communion is our point of contact with our brothers and sisters in Christ. We and they become perfect in Him by His love and goodness to us. We then have His power and strength to love others and be His hands and feet in this world. He shares His body and blood with us for that purpose. It is amazing how tangible Jesus wants to be to us.

Communion is making the great exchange with Jesus. We give up our old self and embrace how he sees us and others and walk in that truth.

> But you are a chosen people, a royal priesthood,
> a holy nation, a people belonging to God that
> you may declare the praises of him who called
> you out of darkness into this wonderful light. (1
> Peter 2:9)

Communion is our point of exchange—the bread was broken, the grapes crushed, the temple curtain torn, and our access to God was made full. We became the temple where the holy of holies lives. We are the priesthood. Laypeople and young believers can offer communion to the bride of Christ, His church.

Give thanks to the Father who has qualified us to share in the inheritance with the saints of life and delivered us from the domain of darkness and transferred us to the kingdom of His beloved Son (Colossians 1:12). Communion is our passport to a kingdom whose citizenship we did nothing to earn.

> For God who said "Let light shine out of dark-
> ness" made his light shine in our hearts to give

us the light of the knowledge of the glory of God in the face of Christ, but we have this treasure in earthen vessels, to show that this all surpassing power is from God and not from us. (2 Corinthians 4:6–7)

Communion is the evidence of our filling that Christ offers us as part of the great exchange. It is so easy to relate to ourselves as earthen vessels; it is more of a challenge to have the faith that in our jars of clay is the living water of the glory of God, who is Jesus Christ our Lord.

# Hope and Trouble

I will make the valley of trouble a door of hope.

—Hosea 2:15

Hope and trouble seem to be unrelated. Yet the Lord says that the valley of trouble will be our door of hope. His word is true, so my thinking must need some work.

We also read in Romans 5:3–5 that suffering produces, among other things, hope that does not disappoint. This challenges me. It is hard to understand that going through trouble and suffering produces the very thing they seem to have destroyed. Yet I am eager to have a hope that does not disappoint.

*Learning to hope in the love of God in the midst of trouble begins to open a hope that does not disappoint.*

Here in the land of Israel, there are many archeological excavations that are constantly in progress. New sites are discovered almost weekly. This land is rich with layer upon layer of life, history, destruction, and then rebuilding. Each layer is waiting to reveal more about the people who had called it home.

The comparison to the Word of God and His character is clear. There is layer upon layer to understand and gain insight about. Until we uncover the upper layer, the lower layers remain closed to us. Learning to hope in the love of God in the midst of trouble begins to open a hope that does not disappoint.

Too often we put our hope in things that do disappoint—relationships, comfort, circumstances, and ease. Hope is not based on these but on applied learning *that the love of God never disappoints us*. It is only by continuing to lift trouble and suffering up to Him and to place our hearts in His hands that can we learn about a hope that does not disappoint. We come to find out that hope is not an automatic response to good fortune but a heart applied to learn of the love of God.

As I began writing these thoughts, Israel was not at war. We left the country on the morning that the bombings began. The areas where we lived have been hit, but there has miraculously been no loss of life there. Once again, my faith is challenged to let trouble lead me to hope. Surely, goodness and mercy shall follow me all the days of my life. God is worthy of our hope!

# I Am a Weaver

### A Love Song of Jesus

My cloth is of purple, gray, scarlet, black, gold, and turquoise.
The strands are wide and twisted or narrow and made of iron.
The pattern is beautiful to my eyes, varied, plain, simple, complex.
When the rain comes, my cloth holds; it blends, binds, and bleeds.

You are my cloth. I see your life as a beautiful, unique combination of strands, colors, pieces, and materials. You may feel the daily warp, the threads under tension; you may not notice the beauty of the weft. I have worked the yarn long before I have shuttled into your life. The piece will be known to you in time to come. The beauty will be exquisite, familiar, and yet unseen. You will feel your representation in it, and you will see my patterns, love, design, and magnificence woven into your life.

# Justice Reigns

Do not be deceived: God cannot be mocked. A
man reaps what he sows.

—Galatians 6:7 NIV

This is a fearful thought, strong and at times invasive. We don't
want to be deceived, but in the secret places of our minds, hearts, and
homes, we have, at times, mocked God. We have judged Him for not
healing the needy, for not preventing an untimely death, or even for
an unanswered prayer. Perhaps in a situation that is beyond our grasp
and understanding, we think God must not be in it. I believe it is safe
to say we have all mocked God.

It is scary and horrifying to realize this.

There is also a feeling of relief. Along with the fear, there is
rest. God is sovereign, big, and He will not be beaten by my petty
thoughts or the ugly words that may have been uttered. There is
justice, and it is sure, evenhanded, and restful. Nobody and nothing
beats God. Ugliness and ruin cannot outweigh His power. His justice
brings joy and even tears of relief.

We have Jesus; He covers our sin, and we are free. And in the
larger sphere, God will never be mocked. Not by me or by anyone
else. He stands firm and strong, unrelenting in His perfection, justice, and glory in every aspect of life.

Our hearts long for justice, not the small daily pining of our
hearts but in the big long picture. We are promised that God will be
strong and sure and will never be mocked, ever.

I am so glad we have a God who stands long, and sometimes
quiet, in His slow justice and His ultimate love.

# Deep Calls to Deep

Deep calls to Deep in the roar of your waterfalls;
all your waves and breakers have swept over me.
By day the LORD directs his love, at night his
song is with me—A prayer to the God of my life.
(Psalm 42:7–8)

Standing on the shore of our great lake, the Spirit of God spoke these lovely words to me. I wanted to share them with you:

As loud as the roar of the water, so is My
acclaim of My children in heaven.
As you see the volume of water before you, this
and far beyond is My love for My own.
Confess freely; empty yourself of that which binds and limits you.
Confess fearlessly; become empty of sin and shame.
As you pour out, so I pour in the deep, secure richness of My love.
My cleansing water, My redeeming blood that
now flows in your veins is your victory.
My victory has become yours; my victory
is installed in your very being.
Let Me transform your body, mind, and
spirit to align with My truth.
You are to live as one cleansed, redeemed, able, and secure,
doing My will, speaking My truth, and trusting moment
by moment in your redemption and My power.

It is hard to imagine that the Lord acclaims us in heaven, much as He did with Job when Satan asked permission to test him. His deep love knows no earthly limits; we can make earth-sized attempts to understand. Our heavenly Father speaks in our language and on our terms to impart His love. What a gracious Lord!

He invites confession, not as a shame to us but as a cleansing release of our spirits, making room in our hearts for His presence to dwell, claiming and reclaiming His victory over sin—a daily washing of truth.

# Leanness of Soul

The hymn "Great Is Thy Faithfulness" is full of majesty and power. It is rewarding to sing, and it inspires us to be thankful. If it is true that "all we have needed" has been provided, then there is something more to be gleaned from this thought.

Could it be true that what we have needed is leanness of soul? In this culture of abundant provision and a continual call for more—huge food portions, support for grabbing all the gusto there is to be had—it is a rare thought that perhaps less is exactly what we need. When we ask and God does not give what we have asked for, rather than thinking He has not heard us or is delaying an answer, perhaps He is giving exactly what we need. Our need may be for a soul that is not dependent on external rewards but for a heart that can sit quietly and wait for the Lord to change our desires to include only Him.

How difficult this is. When we give something up and feel the weight of (even a small) sacrifice, we want to honor our Lord Jesus, the God Almighty, for the sacrifice He made to bring justice to our sin. And that is the cross. All we needed was provided from that reference point. How our longing hearts struggle to settle on that point and that point alone. How free we would become to rest there and be filled.

As we read in Psalm 44:3, "It was not by their sword that they won the land, nor did their arm bring them victory; It was your right hand, your arm, and the light of your face for you loved them."

Our victory is from the light of His face shining down on our lives, and that fact resounds through eternity. He loves us dearly.

# Living in Technicolor

We see through a glass darkly…

—1 Corinthians 13:12

This is a drab time of the year, but the closer we are to Jesus, the more Technicolor we can live in. May we develop the eyes to see what He is doing, who He is reaching out to, and what prayers He has answered. We would see a very different-looking landscape. Learning to live in awareness of what He is doing brings Technicolor to our world.

We pray many prayers but often do not take the time to see, recognize, and respond to each answer. We may move mindlessly through the events of the day and never see the vibrant reality of Christ. To live in a fresh revelation of Jesus and alert to what He is doing brings us a full-color spectrum of life.

It reminds me of going to an art museum and moving quickly from one masterpiece to the next, never slowing down to note the detail and not being moved by anything that we see. Or we can choose one or possibly two masterpieces, sit quietly, look at the detail or the color, and get a sense of the picture and the artist.

As we quietly sit, we begin to absorb the tenor of the artist. The same is true with Jesus. Sitting in His presence, listening to His narration on the world creates a very alive and vibrant world; we absorb the colors of His life. And our life begins to change.

There are times of the year when the barrenness of the surroundings actually cause us to be able to see things we cannot otherwise see. When the trees are full of green, they obscure what is beyond them. When the leaves are down, we can see farther and more. Let this barren landscape be your view of the beyond. We can take the time to see Jesus more clearly, noticing the details He has before us, and live with a broad and deepened view.

To behold the beauty of the Lord and to inquire
in his Temple… (Psalm 27:4 KJV)

# Mercy or Justice

Do you show contempt for the riches of His kindness, tolerance, and patience?

—Romans 2:4

Our hearts are made for the justice that we will have in heaven. We have a built-in "justice meter," and many times a day, it kicks in and picks up the errors in the system of this world.

*Your mercy has played out in our lives when what we deserved was justice.*

There are many days and prayers that are more focused on justice than mercy. Those are the days when I have lost sight of my own need for mercy. I ride the high horse of justice and misapply "a justice meter" to my world when God has graciously applied mercy.

When unforgiveness appears, my sense of justice has trumped my recollection of the mercy of God for me and for others. Grasping the depth of my need for God's mercy causes my desire for justice to fade.

I wonder if that is how it will be in heaven.

Lord, help us to see with spiritual eyes how Your mercy has played out in our lives when what we deserved was justice. It was mercy that caused our Lord to come into this harsh world, live His life in a system of injustice, and respond with sacrificial mercy by dying on a cross. Our earthly justice meter cannot even begin to register this concept.

Thanks be to God for His indescribable gift! (2 Corinthians 9:15)

# Never, God

> Never, God. So my spirit grows faint within me;
> my heart is dismayed. (Psalm 143:4)

Caught in midsentence of the phrase "Never, God," it became obvious to me that some serious soul adjusting was in order. I had lost two husbands and was wrestling with the Lord over possession of my only child, born after seven years of infertility. In my passion, I forgot where my safety was coming from. As if I could protect her by saying, "Never her, God."

Saying "Never, God" is a position of the soul. It is a war between the powerful soul and that of the Holy Spirit that dwells in us. It is a soul against God. I found myself nursing my fears with very convincing arguments. I was offering "anything but" prayers in a bargain with the Lord to leave one thing untouched. I was attempting to protect while keeping my protector at bay. I was fighting the maturing process that God was trying to enact in my heart. I stayed stuck on this argument for about six months. So did God.

Do you have "Never, God" in your vocabulary? I encourage you to start taking down defenses. God isn't as radical as you may think. He is a gentleman; He allows our *no* on certain occasions, yet God is more radical than you think. He knows the power of the soul.

This is an encouragement to shed the power of your soul and walk right into the fire, the fire that burns off the ropes that bind you and hold you back from the freedom of pure, rugged trust in the only One who can protect you and lead you safely home.

> Let the morning bring me word of your unfailing love, for I have put my trust in you. (Psalm 143:8)

# Now Come and Go Back

I have indeed seen the oppression of my people
in Egypt. I have heard their groaning and have
come down to set them free. Now come, I will
send you back to Egypt.

—Acts 7:34

Perhaps this caught my eye because it humored me to see the "come
and go." I love seeing the Lord speak in ways that are meaningful and
funny at the same time. It also caught my eye because I find myself
at a juncture of change in my life.

This passage is about when the Lord is calling Moses to come
back to Egypt from the desert. Moses had fled there after killing the
Egyptian in attempted defense of his people. He had sought refuge
and time. It is okay for us to seek refuge and time. The Lord plans it,
uses it, and helps us get "put back together" as we seek Him. But there
comes a time to "go back" into the previous situation. Perhaps the
going back is in the physical, but more often, it is in our prayer life.

Rarely do we seek the Lord to go back. We are such for-
ward-looking people. I heard a funny statistic that about 90 percent
of the people really believes that next year will be better than this
one. Now we can understand why gambling has such a draw on the
human psyche. We are wired as eternal optimists! It serves us well
and is God's fingerprint on us.

Sometimes going back is going forward. The Lord invited Moses
to "come" and go back. Going back may look painful or difficult, but
when the Lord invites us, we are ready. He will be there, behind us
and before us. He has plans and healing that He wants to accomplish.
He may want to bring healing that only going back can provide. He
will have a chance to speak into a situation to our spiritual ears that
are more healed and able to receive. He can change the backdrop of
the situation with understanding that only He can bring.

When leading on is leading back, we are given the grace to
go there. There is calling and purpose, even if we can't see it at the

moment of the call. My hope is in the love of Jesus. He will be what I need and what you need as well. There is a greater need for trust in Him as we go back. We may remember the pain and difficulty more than the grace and healing. Perhaps it looks like walking into a dark and large forest. Our call is to put out our hand to the living God. You may be asking, "But now Lord, what do I look for?" (Psalm 39:7). The next line is, "My hope is in you." That is where we need to choose to stay. Psalm 48:14 says, "For this God is our God forever and ever. He will be our guide to the end." Sometimes circumstances and situations look more like a forest than an open plain, but God will guide us to the end, and this is the hope we can trust in.

# Points of Brokenness

One of the most disturbing scenes from the end of Jesus's earthly life is when the soldiers mocked Jesus. He wore a crown of thorns and a purple robe and was struck on the head with a staff, and the soldiers bowed down to Him (Mark 15:17–19). All the while, Jesus was silent. Being fully man, He was humiliated and insulted. Yet we know that He also retained His Godhood.

When Jesus comes back to earth and is seated on the throne, we read again about a purple robe (Revelation 1:13), a crown, a scepter that He holds, and that every knee will bow to Him (Isaiah 45:23, Romans 14:11). Jesus knew that all their mocking would be played out in a reality to come. The exact elements of Jesus's humiliation would be used in His rightful glorification.

This applies to our lives as well. We minister best from our points of brokenness. The exact difficulty is often what the Lord uses to reveal more of Himself into our lives and then into the lives of those around us. Our pride would like to minister from our points of strength and growth, which happens to an extent, but our best seems to come from the humility learned in the valley of the shadows.

Our valleys become our training grounds. It would be so much easier to take a class than walk through the valley. We are reminded in Hosea 2:15 that "the valley of trouble becomes our gateway of hope." There is nothing mysterious about how we learn to minister. We have walked through a similar valley, have kept our faith, and have gained authority to minister at the points of our brokenness. There is no showiness in our offerings; they are the salt of the earth, hard-earned through tears and sweat and built on the solid rock.

Once again, our King led the way; His humiliation became the evidence of His kingship! His pain builds the gateway of our hope. Praise His holy name!

# Priorities—Our Training Ground

"Time is the great equalizer," says Dr. Donald Wetmore. Every person living has exactly the same amount of time each day. Each day is a gift.

Priorities have power. We all have 24-7, but our priorities can make us paupers or kings. Priorities set the world ablaze or let it fall in disarray. Priority holds onto integrity, raises up kindness, or slides into backwater living.

Most days in our lives are overly full. Relationships and other wonderful and necessary things call to us. The difference between good and great is the ability to say yes or no to things that call with equal voice to our limited time. What must get done seems to call more loudly than what I would like to do. The must-dos usually win out at the end of the day. That is most often good, but there are times when I wonder if the things that I would like to do that have natural energy behind them may be among the greater calls.

Sometimes it seems a vague sense of Paul's words when he said, "For I have the desire to do what is good, but I cannot carry it out" (Romans 7:18b). It is not so much a result of the sinful nature that Paul writes about but more about the pressures of everyday life and a constant choosing of the priority that best serves the Lord.

Paul writes of the "prisoner of the law of sin at work" in Romans 7:23. This is a different kind of a prisoner. It is a prisoner of the immediate need being substituted for the greater good, which is the more fruitful effort. It brings us to the same conclusion in verses

24–25, "Who will rescue me from this? Thanks be to God through Jesus Christ our Lord." The living relationship with Jesus, the power of the Holy Spirit's daily guidance is what moves us to the priorities that best serve the Lord. It is in the daily choosing that God is revealed in and through us.

> I consider that our present sufferings are not worth comparing with the glory that will be revealed in us. For the creation was subjected to frustration, not by its own choice, but by the will of the one who subjected it…and brought [it] into the freedom and glory of the children of God. (Romans 8:18, 20–21 NIV)

# Red Herrings of Angst

> Do not fear what they fear, do not be frightened, but in your hearts set apart Christ as Lord.

> —1 Peter 3:14–15

Some days it takes a long time to recognize the red herrings of angst. These little distractions can upset us and keep our focus off the peace that could be ours in Christ. Unresolved relationships or areas out of our control tend to be the most frequent distractions.

The red herrings are often legitimate challenges. It may be a piece of new information or an unsubstantiated worry that pops into our mind, and off we go! Our worrisome imagination is in full force, and we are chasing red herrings of angst.

Perhaps it is a poor decision made a long time ago or something that someone did or said that is upsetting your balance. The red herrings intrude and usually contain a lie about self, worries about children, finances, or past failures that we have no power to change.

Prayer appears to have no effect as we watch the red herrings swim around our lives; they are fraudulent diversions that cause us pain and keep our focus off the power of God in the particular area of need. As long as we are looking everywhere but at Jesus, our heart cannot rest.

Once we can identify the red herrings, we can stop looking at them, reorganize our thoughts, and focus on Christ, who calls us to rest and trust in Him.

May the Lord help you net all your red herrings of angst and bring them captive to the obedience of Christ (2 Corinthians 10:5). May you be blessed as you trust Him and lay all your fears at His feet and "in your heart set apart Christ as Lord" and captor of your heart.

# Securing My Lifeline

I have brought You glory on earth by completing
the work you gave me to do.

—John 17:4

When I hear the portion of the airline attendant's speech playing through my head, "Secure your own oxygen mask first before assisting other passengers."

You're right, Lord, I need to secure my own oxygen mask first!
Meditating on Your word,
Talking with You throughout the day,
Listening for Your plans/purposes,
Understanding that the work You set before
me is fulfilling and has eternal impact,
Confessing that the work I choose adds to the
cultural frenzy I want to leave behind,
Only then can I reach out and assist others,
when my lifeline with You is secure.
Wouldn't it be great if we as Christians could each secure
our lifeline and, then as God leads, assist those around us to
turn their focus to the work God has set before them?

With the Lord's help, may we conclude, "Lord, Your Christians have brought You glory on earth by completing the work You gave them to do."

> Jesus gave them this answer: I tell you the truth.
> the Son can do nothing by himself; can do only
> what he sees his Father doing, because whatever
> the Father does the Son also does. (John 5:19)

# Standing in Difficulty

> I will set my face like flint...
>
> —Isaiah 50:7

There are often many clamoring voices in our lives. We must choose whom we will listen to. In the midst of a storm, we often pray for deliverance. Sometimes He delivers immediately. More often, God is in the business of building soldiers for Himself. He wants to deliver you in the midst of the storm. He wants you to sleep calmly in the boat while the storm rages. This is knowing God. This is the challenge of trust.

Most of life is joyful and pleasant. However, the Lord is on a mission. He loves to bless His children, but He also needs able soldiers in His army. Wars are won battle by battle. We often find ourselves on the front line.

Praying effectively into the situation is vital. Praying the scripture is a powerful weapon. Find a scripture that fits the situation, adapt the wording to personalize it, and pray it back to God! This reaps much in the kingdom of heaven. It is rewarding and restful. We know we are in line with His ways.

I remember praying this way about a difficult neighbor situation. At first, I prayed for protection, then to be an effective witness. Then the Lord led us into a more aggressive prayer, "that Jesus would enter their property and lives and that they would respond to Him or move." Unfortunately, they moved. However, I am sure God heard our prayers. He also gave me three long years of boot camp. My face was set like flint; God would have His way in my heart and life. Glad that one is over!

# Terezín

### Sin of the Earth

All men have gone astray each has turned to his own way, but the Lord has laid the iniquity of us all on Him.

—Isaiah 53:6 NASB

Terazin was a Nazi holding camp located in the Czech Republic. I don't know what it means, but to remember the name, I used *tera* (Latin for *earth*) and *zin*, which sounds like *sin*. It was a powerful experience to walk through this place. This is not a camp that has been sanitized or changed at all since the prisoners left in 1945. It was left exactly the way it was found by the Czech people who returned to this area at the end of WWII. Even the toilets still had a stench. No one was trying to make things look better than they were. As we passed through the fortresslike camp, I kept trying to think how the guards could begin to justify what was going on there. The level of self-deception was astonishing. It could have started with convincing speeches that people did not object outwardly to and then moved incrementally forward to the disastrous result of the concentration camps. The human heart's ability to deceive itself has not changed.

*We are offered free grace that no amount of work on our part can achieve.*

The well-remembered Nazi slogan of "Work makes liberty" was written to encourage hard work on the part of the prisoners in the camp. Recognizing that people need hope, the propaganda offered hope that was false. All world religions offer this slogan as well, except for Christianity. We are offered free grace that no amount of work on our part can achieve. The real hope is the opposite of this: grace freely given, the price paid by our Lord.

We are all caught in the "sin of the earth." Since the fall, there is a downward pull on our hearts and minds. Seeing the power of self-deception, which possibly began only as passive disagreement, was horrifying. I don't feel automatically immune to self-deception, not assuming immunity is a first line of protection. It puts the fear of God in my heart that I, too, must follow the safeguards He has given me, lest I should fall.

He has given us His Word, to be personally read, studied, and digested daily with the help of the Holy Spirit. He has given us fellowship of the saints, a place where we can be corrected and challenged to line up our lives with the scripture. He has given us sermons, books, friends, and interests that we choose carefully so that we won't fall into deception. Ignoring the first checks in our hearts is dangerous. Knowing how to respond comes when we request help from the Lord. Let us fear the power of deception, and may that fear cause us to run into the arms of the Lord and stay under the protective measures He has set up for us.

The fear of the Lord is the beginning of wisdom.
(Proverbs 1:7)

# The Fire That Burns

Take off your sandals, you are standing on holy ground.

—Exodus 3:5

The Holy Spirit is our guide, comforter, and counselor. His presence is wonderful, and His help immeasurable. He is also holy, and our relationship with Him should bear that fruit in our lives. We have been enjoying a renewal of His power and presence in the church for a couple decades now. But have we become more holy, more sacrificial in our lives with one another and the body at large? There are some statistics that make Christians look very similar to those who live without the help of the Holy Spirit. Love is self-sacrifice expressed practically, not something squishy and without form. As we walk in the Spirit, the chaff of self needs to burn away and transform our lives to be filled with God's holiness.

Jesus was perfect. He was selfless love, but He was not tolerant of sin. He was the only man who was ever completely holy. We have lost track of holiness. Jesus was an offense to many people of His era, yet He was holy. It is often too easy to think that people-pleasing and tolerance are the hallmark of a Christian. That was not the demonstration Jesus offered. Are we willing to be an offense?

The Holy Spirit is often represented by fire, tongues of fire that came upon the early church. The fiery furnace of Daniel's time burned off only what bound the men, the ropes on their hands, but they were untouched. The burning bush when God told Moses to take off his sandals caused the ground around it to be holy. Joshua (5:13) also stood on holy ground after the fall of Jericho. God's Holy Spirit needs to make an impact in our lives. It needs to cause us to be more holy, more sacrificial in our love, allowing Him to burn off that which binds us. Are we willing to be an offense in our time? Not tolerating sin in ourselves first and others, seeking Him through prayer and devotion and with courage?

Lord Jesus, help us be transformed by Your wonderful Holy Spirit that we would not seek Your power for our own edification but for the building of Your kingdom on earth, in the church, and in our lives. Help us live up to our calling, holy and beloved.

# The Hovering of God's Spirit

Like an eagle that stirs up its nest and hovers over its young, that spreads its wings to catch them and carries them on its pinions.

—Deuteronomy 32:11

The Spirit of the Lord hovers over us and waits to be specifically invited into places of our lives. God is omnipresent in all places at once. Yet at times, He seems to wait for us to invite Him to come closer still. When we ask Jesus into our hearts and lives, He takes up residence and abides with us daily. However, there are times when I have sensed a brooding of the Lord during a time of prayer or in a specific situation. A deeper invitation seems to be needed.

How God can be there and still want to be nearer still is a mystery. God does not overtake us. He allows us to be who we are and even delights in who we are. The existence of God in our lives could be a theocracy. But somehow, He seems to want to make it a democracy of mutual honor. We are undeserving of the amazing God we serve. Yet to shun His willingness to go deeper would be wrong.

There are many wonderful promises in the Bible. God's promise to "never leave or forsake us" (Hebrews 13:5) remains very near to my heart. I really need to know that. Yet this hovering, brooding, waiting God offers yet a deeper gift. "He waits on high to have compassion on us" (Isaiah 30:18). He waits to be called in to bring additional power, love, peace, and patience and to bring each of these to a greater degree than was previously present in the situation.

A majestic, loving God is waiting for our invitation. In this, too, "Lord Jesus, come."

# The Real Big Bang

It is said that scientists can still hear the echo in the universe of the first loud noise. I am not sure how that works, but I believe it. I believe the big bang, and I believe in the One who spoke it. "He spoke and it was done, he commanded and it stood fast" (Psalm 33:9). I relish the fact that scientifically they can still detect the echo of that first loud sound, the echo of God speaking the world into existence.

Our universe is still echoing the sound of God's creative voice. While in Israel, I was able to stand among a land that still rings out the voice of the beloved Son. A land full of rocks! These very rocks have seen the history of mankind unfold. *We can see and touch the rocks that echoed the sound of Jesus voice.* I want to touch them tenderly, stand by them in awe of the God who came to earth and spoke, taught, loved, and gave His earthly life.

The fields of Israel are full of rocks. They build with rocks, and rocks are used and reused from generation to generation in building houses, roads, and city walls. Very likely, Jesus was a stonemason as much as a carpenter.

As the people were praising Jesus during His triumphal entry into Jerusalem, the Pharisees told Jesus to rebuke His disciples. Jesus replied, "If they keep quiet, the rocks will cry out" (Luke 19:40). If the people did not praise Him, the vast number of rocks in Israel would have created a cacophony of praise!

Lift your voice and join in with the echo of praise still ringing from the genesis of the earth.

Let everything that has breath praise the Lord.
(Psalm 150:6)

# The Silent Songs of Heaven

> The Lord your God is with you, he is mighty to save. He will take great delight in you, he will quiet you with his love, he will rejoice over you with singing.

> —Zephaniah 3:17

As a baby comes into the world, we can easily say these things about the baby. God is with this child, mighty to save her or him. The Lord takes great delight in new life. The love of parents and their attentive care will fulfill every need at this time. They will sing over their child, as she or he lies in their arms. When the babe is asleep, they may look on and sing a song of praise to God. We sing over babies naturally, lovingly, calmly. We know it quiets them, and they feel surrounded by the love that is theirs.

It is good to remember there is another parent who is also singing. It is God the Father over us His children. The Father in heaven sings over us and quiets us in His love. We do well to rest quietly and listen for the song He is singing over us.

Are you listening? He has a song of praise and joy He is singing over you.

In the hard and in the sweet, God is mighty to save. In delight, He sings over us and calls us onward and upward to Himself. I hope each one of us will listen to the love song He sings over us. The next time you see a loving parent caring, calming, loving their child, I hope you will remember that as they pour out their love and life into the child's growth, in the same way God in heaven delights over you and pours out His love and His life for you.

# The Wind

And in came a mighty rushing wind.

—Acts 2

The wind blows into the chaos of the world,
Driven by patterns, predictable patterns,
That form and shape the weather, the seas,
the trees, the rocks, the sand.
One day it blows and then it rests.
Chaos is not the wind.
Chaos is unpredictable, scary, mean.
The wind, though strong, is predictable most days.
Even when it forms unpredictable tornadoes or
hurricanes, it still blows in a pattern.
Around and round, damage or not, it tells us its path.
We can move or hide; we can run or buckle in.
The wind, my predictable friend, beautiful,
fierce, creative, powerful,
And soft.

# This Is the One I Esteem

This is the one I esteem: he who is humble and
contrite in spirit, and trembles at my word.

—Isaiah 66:2b NIV

More than anything in life, more than any honor, I want to be esteemed by the Lord. I realize that my esteem is dependent only on the finished work of Jesus on the cross. When He said, "It is finished," my destiny was secured and my relationship with the Almighty was set. I am valued in Him with a value that can never be taken from me. Proof positive: the death and resurrection of Jesus, the finished work of Jesus.

Yet this scripture gives us a clue for our heart's position before Him. Though we were not active participants in the work of Christ on the cross, we are active participants in our sanctification and the usefulness of our service before Him.

Who then is esteemed in this way?

*He who is humble.* We ask, "Lord, forgive me of pride and self-protection. Please forgive any and all boasting, blaming, and attitudes of superiority. Help me remember that I don't know all that is going on in people's thoughts and hearts. Only You can do that with insight, wisdom, and perfect understanding. It is not my job to find fault. Humility is my place."

*And contrite in spirit.* "Jesus, I trade my shame and embarrassment for the safety of being contrite in spirit. Help me to be in the right alignment with You, me on my face before Your throne. Thank You that You bring right order into every situation—Your righteous, right order. As I bring every thought captive as mentioned in 2 Corinthians 10:5, my mind is transformed by Your Spirit as we learn from Romans 12:1. We no longer agree with the enemy of our souls in thought, words, or actions but with Your transformation of our hearts and minds."

*And trembles at my word.* The word was at the beginning of time. His word was spoken, and by His majestic voice, the world and galaxies were created. John 1 tells us that Jesus became the Word here on earth and dwelled among us. As we trembled at the power of His word, both in spoken form and in the presence of Jesus, we can begin to see and understand God's good and perfect presence in this life. A humble, contrite heart positions us to see more clearly. We come through the storms of life, under the shadow of God's protection, in perfect confidence of His mighty arm that saves us and His mighty word that brings forth His will. Standing firm in this leaves no foothold for the enemy in our hearts and lives.

The Lord is relentlessly kind; He guides us to live a gentler, more grace-filled life of faith. Trusting and resting in His position and our position before Him is the picture of one who honors the Lord.

Let us make every effort to walk as a people who are esteemed before Him and who stand before Him in right alignment to His word.

# Tor-Mentors

And we know that in all things God works for
the good of those who love him, who have been
called according to his purpose.

—Romans 8:28 NIV

Recently, at a work conference, this idea was brought forward: What if rather than looking at difficulties and stressors as enemies, they became our mentors? I believe as we apply this concept to the kingdom of God, its clarity and fruitfulness is exponentially increased. The very things that rattle you can show you how to become unrattled. We can let the tor-mentors of life become our mentors.

If there are attributes in a person that quickly get under your skin, ask the Lord how He wants to bring growth and change in you at that very place.

What if you are quickly disappointed? Lean on and learn. Put your ear to the ground and listen to what is being taught by that circumstance. Are you learning to hope in a higher calling than the immediate solution? Perhaps the Lord is redirecting you, and you cannot see the way at the moment. He is faithful. Being curious about those things that bring you angst may be the surest way to get them to settle down. You have learned to live with them as your mentors, tutoring points along the path of life. We are familiar with the passage from Genesis 50:20 NIV, "You intended to harm me, but God intended it for good to accomplish what is now being done, the saving of many." He wants to do that again for you.

Don't let your torments follow you like a stray dog all through life. Turn around, take the dog in, and learn the lesson. Then the dog can stay or go, and you are free in your soul and spirit.

Disappointments and difficulties are as sure as the dawn. Jesus is true to His word: "In this world you will have trouble" (John 16:33 NIV). Let the trouble become your mentor that leads you back to Christ and take up the potential for growth that each situation offers.

The problem is not that troubles exist; it is how we use them for our growth and the furtherance of the kingdom that matters. We turn toward them rather than against them or away.

# Trump Suit

> And we all, who with unveiled faces contemplate the Lord's glory, are being transformed into his image with ever-increasing glory, which comes from the Lord.
>
> —2 Corinthians 3:18a

Playing cards is not something I do often, but as I was listening to a recent sermon, I was thinking about the card game each of us plays in this game of life. In our hands, we hold many suits or ways to handle problems. As the problem is laid out in front of us, we play the best card in an attempt to win the round. We may be strategic and only play what is needed for that round.

The truth in the hand of every believer is not only the trump suit but the trump card. The trump suit would be "hearts," the love of Christ that covers every situation and wins every trick. Love, wisely applied, wins every round. Before we even begin the day, we have won the victory in the situation. Discouragement, disappointment, and conflict all have an answer in the love of God spread abroad. We worry and fret because we try to play the nontrump cards, our own efforts, and worldly ways. They may work for the moment, but we always hold the winning card in our hands and hearts.

It is not fair that victory is ours at the beginning of every game. But that is our inheritance in Christ Jesus. "Love covers a multitude of sins" (1 Peter 4:8), and the love of God trumps the vilest situation. It is ours to wake up confidently deciding to have a song in our hearts when the evening comes. Between our usual behavior and this blessed assurance is living, holding our suit of hearts close to our mind and spirit every moment. What a glorious choice we have, moving from glory to glory, peace to peace, trust to trust! Walk with me in this endeavor.

# Utter Sovereignty

Before a word is on my tongue you know it completely.

—Psalm 139:4

I know that you can do all things; no plan of yours can be thwarted.

—Job 42:2

Understanding these thoughts is like seeing a grain of sand on the seashore. The sum total is beyond our imagination. Yet the meanings of these words have a big impact on our lives. Only a truly sovereign God can allow free choices to His children and still know that His plans will stand to the end of time.

*Only a truly sovereign God can allow free choices to His children and still know that His plans will stand to the end of time.*

I am so glad He is our God. Only a truly sovereign God doesn't flinch when we fail. What a comfort that my actions don't control His ability. We don't have to live in fear of ruining God's plans. His sovereignty isn't interrupted by our error. This is a very big idea. It is not about deliberate rebellion that can impact our effectiveness for Him. It is that He can and is effective in this world because of who He is, not who I am or am not.

Like everyone, I would like to see my life count for the kingdom, be useful to the Lord and His church. I often worry that because of my weaknesses, I will not be very useful to Him. Learning to trust Him to override my sin and be victorious in spite of me is a new ticket to freedom. I don't have to fear my failure but to trust Him to rule and reign. What He begins, He accomplishes. There is no disclaimer in Philippians 1:6, "He who began a good work in you will be faithful to complete it."

Often, I have asked the Lord to help me be faithful to the end. This is a good prayer and needful on one account. However, the truth is, I will stand because He is able to make me stand. It is not about my ability but His sovereignty.

I hope this brings as much relief to you as it has to me. It is truly all about Him. We can rest, trust, love, and live in the truth of His strength. Our Abba Father is our all and all.

> The name of the Lord is a strong tower, the righteous run to it, and they are safe. (Proverbs 18:10)

# Thank You for the Bitter

For all things serve you.

—Psalm 119:91b

Thank you for the bitter things,
They've been a friend to grace.
They've driven me from the paths of ease,
to storm the secret place.

by Florence White Willett

I came across this little portion of a poem about the same time I noticed the above scripture. They seemed to carry a message that deserves our attention: if all things really serve Him, like this scripture suggests, then the bitter things are also His servants. That is life-changing in so many respects. The painful accidents that we attribute to the fallen world suddenly come under His umbrella of protection and purpose. There are no accidents; He is large enough to cover even the ugly and difficult.

This is one of the most difficult weeks of the year for me. I had not necessarily planned to run this devotion on this week. It just "fell that way." This week, I remember the two anniversaries of the deaths of my two husbands; the dates are one day apart. How easily I could have let that be an "accident." Surely a loving God would not place two such life-changing tragedies on subsequent dates. But He did, and I received it from His all-wise hand. This poem becomes the cry of my heart. I want to storm the secret place and dig all those "treasures of darkness" (Isaiah 45:3) out of such events.

There is much growth in our walk when we realize how big the Lord is and we allow Him to be expansive. The bitter things become our friends; the less we understand, the more we trust. If we continue to call on Him as "the Lord who is good and does good" (Psalm 119:68), the more we honor Him and are content with difficulties that are unexplained to us. He is able to love us in, and through, the bitter things. His ability and grace are never outdone.

Loved ones, if you have such events in your life, "storm the secret place!" Call on Him again and again with all your might. He will be there for you and guide you into His secret place of suffering, perhaps, but also into sweet and eternal fellowship.

> See, I have refined you, though not as silver; I have tested you in the furnace of affliction. For my own sake, for my own sake, I do this. I will not yield my glory to another. (Isaiah 48:10–11)

# We Always Have Time

My times are in your hands...

—Psalm 31:15

This scripture has often spoken to me more about life and less about time. Lately, the Lord has been speaking to me about time. My daughter and I are preparing for a return to America after a year in Israel. Life in Israel is more people-centered and less about production. At first, it was a frustration. Now I see it as a benefit.

Pressure, stress, and anxiety seem to be products of our everyday life in the US. Somehow, we have learned to equate busyness with valuable. That is a lie straight from the enemy of our souls. It is simply untrue! As a child, I was praised for going fast, so I learned to rush, cram, and pressure at every turn. As Americans, we idolize efficiency and speed. The Lord sees it very differently.

One thing Israel does very well is to rest on the Sabbath. Everything shuts down; people generally don't go anywhere. "The discipline of rest" has come to be very meaningful. It does not come easily, and sometimes I would rather be moving than resting. Rest is a discipline that needs to be practiced. Hebrews 4:9–11 speaks about this rest, "Therefore, there remains a Sabbath rest for the people of God...let us make every effort to enter that rest."

Seeing our time as belonging to the Lord helps us to enter His rest. *There is actually enough time every day to accomplish what God wants us to do.* This idea seems novel at the writing of every to-do list. Jesus is not the author of stress, anxiety, and pressure. He is the author of peace. With our cooperation, He is able to bring us into His rest. But that rest is a discipline.

Before Lent one year, I asked the Lord what He would like me to give up to help me focus on the upcoming Resurrection Day. By His Spirit, He asked me what was most important to me. My response was time. I chose to dedicate ten minutes a day to praise. No thanksgiving, no other prayers, just praise for who He is. The praise time started slowly with many distractions, but by the end of the disciplined ten minutes, I never wanted to stop. It has been a blessing to this day.

Giving our time into His hands in focused and ordinary ways is our gift of peace from Him. We then have time for loving people and right priorities. Those priorities often include rest and downtime. Growing in the *discipline of rest* has much to offer our busy lives and is a gift we can give back to our loving Savior.

# About the Author

Tasse Swanson has had more than the usual number of blessings and has also known much sadness. She is a child of a divorced family, was raised in a non-Christian home, and became a Christian in her second year of college. Tasse enjoyed the opportunity to work as a missionary in Guatemala and for two years in Nepal at a leprosy hospital. She lived for three years in Israel, in a kibbutz, where she learned to speak Hebrew, and returned years later with her teenage daughter to work in a Christian guesthouse for a year.

Tasse has had three wonderful marriages to three wonderful men, and she has been widowed twice. Her first husband died after a long battle with cancer, and her second husband died suddenly on a morning run. She also worked through seven years of painful infertility, resulting in one precious daughter, who was born almost two months prematurely and needed two surgeries in the first year. Needless to say, she has had many long and tearful nights. She thinks her current husband is a brave soul, among many other loving attributes. She now has had four last names. That was not in her original plan.

On the other hand, the opportunities and experiences Tasse has enjoyed are great. She has been blessed to travel the entire United States and much of the world. Tasse loves to travel. Just the thought of it increases her pulse rate. She loves to hop on her bike and ride wherever the trail takes her. She has enjoyed cycling trips to Germany, Croatia, and the Czech Republic, as well as numerous rides in the States. She has never seen a river she did not want to paddle. She has camped in wonderful, scenic places and has run many races, including several marathons. She loves to ski on water or snow, learned to ride dressage horseback as an adult, and plays the cello for no audience. Having been a national champion gymnast, Tasse learned the drive and the discipline that helped her throughout her life. She has also been blessed to be a speaker at fellowship groups and conferences. Mostly, she loves studying the Word of God during her morning times with Him.

Tasse is a licensed marriage and family therapist and is currently working as the director of her church's counseling clinic. She has retired from a twenty-five-year career in psychiatry as a therapist of various degrees at their county hospital. Currently, she is grateful for her dear husband, daughter, and friends, who have encouraged her to think about publishing the devotionals.

Writing the enclosed devotionals has been a process over fourteen years. Tasse began writing while working at the guesthouse in Israel. She later wrote for the women's ministry at her church. Jeremiah 30:2 says to "write down all that God has spoken to you in a book."

As the Lord has walked with her through these years, He has offered her help and understanding along the way. It is her hope that these words would also minister to you in your life situations.

You may follow the "Through the Fire" Blog for new devotional and inspirational writings at www.faiththroughthefire.com

Lightning Source UK Ltd.
Milton Keynes UK
UKHW010626060223
416537UK00001B/197